HOUSING
ECONOMICS

HOUSING ECONOMICS

GEORGE FALLIS

BUTTERWORTHS
TORONTO

Housing Economics
© 1985 by Butterworth & Co. (Canada) Ltd.

Printed and bound in Canada
by John Deyell Company

Canadian Cataloguing in Publication Data

Fallis, George, 1947–
Housing economics

Includes bibliographies and index.
ISBN 0-409-82940-4

1. Housing – Canada. I. Title.

HD7305.A3F355 1985   333.33′8   C85-098648-6

Sponsoring Editor: Janet Turner
Editing/Design: Robert Goodfellow
Production: Jim Shepherd

The Butterworth Group of Companies

Canada
Butterworth & Co. (Canada) Ltd., Toronto and Vancouver

United Kingdom
Butterworth & Co. (Publishers) Ltd., London

Australia
Butterworths Pty. Ltd., Sydney, Melbourne, Brisbane,
Adelaide, and Perth

New Zealand
Butterworths of New Zealand Ltd., Wellington and Auckland

Singapore
Butterworth & Co. (Asia) Pte. Ltd., Singapore

South Africa
Butterworth Publishers (Pty) Ltd., Durban and Pretoria

United States
Butterworth Legal Publishers, Boston, Seattle,
Austin and St. Paul
D & S Publishers, Clearwater

Contents

Acknowledgements

This book was written while I was a guest of the Institute for Social and Economic Research and the Department of Economics and Related Studies at the University of York, England. Both these places provided an ideal situation for thought and writing. On this side of the Atlantic, S. Bender, R. Murdie, C. Plourde, and L. Smith read various portions of the manuscript. The remaining errors and omissions are of course my own.

Janice Freshney was a capable and cheerful typist, despite my inability to deliver a draft chapter when promised. And to Sheila, Jed, Brooks, and Pearce, thanks for your forbearance when we could have been in the Yorkshire countryside.

1 | Introduction

This is a book about housing economics. It is about the economic theory of how households make housing choices, how suppliers of housing make decisions, of the market that brings the demand and supply sides together, and of how changes in exogenous variables alter the market outcome. It is also about the economics of housing policy – how economists form recommendations on the optimal housing policy and the effects of government programs on prices, outputs, and housing consumption. The field is a lively and fascinating one. In recent years there has been much excellent research published. For the theorist the field offers the latest developments in microeconomics. For the practitioner of applied economics, the econometric testing of the theoretical framework is subtle and challenging. For the policy analyst, the "housing problem" has been and seems destined to remain on the front pages of the newspapers. It is hoped that a sense of the analytical challenge and policy immediacy will be conveyed by this book.

A look at the card catalogue of even a major library reveals that there are few book with the title "Housing Economics." This is perhaps somewhat surprising because economists often develop subfields organized around a specific commodity. For example, there are many books about transportation economics, labour economics, or health economics. Certainly housing is a sufficiently important commodity in our economy to warrant special consideration. Expenditures on housing, furnishings, and household operation are almost thirty percent of personal expenditure; housing equity is the largest single component of household wealth; and residential construction is almost one-third of business gross fixed investment.

Housing analysis has been part of a number of different streams or traditions in the economics literature. There has been a macroeconomic tradition focussing on the national level of housing starts, the role of housing as a component of investment, the role of mortgage finance, and on fluctuations in housing starts especially as influenced by monetary policy. The demand for housing, either rental or ownership, has always been a part of consumer demand analysis. Urban economics has looked at resource allocation in a spatial context and, among other things, sought to explain the spatial pattern of housing prices, housing production, and housing consumption. Urban land economics has studied housing markets as part of the general problem of explaining how land is allocated in urban areas. Local public finance has dealt with residential property taxation, zoning, and the effects of local tax-expenditure patterns on property values. And this list of traditions is certainly not exhaustive. The purpose of this book is to draw upon these diverse contributions and to present the economics of housing as an application of microeconomic theory and welfare economics. It is hoped the application of this framework permits a coherent housing economics to emerge.

There is much that is special or even unique about the commodity housing and the operation of housing markets, as will be discussed in some detail below. The institutional arrangements and government programs that have evolved and now shape the operation of housing and mortgage markets are especially important. Indeed this specialness provides some of the justification for creating the subfield "housing economics." Nevertheless, what is required is the modification and development of the framework of microeconomics rather than a new idiosyncratic paradigm. There may be oligopolistic ownership of developable land, there may be high transactions costs to changing houses, and government regulation may be pervasive in the rental market. But understanding can best be advanced by recognizing that resources are allocated by markets (in which governments may be major participants); that there are demanders for the commodity and suppliers of the commodity, each pursuing their own interests, who interact in a market to determine a price and quantity exchanged. Housing markets are special sorts of markets, but markets nonetheless.

The previous paragraph is obviously directed not so much at economists or students reading about housing analysis for the first time but at people who have been in the housing field for some time – planners, urban geographers, policy analysts, and civil servants – who have tended to ignore or reject microeconomic analysis. Much writing on housing and housing policy is rather *ad hoc*, favouring a general, realistic setting out of a problem over the rigour of fully specified models. Certainly formal microeconomic analysis of housing can be criticized for being on occasion too simplistic and on other occasions for being more concerned with theoretical elegance than with explaining reality. It is hoped, however, to show that economic analysis can be developed to analyse this special commodity, housing, retaining both rigour and relevance to actual markets and actual public policy.

The intended audience for this book goes beyond undergraduate students of economics. It is hoped it will prove useful to many others who share an interest in housing issues. This book cannot be a textbook in the usual sense, in part because of this diverse audience and in part because the field is not sufficiently developed to permit a text on the basic material. Some will find sections of the book quite complicated; others will find sections rather elementary. It is assumed most readers will have had an introductory course in economics, and many will have had an intermediate course in microeconomic theory and welfare economics. Also it is presumed that readers will have some awareness of the participants in housing markets, how these markets operate, and of government housing policies. Wherever possible, ideas will be developed verbally and graphically, but on occasion algebra is the most compact and precise language to use. Results are not derived using algebra and calculus, but the notation of functions and derivatives is used as a language to formally express concepts. It is assumed readers will be familiar, at this level, with this notation. An attempt has been made to provide extensive references to the housing literature, usually in backnotes so the flow of the text will not be disrupted. This literature should be read in conjunction with the text. Certain readings are recommended at the end of each chapter. These readings contain more advanced economic analysis and are intended for the readers with additional background in economics.

Before beginning to think more carefully about the commodity housing, it is useful to recall the standard partial equilibrium analysis of a market from introductory economics. Let us imagine the market for ballpoint pens, illustrated in figure 1.1. A housing market differs from this market in a number of ways, but the standard analysis is a useful reference point. Along the horizontal axis in figure 1.1 is measured the quantity of ballpoint pens; and we have no difficulty in thinking of some standardized pen and so of measuring demand or supply as some number of standardized pens per unit time. Along the vertical axis is measured the price of a pen. The market demand curve is DD, the market supply curve is SS, and the equilibrium price and quantity exchanged are P_1 and Q_1. The market demand curve is the horizontal addition of the individual demand curves of households, and depends upon the number of households, household incomes, and tastes, and other prices. The market supply curve is the horizontal addition of the individual firm supply curves, allowing for increases in factor prices as the industry as opposed to the firm expands, and for differences in efficiency across firms. The supply curve of a firm depends upon the technology of production, and the prices of factors of production. Figure 1.1 shows the equilibrium, and implicitly how many ballpoint pens per unit time each household consumes, the output level of each firm, and the quantities of inputs used in production.

A number of assumptions lie behind the analysis of figure 1.1. It is assumed that the ballpoint pen market and the input markets for metal,

FIGURE 1.1
Equilibria in the Ballpoint Pen Market

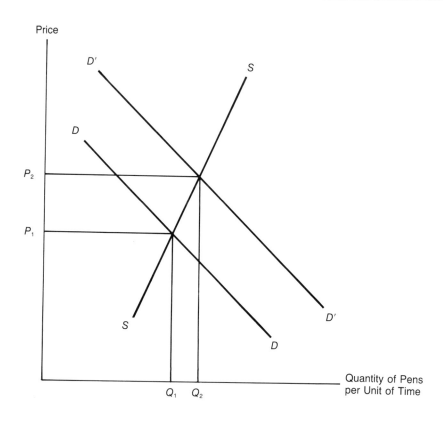

plastic, and ink are competitive: that is, no economic agent, whether demander or supplier, or group of agents can influence prices, and so all agents treat prices as parameters in their decisions. All agents have full information (there is no uncertainty), and there are no transactions costs (costs over and above the price that must be incurred when a transaction is made). Society collectively or the government has little particular interest in the operation of the market.

In figure 1.1, all the other factors except price which influence demand or supply are assumed to remain constant. The demand and supply curves show the relationship between price and quantity, *ceteris paribus*. The influence of these other factors is analysed through the technique of comparative statics (the comparison of two equilibria). Suppose the incomes of households were to increase. Assuming a ballpoint pen is a normal good, each household will demand more pens at any given price, and the market demand curve will shift to $D'D'$. The new equilibrium will be P_2 and Q_2. The increase in income caused an increase in the equilibrium price and quantity exchanged.

The housing market has many differences from the market for ballpoint pens. It is these that make the theoretical and empirical analysis of housing problematic and so challenging. Much of the literature in the economics of housing presented in the subsequent chapters can be seen as analysis that recognizes one of these differences, or even two of the differences, but never all of them simultaneously. The "art" in economic analysis involves dealing with a problem in a sufficiently realistic way to incorporate those differences that are essential aspects of the problems yet retaining a model that is tractable and whose workings are evident enough to aid our understanding. Let us consider some of these differences in turn.

HETEROGENEITY

When thinking about ballpoint pens, it was relatively easy to conceive of what was meant by "one ballpoint pen," and so to measure units along the horizontal axis when drawing a demand or supply curve. It is not so easy in the case of housing, because housing is a very heterogeneous commodity. Both houses and apartments differ greatly. They differ in floor space, design, amount of land surrounding them, age, level of upkeep, and so on. This heterogeneity causes a number of problems.[1] First, it is difficult to define and measure a unit of output or of what is demanded. Two very different dwelling units – a large, run-down, old house and a small bachelor apartment – can command the same rent. And second, it is difficult empirically to establish the price in any transaction because what we observe is the product of price and quantity.

Much of the housing economics literature abstracts from the heterogeneity of housing. Muth (1960) and Olsen (1969) set out clearly this approach. "An unobservable theoretical construct called housing service is introduced" (Olsen 1969, 613). It is assumed in equilibrium that the price per unit of housing service is the same in all dwelling units. One apartment that has twice the rent of another therefore provides twice as many units of housing service as another. A slum dwelling is one that yields few units of housing service per year. In this approach, the notion of quality does not arise – dwellings differ in the number of units of homogeneous housing services they provide. Housing services are an argument in household utility functions, and the household has a demand for housing services, not dwelling units. Firms and other agents supply housing services. Thus the commodity housing is rendered like any other commodity, and the standard framework of microeconomics can be applied. Some researchers feel this approach abstracts too much and misses essential properties of housing. Certainly for some questions it is inappropriate. However it cannot be rejected directly, because a unit of housing service is by definition unobservable; only its implications can be tested insofar as they are observable phenomena. On this basis, the approach has proven very useful.[2]

DURABILITY

A second major difference from the standard commodity is that housing is a durable good. Immediately one must carefully distinguish between the *stock* of housing and the *flow* of housing services per unit of time. Housing services are produced using housing stock, labour, and other inputs such as heating fuel, and electricity. Housing stock is produced using building materials, labour, and land. Housing stock can be augmented either by constructing new buildings or by maintaining or renovating existing buildings. There are thus two housing markets to consider. In one the consumer good, housing service, is exchanged, and the price per unit of housing service is determined. In the other, the investment good, housing stock, is exchanged and the price per unit of housing stock is determined. The two markets are very interrelated. Housing stock is valued because of the flow of services that it yields. In equilibrium in a world of perfect markets, especially perfect capital markets, the price of a unit of stock, P, will be equal to the discounted present value of housing service flows (p_t in time period t) which the stock yields as in equation 1.1. The discount factor for the

$$P = \sum_{t=1}^{\infty} p_t \rho_t (1-d)^{t-1}$$

$$\rho_t = \prod_{s=1}^{t-1} (1+r_s)^{-1} \qquad t = 2, \ldots \infty \tag{1.1}$$

$$\rho_1 = 1$$

service flow in period t is ρ_t, d is the constant annual rate of depreciation, and the interest rate in period t is r_t.

In most of this book, the focus will be on the housing services market and on explaining how the price of the service flow is determined. The stock price can be determined using equation 1.1.

Durability raises the issue of housing tenure. Households demand housing services because they yield utility. But should housing services be acquired by purchasing housing stock or by renting the housing stock owned by someone else? And how should the purchase of housing stock be financed – out of savings, using a mortgage loan, or some combination of the two?

The terminology of housing economics differs slightly here from that of microeconomics, and it is worth pausing to state the differences. When a household rents housing, in common parlance and in housing economics, the rent is equal to the price per unit of housing service times the number of units of housing service yielded by the apartment. In housing economics the term rent is also used as a synonym for the price per unit of housing service when rental markets are analysed. The context makes clear the two usages. These concepts are distinct from the concept of rent or quasi rent in microeconomics, which is payment to a factor above what is necessary to keep it in its current use.

Durability and tenure choice create a host of analytical issues on both the demand and supply sides of the market. On the demand side, explicit purchases are not equal to consumption because many homeowners acquired their homes in previous periods and consume services in the current period. Homeowners are both investors, as owners of housing stock; and consumers, who pay rent for use of the housing stock to the landlord (themselves). These rent payments are imputed or implicit, but in principle are the same as actual rent payments, and the relationship between stock and service prices is as in equation 1.1. The purchase of a house is rather different from the purchase of a standard non-durable commodity and requires special analysis. It is both an investment choice and a consumption choice. Expectations about future price movements and rates of return on alternative investment are important. It is usually not financed solely out of savings but also using a mortgage loan, and is very sensitive to the terms of the loan, especially the interest rate. Wealth and permanent income are important determinants of demand. The purchase is postponable so, in aggregate, purchases may be quite volatile. The purchase is both a discrete choice – to buy or not to buy; and a continuous choice – how much to consume.

On the supply side, housing stock is extremely durable, lasting (with maintenance) thirty, fifty, and even hundreds of years. This durability means that most of the supply of housing services is produced using the existing stock rather than housing stock constructed during that period. Over the last thirty years in Canada, annual housing starts have varied between 2 and 4 percent of the housing stock and are currently below 2 percent. Supply of new stock also comes from maintenance and renovation by landlords and owner-occupiers; demolition and conversion of dwelling units reduce stock. Disinvestment in housing stock is relatively slow. Past decisions about the amount, type, and location of housing stock are significant determinants of current prices and so current outputs. As housing stock depreciates it becomes qualitatively different from new housing stock. The market establishes the price of quality levels as part of a complex equilibrium across quality levels. The production function which shows how housing services can be produced using housing stock and other inputs will be a function of the quality of stock, and intertemporal relationships arise where current production choices depend on past choices.

In most housing economics, durability is dealt with in a very simplified manner. The assumption of a homogeneous unit of housing service is retained, and there is also assumed to be a homogeneous unit of housing stock. One unit of housing service is the quantity of service yielded by one unit of stock per unit of time. Implicitly, this assumes either that housing stock is the only input into producing housing services, or that there is a fixed coefficients production function. The idea of the quality of housing stock does not arise; depreciation is a using up of homogeneous units. The intertemporal issues are dealt with in stock-flow models or standard partial equilibrium models with appropriate attention to the distinction between short and long run.

The cost of obtaining housing services through ownership of housing stock is referred to as the user cost. If there are no price changes over time, no depreciation, and no operating costs, the user cost of a unit of housing stock is Pr – its price times the rate of interest. This relationship holds whether the stock is purchased with cash, and so the cost is the opportunity cost of interest earnings foregone, or the stock is purchased with a loan, and so the cost is the interest on the loan (assuming the rate of interest on alternative investments and the mortgage rate of interest are equal). In the slightly more complicated case of price changes and depreciation the user cost is as in equation 1.2,

$$P_1 r - [P_2 (1-d) - P_1] = \text{user cost} \tag{1.2}$$

where d is the constant annual rate of depreciation and P_1 is the price per unit of housing stock at the beginning of period 1.[3] User cost is the opportunity cost (or loan cost), plus depreciation, less capital gains.

In equilibrium with perfect markets, the relationship between rents and capital values in equations 1.1 holds. This is restated in equations 1.3. Multiplying the second equation in 1.3 by $(1-d)/(1+r_1)$ and subtracting the second equation from the first produces equation 1.4. The

$$P_1 = p_1 + \frac{p_2(1-d)}{1+r_1} + \frac{p_3(1-d)^2}{(1+r_1)(1+r_2)} + \dots$$

$$P_2 = p_2 + \frac{p_3(1-d)}{1+r_2} + \frac{p_4(1-d)^2}{(1+r_2)(1+r_3)} + \dots \tag{1.3}$$

$$\frac{P_1 r_1 - [P_2(1-d) - P_1]}{1+r_1} = p_1 \tag{1.4}$$

user cost is equal to the rent; the cost of obtaining housing services as a renter is the same as the cost as an owner. In this discrete time frame rent is paid at the beginning of the period while user cost, as defined in equation 1.2, is borne at the end of the period; to make them comparable one must evaluate the present value of each as in equation 1.4. The household is thus indifferent between consuming housing services as an owner or as a renter. The issue of tenure choice does not arise. The housing demand functions of owners can be specified and estimated in the usual way using the user cost of capital as the price of housing services.[4]

Thus even when housing is recognized as durable, the introduction of the user cost concept and the assumption of perfect markets implies that the distinction between ownership and rental markets vanishes. Tenure enters the analysis when some of the above austere assumptions are removed; for example when people do not have perfect access to capital markets or when non-neutral income taxes are introduced.

SPATIAL FIXITY

A third important special characteristic of housing is that it is spatially fixed. In contrast to most other goods purchased by consumers, a housing unit cannot be moved from one location to another (except at prohibitive cost). When a household buys a dwelling unit it also buys a "location" and therefore accessibility to other locations, a neighbourhood, and a local government. Travel from home to other locations such as one's job, stores, parks, restaurants, or the homes of friends takes both time and money. Households will pay to reduce these costs of travel and so, for example, dwelling units near centres of employment will command a higher price than those farther away. The price per unit of homogeneous housing services will vary across space. Much work in urban economics has been devoted to analysing the trade-off between access and house prices in a spatial equilibrium. Many characteristics of the neighbourhood influence the utility of the household, from the adjacent land uses, and the socioeconomic and racial characteristics of other residents of the neighbourhood, to the level of noise and air pollution. This is simply another way of saying that externalities will be very important in spatial housing markets. Another aspect of a site is that it locates a dwelling within a local government jurisdiction. The owner-occupier or landlord must pay residential property taxes, and the residents can consume the public services that are provided. Of particular importance to many households are the primary and secondary schools and the level of police protection. Households will be influenced in their choice of a dwelling unit by the tax-expenditure pattern of the jurisdiction.

Spatial fixity also implies that markets adjust by way of the movement of people to dwelling units rather than goods to people. When demand patterns change, for example, and people move to the suburbs or other cities, housing units cannot follow them to their new locations. People face high transactions costs in moving, and supply is quite inelastic, so housing markets take a long time to adjust.

A good deal of housing economics ignores the spatial issue and treats housing in the aspatial way of standard microeconomics. When space is introduced, the other complexities such as heterogeneity and durability are usually not incorporated.

These three characteristics of housing – its heterogeneity, durability, and spatial fixity – have strongly influenced the directions of housing research. They have provided many of the challenges for theorists attempting to explain the operation of housing markets and econometricians attempting to estimate such things as the price and income elasticities of demand.

Housing markets have several other special characteristics. They are characterized by high transactions costs and imperfect information – unlike the simple world of figure 1.1. It is costly for householders, especially homeowners, to change the quantity of housing consumed. It is expensive to move in terms of time, money, and the emotions. As a result, housing markets adjust slowly to changes in consumer income, and for long periods of time households consume a different quantity of housing than they would if they could costlessly recontract at that moment. Households do not have complete information on the characteristics of units for sale or rent and so do not have true information on price. Sellers likewise do not have full information on the bids of households and the prices of other sellers. A dispersion of prices may exist in such markets; it may take agents a long time to become aware of exogenous changes; and both buyers and sellers will have to devote resources to acquiring information. There is now a literature formally analysing the behaviour of buyers, sellers, and markets when there are high transactions costs and imperfect information; but although the importance of these issues for housing markets is evident, relatively little of the literature deals specifically with housing.

Another important characteristic of housing markets relates to government involvement. Society clearly has a special concern about housing consumption that goes much beyond simply considering it as one of many items on which households spend their money. Society wants to ensure that all households have adequate housing; that housing is affordable; and that households have security of tenure. These concerns can be grouped under the heading of equity. The usual efficiency and stabilization issues also arise in housing matters. The analytic problem for housing economics is to define the objective of intervention in an operational way and to design the optimal policy.

Besides studying the optimal policy, housing economics also examines the effects of actual policies. There are an enormous number of government housing programs. There are programs of mortgage lending, mortgage insurance, of subsidies to demanders, and of subsidies to new construction and renovation. The income tax laws contain many special provisions for homeowners and landlords. There is public housing. There are rent controls. The location, density, and construction of housing are heavily regulated. All governments – federal, provincial, and local – have programs with significant effects on housing markets.

To this point, the introduction has tried to suggest the nature of housing economics and why the standard microeconomic models will have to be modified. The next introductory sections attempt to supply some context for the more formally analytic chapters that follow. How many housing starts are there annually in Canada? How has the price of housing services varied over time? What is a mortgage loan, and which financial intermediaries supply mortgage funds? The answers provide a quantitative and institutional context for housing analysis. These details are in part stylized facts which will be explained in later chapters and in part background material. Many of the data are drawn from *Canadian Housing Statistics*, the *Bank of Canada Review*, and Statistics Canada's *Census of Canada*, *Survey of Consumer Finances*, *Family Expenditure in Canada*, *National Income and Expenditure Accounts*, and *The Consumer Price Index*. These in conjunction with a few special surveys by Statistics Canada and Canada Mortgage and Housing Corporation (CMHC) provide the main data sources for empirical analysis. They provide data for cross-section analysis, which are consistent across housing markets, and data for time series analysis, which are consistent over time. Obviously these publications should not be read from cover to cover. But any serious students of housing economics ought to browse through them, especially *Canadian Housing Statistics*, as part of their introduction to the field, and then gradually develop more detailed knowledge as the need arises and their study proceeds.

HOUSING STARTS

Housing services are produced in any time period using housing stock that remains from previous periods and housing stock that is constructed during the period. The production of new stock by the building industry has always been the main focus of government housing policy and of central concern to the macroeconomic side of housing economics. But it is well to remember that housing starts measure output in the capital goods market, not the output of the market that produces housing services; and starts measure only part of the gross new investment. Owners of existing dwellings renovate premises and increase the capital stock. There are almost no data to adequately measure this latter sort of new investment, although many believe it is significant and will grow more so over the coming years.

The production of new housing stock through new construction is usually measured by the number of dwelling or housing starts. A dwelling unit is defined as "a structurally separate set of self-contained living premises with a private entrance from outside the building or from a common hall, lobby or stairway inside the building. Such an entrance must be one that can be used without passing through another separate dwelling unit" (CMHC 1982, 88.) A single detached house is one dwelling unit, and an apartment building with ten separate apartments is ten dwelling units. Housing starts data do not consistently measure the production of housing stock because the number of units of housing stock in the various types of dwellings will vary.

Table 1.1 gives the annual level of housing starts in Canada from 1951 to 1982; and also the total population and number of dwelling units in census years. There is considerable variation from year to year, but the basic pattern is: growth in the annual level of starts until 1976, and then decline after 1976. Housing starts have varied between 1.9

TABLE 1.1
Housing Starts, Population, and Housing Stock

Year	Housing Starts	Total Dwelling Units[1]	Population	Year	Housing Starts	Total Dwelling Units	Population
1951	68,579	3,522,162	14,009,000	67	164,123		
52	83,246	(.019)[2]	(3.98)[3]	68	196,878		
53	102,409			69	210,415		
54	113,527			70	190,528		
55	138,276			1971	233,653	6,324,685	21,568,000
1956	127,311		16,081,000	72	249,914	(.037)	(3.41)
57	122,340			73	268,529		
58	164,632			74	222,123		
59	141,345			75	231,456		
60	108,858			1976	273,203		22,993,000
1961	125,577	4,744,715	18,238,000	77	245,724		
62	130,095	(.026)	(3.84)	78	227,667		
63	148,624			79	197,049		
64	165,658			80	158,601		
65	166,656			1981	177,973	8,756,675	24,205,000
1966	134,474		20,015,000	82	125,860	(.020)	(2.76)

1. This excludes vacancies.
2. Figures within parentheses below total dwelling units are the ratios of starts to total dwelling units in those years.
3. Figures within parentheses below population are the ratios of population to dwelling units in those years.

SOURCES: CMHC (various years), *Canadian Housing Statistics*; Canada (various years), *Census of Canada*.

FIGURE 1.2
Fluctuations in Housing Starts and in the Economy Expressed as Deviation from Trend

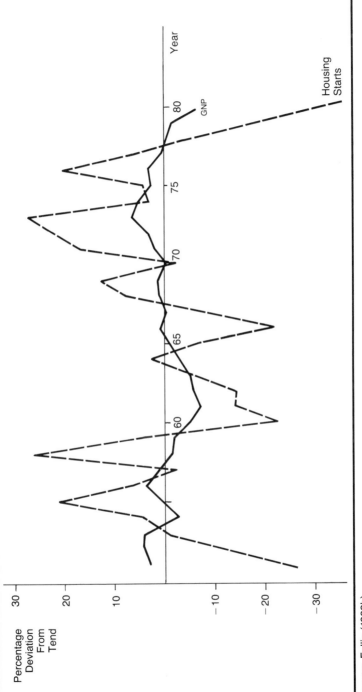

SOURCE: Fallis (1983b)

and 3.7 percent of the total stock. The increase in the number of dwelling units has been much larger than the increase in population with the result, that, even with demolitions, the average number of persons per dwelling has fallen from 3.98 to 2.76. In this sense, Canadians have become much better housed over these thirty years.

The annual variation in starts is made more evident in figure 1.2. An exponential function was fitted to the annual data to establish the basic underlying trend. Figure 1.2 graphs the percentage deviation of annual starts from the estimated long-run trend. The deviation of real gross national product (GNP) from its long-run trend has been placed on the same graph for comparison. Housing starts are clearly much more volatile than the entire economy.

HOUSING CONDITIONS

How well housed are Canadians? Has their situation been getting better or worse? Ideally, to answer these questions we would like data on the number of homogeneous units of housing service consumed each year, for a number of years. But a unit of housing service is an unobservable theoretical construct so we are forced to fall back on a series of proxies. Even in the ideal world there is the problem of deciding what to include under the general heading of housing conditions. When a household buys or rents housing, it also acquires accessibility, a neighbourhood, and a local government. Some would include measures of these components in representing housing conditions. Partly because of lack of consistent data, they will not be included here, although they evidently influence the welfare of households.

We have already seen from table 1.1 that the average number of persons per dwelling unit has fallen. Other related proxy measures of housing consumption are presented in table 1.2 The number of families not having their own separate dwelling unit has fallen considerably. In 1981, just under 100,000 families were doubled up, which is less than 2 percent of all families. In 1951, over 10 percent of families were doubled up. An arbitrary index of crowding is often established as more than one person per room in the dwelling. The absolute number of crowded units rose from 1951 to 1961, although falling slightly as a percentage of the stock, but the absolute number fell significantly by 1971. Data from CMHC (1981) indicate that by 1978 only 3.5 percent of households had more than one person per room.

These proxies suggest that the consumption of housing services per person has risen over the last thirty years. The rise is even more significant when it is remembered that as time passes, more and more of the dwelling units are new and yield more units of housing service per dwelling. Now almost fifty percent of the dwelling units have been built since 1961. Some measure of this improvement is supplied by

TABLE 1.2
Households, Doubling and Crowding

Year	Number of Households Family	Non-Family	Families Not Maintaining Own Dwelling Unit	Crowding[1]
1951	3,024,285	385,010	320,645	641,820
1961	3,948,935	605,801	235,915	750,942
1971	4,933,440	1,107,840	172,395	569,485
1981	6,231,490	2,050,045	96,595	not available

1. Households that have more than one person per room.

SOURCE: Canada (various years), *Census of Canada*.

table 1.3. The percentage of dwellings without basic plumbing and heating facilities has dropped dramatically since 1951.

A special computation (CMHC 1981) using a survey that collected data on whether dwellings were in poor condition revealed that 11 percent of renters in Census Metropolitan Areas in 1978 had inadequate housing (defined as in poor condition, or crowded, or without basic plumbing and heating facilities). Extrapolating this to all owners and other renters suggests that well under 10 percent of Canadian households have inadequate housing.

Though small in percentage terms, a large absolute number of households still have very poor housing: a fact that these aggregate data tend to disguise. In the minds of many Canadians this absolute number remains unacceptably high, given the income and wealth of our society. Most of the poorly housed have low incomes, although by no means all low-income households have poor housing. The incidence of poor housing is higher in rural areas, among the single elderly in large cities, among native peoples, and among single-parent families.

TABLE 1.3
Proxy Measures of Housing Quality

Year	Percentage of Dwelling Units No Central or Electrical Heating	No Piped Hot and Cold Water	No Exclusive Use of Flush Toilet
1951	52.0	43.1	35.9
1961	32.5	19.9	21.0
1971	18.9	7.3	6.9
1974	10.9	4.2	3.0
1978	not available	1.9	1.7

SOURCE: CMHC (1981)

THE PRICE OF HOUSING

There can scarcely be a more central concept than price to economic analysis, whether theoretical or applied, yet in housing economics the price of housing is hard to measure. The problems have already been alluded to. In rental and ownership markets, the price is hard to conceptualize because the commodity is so heterogeneous; and in ownership markets, the price concept is further complicated because housing is durable, and there are no explicit transactions for many households although they obviously consume housing. Empirically, the problems arise because all data are the price multiplied times the quantity; we cannot separately observe each.

In rental market analysis, the conceptual problem is solved by creating the abstract concept of housing services. Changes in the rent on identical dwellings can be used to create an index of price change. Alternatively, one can think of an apartment as containing a bundle of measurable characteristics which is what households are actually purchasing. Data on rent and characteristics can be used to generate measures of the implicit marginal prices of characteristics and their changes over time.

In ownership markets, both the homogeneous commodity and characteristics approach can be used to conceive of and measure the price of a unit of housing stock. But what of the price of housing services faced by homeowners? Homeowners rent the stock that they own, from themselves. Assuming the existence of a homogeneous unit of housing service, and that one unit of stock produces one unit of service, the owner's price of housing service is the user cost of a unit of stock. This price has already been set out in equation 1.2. A more realistic and complete measure of the price of services follows from extending this equation in two ways. Most homeowners pay the price of a house using some accumulated savings and the proceeds of a mortgage loan. The interest rate that could be earned on the savings, r, is usually less than the rate that must be paid on the mortgage, m. Also there are other costs incurred in producing the housing services such as property taxes, necessary maintenance, and insurance. The more complete expression for the price of housing services to homeowners is shown in equation 1.5, where E is their equity and M the mortgage loan per unit of stock, and a is the rate of maintenance, i the rate of insurance and t the rate

$$Er + Mm + P_1(a+i+t) - [P_2(1-d) - P_1] = \text{user cost} \qquad (1.5)$$

of property taxation (assuming these expenses per unit of stock are some constant ratio of the price of the stock). Thus the price of services to a homeowner is the opportunity cost of his equity, the mortgage interest, associated out-of-pocket costs, depreciation *minus* any capital gains from owning the stock. Even this measure of user cost is not complete. For demand analysis, one should speak of the expected user cost and so of expected costs and expected capital gains. Also one should incorporate the income tax system into the measure: in Canada this means recognizing that the opportunity earnings of equity would be taxed and that capital gains when realised would not be taxed.[5]

There has been much confusion in the public debate about the cost of housing services to owners. The emphasis has been on explicit out-of-pocket payments, $Mm + P_1(a + i + t)$, particularly the mortgage interest payments, ignoring the capital gains from holding the stock. Many commentators have greatly overstated the rise in the cost of housing services through ownership – until very recently nominal mortgage interest rates were very high, but of course interest rates were high because of inflation, and nominal capital gains on houses were also high. Households did not fall victim to the commentators' confusion and continued to consume housing services through ownership.

Reflecting on the measure of housing price set out in equation 1.5 raises a number of interesting issues. The price of housing services can vary from person to person depending upon the financing of their house and the capital gains on their house. There can be a considerable difference between the expected price of services and the actual price because of the capital gains. On several occasions in the last decade, actual capital gains were far greater than expected gains; and the actual price of housing services was even negative on occasion. In the early 1980s, actual gains were much less than anticipated gains, and the actual price was extremely high. This measure of price proves extremely volatile, yet consumption patterns do not show a corresponding volatility. This suggests that transactions costs, which we know to be large, play a key role in explaining demand. Finally, there are different sorts of costs in equation 1.5. The mortgage interest cost must be paid each month, while the capital gains are not realised unless the household sells the house. In a frictionless world of perfect capital markets, this would not make any difference because households could borrow against the capital gains to pay the mortgage interest. But our world is not frictionless and does not have perfect capital markets. The high inflation rate which has meant high nominal interest rates and usually high offsetting capital gains on housing has caused many problems in our system of housing finance. New mortgage instruments have been developed to deal with the unrealised capital gain problem.

In time series analysis, it is necessary to know how the price of housing services has changed over time. This change has also been central to public policy discussions over the last ten years. There was a widespread perception that the relative price of housing services had risen sharply, far faster than incomes, and this led to several new government housing programs. The development of public policy over this period can be seen as a response to our evolving understanding of the effects of inflation on housing and mortgage markets.

Price change over time is usually measured using a price index. For a single commodity, this price index in any period is simply the ratio of the current price to the base period price multiplied times one hundred. If one wishes to measure the price change of a group of commodities, some sort of average of the changes in the individual prices is required. The Laspeyres price index can be thought of as the sum of the price indices of the separate commodities weighted by the share in total expenditure of each commodity in the base period.

An index of the change in the price of housing services through rental is an index of price change of a single commodity assuming there is a homogeneous good called housing services. The consumer price index (CPI) rent component measures the change in price on a group of apartments rented by the target group in the base year. Table 1.4 shows the CPI rent component and the total CPI (including rent and ownership components) since 1961, and reveals that rents have risen less than other prices. The CPI component, however, is subject to downward bias. The price change is not computed by monitoring the rent on a given group of apartments but rather the rent on a sample of apartments within which the apartments change. The procedure correcting for quality improvement is widely regarded as causing downward bias. The index of actual rents paid, from the Labour Force Survey, has risen far more than the CPI rent component, and the divergence seems much larger than what could be attributed to quality change. A revised CPI rent index is presented in the third column of table 1.4. Contrary to popular belief, rents have risen less than other prices, indeed to a startling degree. No doubt there have been large rent increases in a single year on specific apartments in specific locales, but even there the increases often reflected a one-period adjustment. Over a longer period the annual change was not large. The data simply do not support the idea that rents have risen greatly. In many provinces rent controls were introduced with wage and profits controls in 1974, and in some provinces they remain.

An index of the price of housing services through ownership is an index of price changes on several commodities: mortgage interest, insurance, maintenance payments, and so on. Computation of the index requires price indices on the various components and weights that are derived from the expenditure pattern of some group in the base period. For behavioral analysis such as estimating demand functions, the appropriate index would be of expected price; whereas for other purposes such as a consumer price or cost-of-living index the actual price is of interest. The ownership component of the Canadian CPI does not measure ownership cost as in equation 1.5. The CPI index ignores capital gains and the opportunity cost of equity. In computing the price indices on the mortgage, depreciation, maintenance, insurance, and property tax components, it is recognized that expenditures will rise on a "stand-

TABLE 1.4
Indices of the Price of Housing Services and Per Capita Income

Year	CPI Rent Component[1]	Revised Rent Index[2]	CPI Ownership Component[1]	Revised Ownership Index[3]	All-Items CPI[3]	Per Capita Income[4]
1961	100	100	100	100	100	100
62	100.3	99	102.8	109.2	101.2	106.8
63	100.6	100	105.9	91.2	102.9	111.4
64	101.2	101	110.4	75.6	104.8	117.1
1965	101.9	104	115.0	69.5	107.3	126.7
66	103.6	108	120.1	51.0	111.3	139.5
67	107.1	114	126.9	92.8	115.3	150.3
68	111.8	119	136.1	86.8	132.0	162.9
69	116.3	123	148.3	93.7	125.3	178.3
1970	120.3	130	161.3	170.4	129.6	189.5
71	122.5	135	174.3	141.2	133.3	208.1
72	124.3	138	188.3	117.9	139.7	232.7
73	126.4	142	207.0	77.7	150.3	268.8
74	130.1	148	227.1	−3.5	166.7	316.5
1975	137.2	157	250.3	4.2	184.7	363.5
76	147.0	168	284.8	114.6	198.5	409.2
77	154.7	176	315.8	−	214.4	446.1
78	162.8	186	341.8	−	234.4	490.4
79	170.2	194	363.1	−	254.9	540.1
1980	178.2	203	390.2	−	280.8	600.4
81	189.6	216	440.3	−	315.9	704.6
82	206.7	236	499.9	−	350.0	−

SOURCE: 1. CMHC (various years), *Canadian Housing Statistics.*
2. Fallis (1980), with extension.
3. McFadyen and Hobart (1978).
4. Canada (various years), *National Income and Expenditure Accounts.*

ard" house in part because the price of these components rise, and in part because the value of the standard house rises. Correction for the latter is made using an index of building materials and labour costs. This approach omits land costs and any short-run house value changes; these could be captured by using an index of actual price change on a standard house. Because the CPI's emphasis is on the actual prices faced by homeowners, the mortgage interest rate used is not the current rate but an average rate, reflecting the actual rates on outstanding mortgages. Although one is often tempted to label one index right and another wrong, it is better to regard each as appropriate for certain types of analysis and to take care to understand how an index is computed before using it.

The CPI ownership component is presented in the fourth column of table 1.4. McFadyen and Hobart (1978) recomputed the homeownership component including capital gains, the opportunity cost of equity, and measuring the mortgage component using the current mortgage rate of interest, and using an actual dwelling price index rather than a construction and labour price index. The differences between the indices are significant: the revised index is considerably more volatile and in every year lower (except 1970) than the CPI ownership component. The CPI index has risen considerably more than the all-items index; but the revised ownership index rose much less.

There was considerable income growth over most of the 1961–1982 period (last column of table 1.4). The index of nominal per capita income stood as at 705 in 1981. Thus while ownership costs as measured in the CPI rose faster than the CPI, incomes more than kept pace with this price increase.

There has been an enormous amount written on the housing expenditure to income ratio of households, much of it connected with the so-called affordability problem. If a household spends more than twenty-five per cent of its income on housing, it is said to have an "affordability" problem. It is argued, in some detail, in chapter seven that the housing expenditure to income ratio should not be used to define housing problems because it is really a proxy measure for whether a household consumes all of life's necessities, and a poor proxy at that. It is however important to recognize that housing expenditure is a large part of the household's budget and therefore any change in the price of housing service will significantly alter the real income of consumers. We do not have data for a proper measure of housing expenditure. In the case of renters, data are available – expenditure is the rent paid to the landlord. In the case of homeowners, however, true expenditure is the rent paid by oneself as tenant to oneself as landlord. Measuring this has the same problems as measuring the price of housing services for owners; it must recognize the capital gains and the opportunity cost of equity. Available data only record out-of-pocket expenditures of owners. Using out-of-pocket data, Canadians on average spend slightly less than 20 percent of gross income on housing; although the percentage is higher among low-income households.

MORTGAGES AND THE MORTGAGE MARKET

We now deal with a final bit of background: the mortgage market. A mortgage is simply a loan – a form of contract specifying the manner in which loaned funds are to be repaid. Real property such as a house or an apartment building is offered as security on the loan. If the borrower does not repay the loan, the lender takes possession of the property. Mortgages are enormously important in housing markets. Most new construction of apartments and new houses is financed by mortgages rather than the retained earnings of the builder or bank loans or bonds. Most households finance the purchase of a house using a mortgage.

The mortgage contract sets out certain things: the amount of the loan which is called the principal, the interest rate which will be applied to the unpaid principal, the term which is the length of time that the interest rate will be held constant, the amortization period which is the length of time over which the principal is to be paid off, the method of computing the monthly payments, and any prepayment privileges. Each of these terms of the loan can, for a loan of a given size, alter the amount and timing of payments, which can alter the demand for and supply of mortgage funds.

Until the mid-sixties in Canada, most residential mortgages were what have been called "standard" level payment mortgages. Some feeling for the nature of a mortgage can be gained from looking at this particular form in detail. The monthly payment remains constant over the amortization period of the loan which can be as long as twenty to twenty-five years. The loans are fully amortizing in the sense that at the end of the period the entire principal is paid off (as opposed to there remaining a lump sum). The term of the loan is the same as the amortization period so that the interest rate established when the loan is made applies throughout the loan. Because the monthly payments are constant, in the early years of the mortgage the payments barely cover the interest cost on the outstanding principal. The amount of principal that remains to be paid off declines only slowly. However in the last years of the mortgage the principal outstanding is small so the monthly payment easily covers the interest and largely goes to paying off the principal. Figure 1.3 illustrates the amount of principal outstanding over a twenty-five year standard level payment mortgage (interest rate ten percent).

The effect on the monthly payment of changes in the characteristics of the standard level payment mortgage are illustrated in table 1.5. Changes in the principal yield proportionate changes in monthly payments across all amortization periods. Increases in the interest rate increase the monthly payment but less than proportionately. The longer the amorization period the larger the percentage increase in monthly payment with a given increase in the interest rate. Lengthening the amortization period at first greatly reduces the monthly payment, but as the amortization period gets longer this reduction becomes quite small. The monthly payment is of great import to both the borrower and the lender, although it should be recognized that the present value of the constant monthly payments is always equal to the principal.

Since the mid-sixties, the Canadian economy has experienced high and unpredictable (unanticipated) inflation. This has led to changes in the mortgage contract. Level payment mortgages have terms as short as one year, some mortgages have variable interest rates, and some have varying rather than constant monthly payments.

The demand for residential mortgage finance is a derived demand –

FIGURE 1.3
Principal Outstanding by Year
Standard Level Payment Mortgage
(10% interest; 25-year amortization)

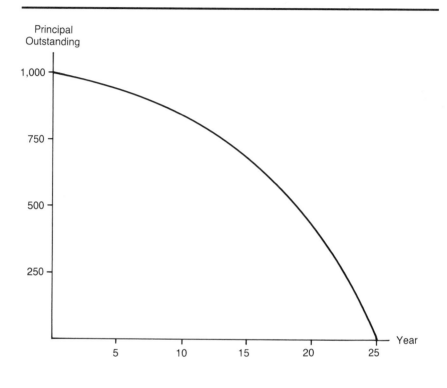

SOURCE: Data from Financial Publishing Company (1966).

derived from the demand for housing services. Demand for finance is also closely related to new construction, because new buildings whether for sale or rental are primarily financed by mortages. The ratio of the mortgage principal to the market value of the building – the loan-to-value ratio – can be as high as 0.9. Demand also arises in the existing housing market. When houses or rental buildings are sold, often the old mortgage is paid off and a new one arranged. Exisiting owners also refinance to pay for housing renovations or expenditures in other areas.

The supply of residential mortgage finance comes from a number of diverse sources. The principal suppliers are private financial institutions such as banks, trust companies, life insurance companies, mortgage finance companies, and other institutions such as the Quebec

TABLE 1.5
Monthly Payments on a Standard Mortgage

	Amortization Period in Years					
	5	10	15	20	25	30
Principal						
(5% interest rate)						
10,000	188.48	105.82	78.82	65.72	58.17	53.37
20,000	376.96	211.63	157.63	131.43	116.33	106.74
40,000	753.92	423.26	315.26	262.86	232.66	213.48
Interest Rate						
(10,000 principal)						
5	188.48	105.82	78.82	65.72	58.17	53.37
6	192.99	110.66	83.99	71.22	63.99	59.49
7	197.55	115.60	89.33	76.94	70.05	65.87
8	202.15	120.65	94.82	82.84	76.33	72.48
9	206.79	125.79	100.46	88.92	82.80	79.79
10	211.48	131.04	106.23	95.17	89.45	86.27

SOURCE: Financial Publishing Company (1966).

savings banks and fraternal and mutual benefit societies. These inter-mediaries gather savings and invest them in mortgages, government bonds, and other financial instruments. These suppliers provide well over half of all new mortgages initiated and a still higher percentage of mortgages to finance new residential construction. The second major supplier is the government sector. At the federal level, Canada Mortgage and Housing Corporation (CMHC) is a Crown corporation created to administer the National Housing Act (NHA) and initiates most of the federal residential housing loans. Most provinces have created similar special-purpose bodies for mortgage lending. Almost all government mortgage loans have been to finance new construction, often of housing for low-income households. Annual government lending varies con-siderably from year to year according to the dictates of social and eco-nomic policy; in recent years federal lending has been sharply curtailed. Government funding has been the principal source of finance for as high as 30 percent of housing starts in 1970, and as low as 1.3 percent of starts in 1982. The third group of suppliers includes individuals; small loan and other corporations for whom mortgage lending is peri-pheral to their main activities; estates, trusts, and pension funds; and co-operatives, credit unions, and caisses populaires. This group held about 10 percent of outstanding mortgages in 1969 (Smith 1974, 82). The motivations and determinants of lending by this group are as di-verse as the members of the group. For example, much individual mort-gage lending is in connection with the sale of a home – the vendor "takes back" a mortgage. Many corporations provide mortgage loans to their employees as part of their remuneration package. And credit unions are institutions created to channel the savings of members to other members who wish to borrow.

Since 1954 in Canada, the public sector has offered mortgage insurance under the National Housing Act (NHA). The borrower pays a premium (approximately one percent of the loan which is added to and amortized with the loan), and the lender is insured against capital and interest losses. Mortgage loans by certain "approved" lenders, mainly chartered banks, life insurance, loan, and trust companies are eligible for NHA insurance. Canada Mortgage and Housing Corporation sets out the terms of mortgages eligible for insurance, the maximum house value eligible, and set the mortgage interest rate until 1969 when it was freed to be set in the private market. National Housing Act loans are an important part of the lending by large financial intermediaries and of the financing for new residential construction. Although the interest rate is now free, NHA lending cannot be regarded as purely market determined because CMHC still controls the other terms of eligible loans. During the 1970s several private mortgage insurance firms were established, and now most high-ratio, conventional (non-NHA) loans are insured.

Table 1.6 shows the mortgage assets of a large group of mortgage suppliers; the figures in parentheses show the share held by each type of institution. The flow of mortgage credit grew rapidly from 1960, and the total value of loans outstanding doubled almost every five years.

TABLE 1.6
Mortgage Loans Outstanding to Certain Mortgage Suppliers[1] ($000,000)

Year	Life Insurance Companies	Chartered Banks	Loan Companies	Trust Companies	Credit Unions	Governments	Corporate Lenders	Other Companies	Pension Funds	Estates, Trusts
1960	3,412	971	698	472	390	1,995	524	97	299	534
	(36)[2]	(10)	(7)	(5)	(4)	(21)	(6)	(1)	(3)	(6)
1965	5,662	810	1,839	1,975	695	3,222	1,930	276	623	1,586
	(30)	(4)	(10)	(11)	(4)	(17)	(10)	(1)	(3)	(9)
1970	7,723	1,481	2,868	3,829	1,353	7,221	2,052	382	1,022	2,714
	(25)	(5)	(9)	(12)	(4)	(24)	(7)	(1)	(3)	(9)
1975	10,364	8,039	6,560	10,542	5,205	11,100	2,518	581	2,479	4,983
	(17)	(13)	(11)	(17)	(8)	(18)	(4)	(1)	(4)	(8)
1980	16,319	19,105	12,956	26,814	15,619	13,770	3,543	1,192	5,738	10,525
	(13)	(15)	(10)	(21)	(12)	(11)	(3)	(1)	(5)	(8)

1. This is not a complete listing of suppliers.
2. Figures within parentheses are the percentage of the row total.

SOURCE: CMHC (1982, 64).

There have been major changes in the suppliers of funds over the years; in 1960 more than half of the mortgages were held by the life insurance companies and governments, but by 1980 their share had fallen to less than 25 percent. The new major participants were the banks, trust companies, and credit unions. The chartered banks had been permitted to make NHA loans in 1954 and were dominant in that market until about 1960 when the NHA mortgage rate rose above the 6-percent ceiling on bank lending rates. From 1960 to 1967, the chartered banks withdrew almost completely from mortgage lending. In 1967, banks were permitted to make conventional mortgage loans and the 6-percent ceiling was removed; in 1969 the banks were permitted to issue 5-year debentures which could be matched with the 5-year term on mortgages; and

FIGURE 1.4
Conventional Mortgage Rate and Corporate Bond Rate

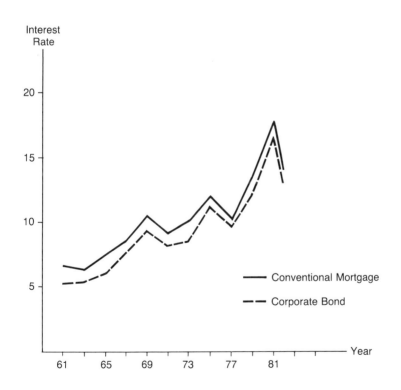

SOURCE: CMHC (various years), *Canadian Housing Statistics.*

since then, banks have been active participants in the mortgage market. Not shown in table 1.6 is the personal sector which has declined steadily in importance.

Demanders, suppliers, and governments together determine the mortgage interest rate; this rate is graphed in figure 1.4. For comparative purposes the corporate bond rate is also graphed. The mortgage rate shows considerable variability and a long-term, secular rise culminating in September 1981 when the rate on conventional mortgages hit 21.46 percent. The NHA rate has been about one-half to one percentage point below the conventional rate.

SUGGESTIONS FOR FURTHER READING

Canada Mortgage and Housing Corporation (current year) *Canadian Housing Statistics* (Ottawa: Canada Mortgage and Housing Corporation).

Gillingham, R. (1983) "Measuring the Cost of Shelter for Homeowners: Theoretical and Empirical Considerations," *Review of Economics and Statistics* 65:254–65.

Olsen, E. O. (1969) "A Competitive Theory of the Housing Market," *American Economic Review* 59:612–22.

Smith, L. B. (1974) *The Postwar Canadian Housing and Residential Mortgage Markets and the Role of Government* (Toronto: University of Toronto Press). Chapters one, two, and five.

2 | The Demand for Housing

The purpose of this chapter is to study the demand side of the housing market. As with traditional microeconomic analysis, the starting point is the theory of consumer or household choice. From there individual demand curves are derived, which can be aggregated to form the market demand curve, and then combined with a market supply curve in models of market adjustment and equilibrium. The special characteristics of the commodity housing – its heterogeneity, durability, and spatial fixity – each require modification of the standard consumer choice model. After setting out the standard model, subsequent sections present these modifications.

The demand for housing embodies three distinct choices by consumers. One is the decision to form a household and about how many members that household should have. The demand for housing services arises not from individuals but from groups of individuals sharing a dwelling unit; that is, from households. The demand for housing services is not strictly proportional to the number of people, but depends on how they group themselves into households. A second decision is whether to own or rent housing. And a third decision is how much housing to consume.[1] These are in principle simultaneous decisions, although the structure of preferences may imply they are separable. In this book, household formation is assumed to be exogenous and existing households are the decision-making agents.[2]

To a certain extent, of course, the demographic make-up of households is endogenous to the housing market. If the price of rental accommodation is relatively low, young people will be more likely to leave their parents' homes, and elderly people will be more likely to stay in their own apartments. If the price of detached houses rises, people may postpone marriage or postpone having children.

HOUSING AS A STANDARD COMMODITY

Assume that there is a homogeneous good called housing services, that the household is indifferent between owning and renting housing stock, and that the concept of location may be ignored. Assume that the household has preferences that can be represented by a utility function (with all the usual desirable properties), and that the household has exogenously established income y, all of which is spent in the current period. There are no choices to be made between work and leisure, or between consumption today and consumption tomorrow. The household maximizes utility function (equation 2.1), subject to the budget constraint (equation 2.2). From the first order conditions for a maximum can be derived the household's demand function for housing services (equation 2.3), where x_2 is housing services. Demand is a function of

$$U = U(x_1, x_2 \ldots x_n) \tag{2.1}$$

$$p_1 x_1 + p_2 x_2 + \ldots + p_n x_n = y \tag{2.2}$$

$$x_2 = f(y, p_1, p_2 \ldots p_n) \tag{2.3}$$

income, the price of housing services, and all other prices and tastes. Figure 2.1 represents the choice problem and its solution graphically. The household faces budget constraint AB and chooses point I which represents a level of consumption of a composite good and consumption of housing services that yields utility level U_2. By varying the price of housing services in figure 2.1 and again solving for the point of maximum utility, a locus of points called the price-consumption curve can be derived. The quantity of housing services at these points and associated prices can be redrawn as DD in figure 2.2, which is of course the household's ordinary demand curve for housing services. The influence of other variables on quantity demanded can be illustrated by showing how these variables shift the demand curve. First the variable is changed in figure 2.1, then a new price-consumption curve is derived and then a new demand curve is drawn. For example, an increase in income might shift the household's demand curve from DD to D'D' in figure 2.2.

The own-price elasticity of demand for housing services is the percentage change in quantity demanded of housing services with a one-percent change in the price of housing services. Graphically, this is a movement along a demand curve. The income elasticity of demand for housing is the percentage change in quantity demanded of housing services with a one-percent change in income. Graphically, this is a movement from one demand curve to another, holding p_2 constant.

As an illustrative example, consider the familiar Cobb-Douglas utility function (equation 2.4) from which may be derived the demand function for housing services (equation 2.5). It is immediately evident that

$$U = Ax_1^{\alpha} x_2^{1-\alpha} \qquad 0 < \alpha < 1 \tag{2.4}$$

FIGURE 2.1
Household Consumption Choices

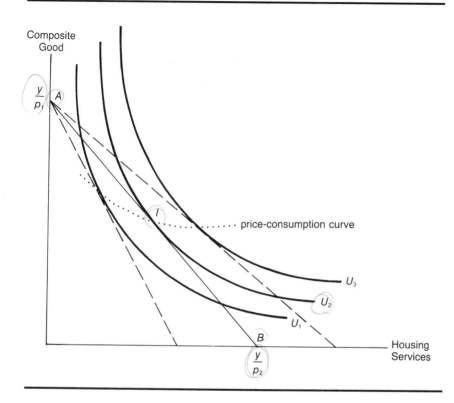

$$x_2 = \frac{(1-\alpha)y}{p_2} \qquad\qquad (2.5)$$

the Cobb-Douglas utility function implies a very restricted class of demand functions. Total expenditure on housing is a constant share of income $(1-\alpha)$. This can be stated another way: the income elasticity of demand for housing services is one. The price elasticity of demand is minus one, and the demand for housing services is independent of other prices (the cross-price elasticity is zero).

If the econometrician believed this were the true model, he would regress housing expenditure on income to obtain an estimate of $(1-\alpha)$. No estimate of the income or price elasticity of demand for housing services would emerge from his work; only an estimate of the share of income that is spent on housing. But of course no estimate is required because the underlying model assumes that these are known to be one and minus one.

FIGURE 2.2
Demand Curves for Housing Services

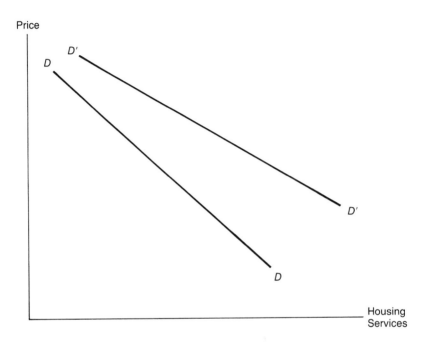

The point here is to show the relationship between the underlying theory of consumer behavior and econometric work. The theory should be used to derive a specific estimating equation. In almost all empirical work on the demand for housing, the estimating equations have not been derived from an explicit consumer choice model. The equations have been specified in a rather *ad hoc* fashion. However every equation to be estimated is implicitly generated by some model of behaviour. Most recent econometric work in the demand for housing has been devoted to exploring the implicit models behind *ad hoc* specifications, and to identifying the assumed true model, and then using it to explain why two different *ad hoc* models yield apparently conflicting results.

The earliest empirical studies of consumer demand considered the relationship between housing and income.[3] Writing over one hundred years after the first of such studies, Margaret Reid (1962) could write that "a wide range of tendencies has been observed," and in her book *Housing and Income* attempted a reconciliation. Twenty years and dozens of papers later this reconciliation is still proceeding. The literature offers a fascinating case study of both theoretical and empirical demand analysis and of the progress of economics. Unfortunately it is not possible to properly survey this literature. Many references will be provided in the text and the backnotes, and these sources provide further references. What will be offered is a stylized picture of the diversity of estimates that have been published, and the sorts of explanations that have been offered to explain them, and the consensus that seems to be emerging. The explanations that have been offered can be interpreted as pointing out how the econometric work has ignored the special characteristics of the commodity housing. It is hoped this stylized picture will convey the flavour of econometric analysis of housing demand.

Let us start by assuming that we seek to estimate the demand function of an individual household for housing services. It is possible to be interested in some aggregate demand function, but most researchers even when using aggregate data have sought to estimate the household demand function or the demand of a "representative" consumer. Many researchers have assumed that there is a constant income elasticity and a constant price elasticity, and that the true household demand function is as in equation 2.6.[4] The parameter β_1 is the income elasticity, and the parameter β_2 is the own-price elasticity. Since there is more than one other good consumed besides housing services, p_1 is an index of other

$$\log x_2 = \beta_0 + \beta_1 \log y + \beta_2 \log p_2 + \beta_3 \log p_1 \qquad (2.6)$$

prices. To avoid the problem of defining a unit of housing service, log p_2 is usually added to both sides. Equation 2.7 is estimated, regressing housing expenditure on income and other variables.

$$\log p_2 x_2 = \beta_0 + \beta_1 \log y + (1 + \beta_2) \log p_2 + \beta_3 \log p_1 \qquad (2.7)$$

Table 2.1 presents the estimates of the income elasticity of demand for housing services from representative studies: the estimates range from 0.35 to 2.05. Three main explanations have been offered to reconcile this diversity. The first relates to the income variable, the second to the price variable, and the third to aggregation bias. Not all would necessarily apply to reconciling the difference between any two studies.[5]

The incomes of households do not follow a smooth path over time but are subject to fluctuations. For example, a government subsidy program might increase the income of a worker for a short period; a factory worker might not be able to work the overtime he expected; a spouse might decide to change jobs and spend two months searching between jobs. The measured income of households can be thought of as having two components. One is referred to as permanent or normal income and the other transitory income. The terminology has been

TABLE 2.1
Estimates of the Income Elasticity of Demand for Housing

Study		Income Elasticity Estimate
Rosen (1979)	Owners	0.35
Hanushek and Quigley (1981)	Renters	0.5
Lee (1968)	Owners	0.8
	Renters	0.65
Carliner (1973)	Owners	0.6–0.7
	Renters	0.5
Maisel, Burnham, and Austin (1971)	Owners	0.46–0.9
Smith and Campbell (1978)	Owners	0.5–0.7
Polinsky and Ellwood (1979)	Owners	0.8
Winger (1968)	Owners	1.05
de Leeuw (1971)	Owners	1.1–1.5
	Renters	0.8–0.10
Reid (1962)	Owners	1.55–2.05
	Renters	0.8–1.16

adopted from Friedman (1957), although his work dealt with the aggregate consumption function rather than the household demand for individual commodities. Permanent income is a long-run concept; it is an expectation of what income will be and is basis for some consumption decisions; empirically it tends to be estimated as a weighted average of past years' incomes. Because housing is a durable good and there are high transaction costs to changing one's level of housing consumption, it is argued that households make decisions on the basis of permanent income rather than measured or actual income. Measured income is the sum of permanent and transitory income. Transitory income can be positive, negative, or zero. An estimate of β_1 using individual data involves regressing the housing expenditure of single households on their measured income. An estimate using aggregate data, for example, might involve regressing the average housing expenditure in census tracts on average measured household income. However because some households will have positive transitory income and others negative, these will tend to cancel out, and average measured income will approximate average permanent income. The elasticity of housing demand will be higher with respect to permanent income than with respect to income in any one year. This, it is argued, helps to explain the fact that individual data give lower elasticities than aggregate data (see for example Muth [1960] and Reid [1962]).

Several housing demand analyses have been based on data, either individual or averages by census tract, taken from one metropolitan area. Because the observations all came from one housing market it was assumed that the price per unit of housing service was the same throughout the market, and therefore the regressions ignored the housing price term. This had the further appeal of avoiding the problem of how to measure the price of housing services. However, this assumption ignores the spatial fixity of housing. When a household purchases housing they buy a house and a location; the price of housing services will be higher in the more accessible, central locations (see chapter four). Higher-income persons tend to live further from the city centre so that in a metropolitan area high-income households face a lower price of housing services. Studies that are based on a single metropolitan area and ignore the price term will produce estimates of the income elasticity that are biased downwards, assuming the demand for housing is price elastic (see Polinsky [1977]).

The third explanation deals with what is called "pure aggregation bias" (Smith and Campbell 1978). If the data are aggregated by an independent variable – for example the top five percent of households by income are averaged, the next five percent, and so on – and the averages are used in the regression, this regression produces unbiased estimates of the parameters of the household equation. However if the data are aggregated by the dependent variable – for example, the top five percent of households by housing expenditure are averaged, the next five percent, and so on – this regression will produce biased estimates of the parameters of the household equation. And the bias will be upward. It is argued that using census tract averages in a housing demand study is in effect aggregating by the dependent variable because census tracts are far more homogeneous in terms of housing consumption than the population as a whole. Thus, this pure aggregation bias can help to explain further why studies based on individual data have produced lower estimates of the income elasticity of demand for housing than studies using aggregate census tract data.

Research into the income elasticity of demand for housing services is by no means finished. New estimates will likely be based on models that more explicitly deal with the price of housing services taking into account the spatial fixity, expectations, and the tax treatment of housing. There does however appear to be a rough consensus emerging that the demand for housing is inelastic with respect to permanent income. Most researchers would place the elasticity in the range of 0.5 to 0.8; but there is still considerable diversity of opinion about the precise value.

There have been somewhat fewer studies that estimate the price elasticity of the demand for housing services, although one would think looking at equation 2.7 that price and income elasticities would be generated together. As noted above, in many studies using intrametropolitan data price, elasticities were not estimated because it was assumed that the price of housing was constant across all observations. Table 2.2 surveys some representative studies, and again a considerable range is indicated. The emerging rough consensus is that demand is price inelastic; and that the precise value is somewhere in the range −0.7 to −0.9.

TABLE 2.2
Estimates of the Price Elasticity of Demand for Housing

Study	Price Elasticity Estimate
Cross-Section of Cities	
de Leeuw (1971)	−0.7 to −1.5
Maisel, Burnham, and Austin (1971)	−0.81 to −1.03
Carliner (1973)	0.0 to −0.8
Intrametropolitan	
Muth (1971)	−0.7
Polinsky and Ellwood (1979)	−0.7

We cannot observe the price of housing services, only transactions which are the product of price and quantity. There are several approaches to measuring prices in these studies. One is used in connection with data that are a cross-section of cities. City-wide averages of rents or house values and incomes are gathered, and the price of housing services is measured using a city-specific index of construction costs. Implicit is the assumption that city housing markets are in equilibrium, and that price is equal to the cost of constructing a house at the margin.[6] A second approach to measuring the price of housing services arises in connection with intrametropolitan data. The assumption of constant price is rejected, and procedures are applied to generate an estimate of price for each observation within the metropolitan area. The procedure is to first estimate a production function for housing services (see chapter three), then derive the cost function, and finally generate a price index on each house using data on the inputs used in producing the housing services (land and buildings). These approaches both presume that markets are in long-run equilibrium and use input costs to generate prices. A third approach relies less on the equilibrium assumption, and when analysing the demand by owners takes the user cost, as in equation 1.5, as a measure of price. This draws out the importance of expectations, mortgage interest rates, and the income tax treatment of housing on the demand for housing.[7]

HOUSING AS A HETEROGENEOUS COMMODITY

To treat housing as a standard commodity is obviously an extreme simplification and causes problems for demand analysis. However to model it as a heterogeneous commodity is not without its own difficulties. The most general approach assumes that any dwelling unit can be represented by a vector $(z_1, \ldots z_n)$ of objectively measurable characteristics. These characteristics are such things as the number of rooms, the number of bathrooms, the age of the dwelling, the size of the lot, the adjacent land uses, and so on. There is a price in the market, $p(z)$

as in equation 2.8, associated with this vector of characteristics. In the rental market it would be the contract rent; in the ownership market it would be the sales price of the house (which is implicitly assumed to be some multiple of annual imputed rent). Households can shop around and in the market see prices associated with various bundles of characteristics. The $p(\mathbf{z})$ is the minimum price at which a given bundle may be purchased.

$$p(\mathbf{z}) = p(z_1, \dots z_n) \tag{2.8}$$

Rosen (1974) showed how to introduce this **n**-characteristic commodity into the theory of consumer choice; the following is based on that paper. It is assumed that consumers purchase or rent one dwelling unit, spending the remainder of their income on a composite good x_1. The characteristics of housing yield utility, so that consumers maximize the utility function (equation 2.9) subject to the budget constraint (equation 2.10).

$$U = U(x_1, z_1, \dots z_n) \tag{2.9}$$

$$y = p_1 x_1 + p(\mathbf{z}) \tag{2.10}$$

The solution to this problem can be extremely complex because $p(\mathbf{z})$ may be non-linear; however the nature of the consumer's maximum can be shown graphically. A bid function can be defined (equation 2.11), which indicates how much the household is willing to pay for

$$\theta(z_1, \dots z_n \mid U, y) \tag{2.11}$$

the bundle of characteristics $(z_1, \dots z_n)$, given a utility level and an income level. Part of this bid function is illustrated graphically in figure 2.3. It shows how much the household would be willing to pay for different levels of characteristic z_1, holding the level of all other characteristics constant and at a given utility level and income. A family of such indifference curves would exist for various utility levels and income levels. Under plausible assumptions, the bid function has the concave shape illustrated. The slope of the function is the household's marginal rate of substitution between characteristic z_1 and other things. Part of the market $p(\mathbf{z})$ function can also be graphed in figure 2.3. It shows the cost of various quantities of z_1, given a level of all other characteristics. The slope of this price curve is the marginal rate at which the household can substitute z_1 and other things in the market. At the utility maximum the bid curve will be tangent to the price curve. The household's valuation of a marginal unit will just equal its cost. Consumers with different tastes or incomes would be tangent at different points.[8]

FIGURE 2.3
Household Utility Maximum
Characteristic z_1

To reiterate, the consumer values housing characteristics, but must buy them in bundles (dwelling units). The consumer is a price taker in the market; the market reveals a $p(\mathbf{z})$ function that relates prices and bundles of characteristics. The $p(\mathbf{z})$ function is a market equilibrium function and so depends on both demand and supply side factors. There is no a priori reason to assume it is linear.

In principle, demand functions for characteristics can be estimated. The data on housing characteristics which have been used in the various studies so far are too diverse to permit comparison of estimated income and price elasticities of demand for characteristics, or subbundles of characteristics. Nevertheless, studies do show that households substitute characteristics for one another in response to price changes; which is as the theory would predict. They also suggest substantial differences in the income elasticity of demand for various components of the housing bundle.[9] A more detailed discussion of how to estimate the demand for characteristics is presented in chapter four. There, it is preceded by an interpretation of the market equilibrium p(z) function which is needed before further demand analysis can be discussed.

TENURE CHOICE

An important part of the household's demand for housing is the decision about whether to acquire housing services through rental or through ownership. The standard model of consumer choice will evidently have to be modified to provide a theory of tenure choice. The choice is discrete – to own or not to own – rather than continuous as in standard analysis. Durability will have to be introduced and the assumptions relaxed of perfect markets and no government, because the question of ownership versus rental only arises in such cases. And finally, there is a fundamental intertemporal aspect to the choice of tenure, therefore a model of more than one period is required.

A formal model with the required modifications is beyond the scope of this book, but it can be discussed at an intuitive level. The discrete nature of tenure choice can be analysed by modelling the household as solving several maximization problems rather than just one. The household maximizes utility as a renter, choosing the quantity of housing services and other goods to consume, facing the rental price of housing and other prices. Then the household maximizes utility as an owner, choosing the amount of housing services and other goods to consume, facing the user cost of housing and other prices. The household chooses the tenure (and consumption bundle) that yields the highest utility – the best of the maximums.

The model must be extended beyond one period because of the high transactions costs of changing houses, and because a household as owner of housing stock will consider the value of the housing stock in future periods when making a tenure and consumption choice. Households can be thought of as maximizing not a one-period utility function but rather a utility function defined over several periods. Today's consumption, tomorrow's consumption, and so on all yield utility. An essential part of the household's problem is to decide between consumption today and consumption tomorrow; the household's tastes include their rate of time preference. Today's consumption choices are the outcome of intertemporal utility maximization; that is, households in each time period formulate consumption plans to maximize lifetime utility subject to a lifetime budget constraint. The budget constraint is established not simply by current prices and income but also future prices and future incomes as well.[10] This intertemporal utility maximization framework is sometimes called life-cycle analysis. In principle, consumers consider all possible patterns of consumption and tenure over time and choose the intertemporal plan that maximizes the intertemporal utility function. Current choices are the first period of the lifetime plan.

Fundamental results[11] of life-cycle models are that the timing of income affects consumption only insofar as it affects the discounted value of lifetime income, and that if the rate of time preference is less than the market rate of interest then consumption of housing will increase over time, assuming there is no change in relative prices, and housing has a unitary income elasticity of demand. The latter result has an important implication for the interpretation of observed housing expenditure to income ratios. The normal pattern of real income over the life-cycle is an inverted saucer shape – income rises as the worker gets older and more experienced, and then falls at the end of the period in the labour force and through the retirement years. The optimal consumption pattern may be continually increasing housing consumption with the result that the housing expenditure to income ratio will be relatively high for the young, relatively low for the middle-aged, and relatively high again in old age. These differences would occur among households of different age although they all had the same lifetime income streams.

Comparative static analysis can be done in the usual way in life-cycle models except that there will be both intraperiod and interperiod effects. The income effect of an increase in the current price of housing services depresses both current and future consumption. The substitution effects cause a substitution in the first period from housing to the composite good, and a substitution away from current consumption to future consumption. The demand for housing services in the current period falls, but the effect on future periods is ambiguous. This analysis makes the usual *ceteris paribus* assumption; that is, the current price changes and all other things remain the same. However, a change in the current price may affect what one expects housing prices to be in the future; or what income will be in the future. A model incorporating an expectations process could produce different results.[12]

Tenure choice is introduced into life-cycle models by recognizing that in each period the household pays the rental price of housing services if it chooses to rent housing and user cost if it chooses to own housing stock. The optimal consumption plan under all possible tenure patterns is computed and then the package of consumption and tenure that yields the greatest utility over the life-cycle is selected. However, in equilibrium, the rental price and user cost are equal, which implies that tenure choice is not significant. Tenure choice becomes important either in disequilibrium or when the assumptions of no taxes, or perfect capital markets, or no transactions costs are removed.

Modelling consumer choice in an intertemporal framework, and removing these assumptions is extremely complicated, often requiring dynamic programming. However insight can be gained using a traditional graphical presentation of a one-period model, retaining some essential aspects of the more complex problem (this discussion is based on Fallis [1983a]).

The household maximizes the utility function (equation 2.12). The

$$U = U(x_1, x_2) \tag{2.12}$$

household has earned income y in the current period and savings S accumulated from past periods. The household cannot increase or decrease savings over the period. Savings may be invested in owner-occupied housing or in a financial asset yielding return r per period. The earnings from savings are consumed in the period. These assumptions permit the role of savings and alternative investments to be considered without the complexity of an intertemporal model. There are no capital gains, no transactions costs and, initially, no income taxes.

If the household were to rent housing services, it would face the budget constraint (equation 2.13). If the household were to purchase

$$p_1 x_1 + p_2 x_2 = y + Sr \tag{2.13}$$

housing stock, it would face constraints (equations 2.14), where E is the down payment on the house, M is the mortgage principal, m is the mortgage rate of interest, and c is the annual rate of maintenance, insurance, property taxation, and depreciation. Assuming that the mortgage rate of interest is equal to the rate of interest on alternative invest-

$$p_1 x_1 + c P_2 x_2 + Mm = y + (S - E)r$$
$$P_2 X_2 = M + E \tag{2.14}$$
$$E \leqslant S$$

ments, the owner is indifferent between using savings to reduce the mortgage (and so foregoing investment income) and using savings to earn income (and make mortgage payments).

In equilibrium the rental cost of a unit of housing service is the same as the user cost as in equation 2.15. Using this relationship, the indifference curves and budget lines as owner and as renter could be

$$p_2 = P_2 (m + c) \tag{2.15}$$

drawn on the same set of axes. The budget lines would be coincident

– the household is indifferent between owning and renting. This model, despite offering no explanation of tenure choice, is a benchmark. The assumptions can now be varied to show their effect on tenure choice.

Consider as an example, the introduction of income taxes. In Canada, the income tax law contains several provisions for housing, especially for homeowners. An owner of an asset receives an annual flow of benefits. If it is a financial asset the flow of benefits is interest payments or dividends. These flows are subject to income tax (the first $1,000 of interest earnings and dividends from Canadian corporations are exempt). If it is a real asset the flow of benefits is the value of the services realised in using the asset. For example, the flow from owning housing stock is housing services. If the owner of the asset rents it to someone else (who enjoys the service flow), the return to the owner becomes a financial flow. If the owner of the asset uses it himself and enjoys the service flow himself, this flow is called imputed income. In principle, a neutral tax system would tax both cash income and imputed income. However in Canada, cash income is taxed and imputed income is exempt. If imputed income were to be taxed, deduction of expenses incurred for the purpose of earning this income would be permitted. Homeowners would be able to deduct mortgage interest paid, depreciation, property taxes, maintenance expenditures, and insurance premiums – they would be treated analogously to landlords. The net imputed income that would be added to taxable income is roughly approximated by the homeowner's equity times the rate of interest.

It will be assumed that the household faces a constant average and marginal tax rate of t, and that earned income and cash income from savings are taxed, but net imputed income is exempt. In order that only one assumption be varied at a time, it will be assumed that landlords do not face taxation. The equilibrium condition (equation 2.15) continues to hold.

The two budget lines may again be derived and placed on the same set of axes. The renter's budget constraint is as before, except expenditures come from after-tax income. The price for an owner is $P[r(1 - t) + c]$ if savings are used to purchase housing and $P(m + c)$ if a mortgage is used. The price is lower using savings (assume $m = r$) because the foregone cash income would be taxed. The budget line has the kinked shape ABD as in figure 2.4. The location of the kink depends on the amount of savings the household has accumulated from past periods. If a household has any savings, it will choose to own housing. The exemption for imputed income is an example of the more general issue of how the rates of return on alternative investments influence tenure choice.[13]

This simple, one-period graphical model conveys some idea of why some households choose to rent housing and others choose to own. But there are other reasons besides non-neutral income taxes. Savings and

FIGURE 2.4
Household Choices as Owner and Renter Imputed
Income Exemption

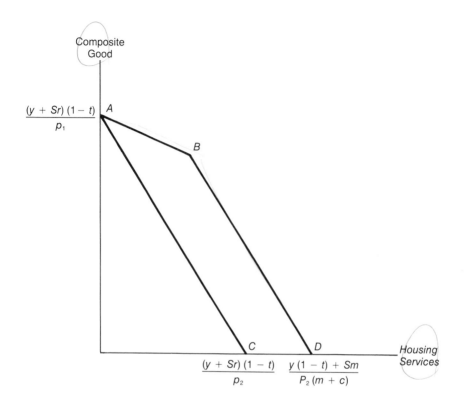

SOURCE: Based on Fallis (1983a).

income limit the size of mortgage that can be obtained. Transactions costs are important: homeowners face higher transactions costs of selling and moving than renters. Therefore, households that will move frequently, for example the young, will tend to be renters. Elderly homeowners may remain in their homes because of the very high dislocation costs of shifting to a rented residence. The concept of self-production also plays a part. If you own a house, you have chosen to produce housing services yourself rather than purchase market-produced housing services (that is, rent housing). People differ in their abilities to do maintenance, repairs, and grounds keeping, or differ in their abilities to subcontract these activities. For some people doing such things may even be a consumption good. People also differ in the opportunity cost of time that must be devoted to such things. So people will differ in the efficiency of self-production of housing services, and those who are efficient producers will own. Investment issues are also an important part of an explanation of tenure choices. To own housing is to place some of your savings in the asset housing stock as opposed to other assets such as government bonds or stocks or your own business. These different investments have different characteristics – they differ in rate of return, in riskiness, and in liquidity. Ownership of housing is in part a portfolio allocation decision, and so a household's attitude to risk or need for liquidity will influence its tenure choice. But housing as an investment has a special characteristic that it shares with few others – the annual income from it is not cash but a flow of housing services. Housing ownership is therefore a joint consumption and investment decision – housing stock appears in both the utility function and the budget constraint. Finally, tenure choice is in part explained by the desired pattern of consumption over the life-cycle. In the absence of any capital market constraints, life-cycle models of the sort discussed above may be solved to yield the optimal path of consumption and saving over time. Now suppose that for some reason, for example the income tax law, it is cheaper to acquire housing as an owner than as a renter, but because of mortgage market constraints one must save a down payment and borrow using the standard level payment mortgage. Thereore in order to become a homeowner one must save first (for a down payment) and then agree to a certain pattern of further saving over time (repaying the mortgage). Some households may find lifetime utility higher as a renter than as an owner having to distort their savings pattern, even though housing services are cheaper for owners. This explanation may seem rather arcane but it is perhaps more important than is first evident. One of the great attractions of homeownership for many households in the past has been that under the standard level payment mortgage a savings pattern was set up that matched their optimal savings path. In the early years of the mortgage, payments go mainly to interest and savings are relatively low. In the last years of the mortgage when the head of the household is about fifty years old, mortgage payments imply a high savings rate. Part of the disruption caused by inflation in recent years is that it has altered the real savings pattern of a standard level payment mortgage (see chapter five).[14]

While our theoretical understanding of the tenure choice decision has developed in recent years, there has been relatively little testing of the predictions of the models or of measurement of the parameters of the models. The broad stylized facts – that the incidence of homeownership rises with the age of the head of the household until late middle age and then declines, and that the incidence of homeownership rises with income – are consistent with the theory. And what empirical work that has been done does support the idea that the relative price of housing services under different tenures does affect choice, that income taxes are especially important in determining relative prices, and that portfolio considerations influence tenure choice.[15]

HOUSING IN A SPATIAL CONTEXT

The standard model of consumer demand treated housing aspatially. The idea of where the house was located was not part of the model. Now let us consider a spatial housing market – the housing market of a city. The term "city" includes any urban area, whether large or small. At an exogenously given point at the centre of the city, all employment is located. Housing is a homogeneous commodity and is located on the land around the central point. Assume that transportation costs money and takes time, that transportation is equally easy in all directions around the central point, and that both money and time costs are directly proportional to distance travelled. Households live in the housing around the central point and commute from their homes to work in the central business district and back again. What does the consumer's choice problem look like in this spatial model, and how can the utility maximum be characterized?

It will be assumed as before that households maximize utility by choosing how much housing and a composite good to consume; and now households must also choose a location. Because transportation is equally easy in all directions, and because the only spatial issue that matters to a household is the journey to work, location may be expressed simply as distance from the centre of the city. The household is indifferent between locations on a circle centred on the central business district. The household's choice problem may be set out as below. The household maximizes the utility function (equation 2.16) subject to the budget constraint (equation 2.17). $x_1(u)$ and $x_2(u)$ are the quantities of com-

$$U = U [x_1(u), x_2(u)] \tag{2.16}$$

$$p_1 x_1(u) + p_2(u)x_2(u) + tu = wT \tag{2.17}$$

posite good and housing services consumed by the household if it lives u units of distance from the centre of the city. The price of the composite good is the same everywhere, but the price of housing services $p_2(u)$ varies with location. The round-trip commuting cost per unit of distance is t. This cost of travel is both a money cost and a time cost; in the formulation above, time has been implicitly valued at the wage rate: that is, the consumer would be willing to pay an amount equal to his hourly wage rate in order to reduce his commuting time by one hour. Most studies of how consumers value time indicate that time cost is the largest component of total travel cost, and that people are willing to pay more to reduce time spent walking and waiting than to reduce time spent travelling in a vehicle.[16] In the budget constraint, T is the total time available to the household and w is the wage rate.

For a utility maximum (and an equilibrium), the household must not be able to increase its utility by changing the quantities of the composite good or housing services consumed, or by changing its location. Given some $p_2(u)$ function, the household could choose its preferred consumption and location package. However to facilitate subsequent combining of the supply side with the demand side in a spatial model of a housing market equilibrium, it is interesting to ask what $p_2(u)$ function would leave a household indifferent between living at any distance from the employment centre? The answer can be shown graphically as in figures 2.5 and 2.6. Consider any arbitrary utility level U^* that the household might attain, and then select some location u'. At this location, total commuting costs are known and so one can calculate how much composite good the household could buy if it were to spend all of its post-commuting income on the composite good. This is one point on the household's budget constraint at u' and is shown as A on the vertical axis in figure 2.5. Given A and utility level U^*, one can solve for the price of housing at u' that is consistent with utility maximizing behaviour. Graphically, a straight line through A is rotated until it is tangent to indifference curve U^*. The intersection of the tangent line with the horizontal axis at B establishes how much housing the household could consume if it were to spend all its post-commuting income on housing; and from this amount may be calculated a price of housing services at u'. Thus, given a utility level and a location, a price of housing services is calculated that is consistent with a utility maximum. This procedure can be repeated for another location. In figure 2.5, the budget line CD for location u'' has been established where u'' is further from the centre of the city than u' (u''>u'). Repeating this for all u, the calculated price of housing services at each location has been graphed in figure 2.6, which shows the $p_2(u)$ function that implies utility-maximizing households are indifferent as to location. Whatever u the household selects, it will achieve utility level U^*.

The $p_2(u)$ function in figure 2.6 is analogous to the bid function in equation 2.11. Here the household is buying simultanously housing and location, and the bid function shows how much the household is willing to pay per unit of housing services at each location given U^*. The analogy is not surprising for the work on hedonic pricing built upon spatial models.

The nature of the spatial equilibrium can be given further economic content. For a small move away from the city centre, the household

FIGURE 2.5
Consumer Choice with Commuting

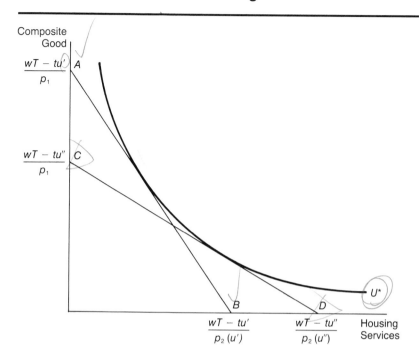

faces a decrease in the price of housing services and an increase in commuting cost while remaining at the same level of utility. The price decrease has both an income and a substitution effect; the income effect of the change in housing prices is just offset by the change in commuting cost. Algebraically, this may be stated as in equation 2.18. Recalling how

$$\frac{dp_2(u)}{du} x_2(u) = -t \tag{2.18}$$

an income and substitution effect can be illustrated graphically, this interpretation is evident in figure 2.5. The change in housing consumption as a result of a move is the pure substitution effect of the change in the price of housing services.

Equation 2.18 is a central relationship in all spatial housing models. It establishes how the price of housing services must *vary* over space in order for consumers to be in equilibrium. However, this is not a pure demand side model for the equation does not establish *the* price of housing services.[17] In order to establish the price of housing services, a supply side must be added.

FIGURE 2.6
Price of Housing Function

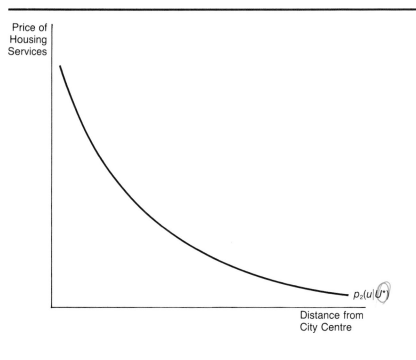

In a spatial model, consumers are choosing both housing services and location; and both the price of housing services and commuting costs vary with location. It has already been discussed that ignoring the spatial variation in house prices can cause problems in econometric work estimating the income elasticity of housing demand. A significant implication of spatial models is that identical, equally well-off households can have different consumption patterns. As the household moves closer to the centre of the city, it faces higher housing prices and lower commuting costs and consumes relatively fewer housing services; as the household moves farther from the city centre it faces lower housing prices, higher commuting costs, and consumes relatively more housing services.[18]

Obviously, the model is a highly abstract conception of a spatial housing market. Travel is not equally easy in all directions nor are costs directly proportional to distance travelled. There is not one workplace in the centre of a city but many spread across the city. Households not only make trips to work but also to shops, restaurants, schools, the homes of friends, and to recreation sites outside the city. The model is implicitly a long-run equilibrium model taking no account of the spatial configuration of already-built housing stock. Considerable progress has been made in introducing some of these complexities into spatial models, but they remain far from realistic. However the unreality only argues against their cavalier use in applied or policy work; but it should not hide their fundamental contribution to analysing the equilibrium relationship between housing consumption, housing prices, and location.[19]

Another variant of spatial housing analysis is associated with Tiebout (1956). Tiebout's work has both a normative orientation exploring the desired spatial arrangement of people and local governments in a metropolitan area and a positive orientation explaining how people arrange themselves in a metropolitan area. The positive side is of concern here (the normative side is taken up in chapter eight). Suppose a large metropolitan area has many separate local governments, and that households have already decided to live in the area and now are choosing which jurisdiction in which to live. The purchase of a house or renting of an apartment is also the choice of a local government with its tax and local public expenditure package. Taxes for local government are raised through the residential property tax which in theory is a tax in proportion to the market value of property (although in practice rates differ by property). If all houses in a community are of the same value, each household will pay the same taxes and obtain the same level of local public services. Tiebout suggested that people differ in their demand for local public services, and that people will choose to live in a jurisdiction with a tax-expenditure package that suited them. Thus people with similar demands for local public expenditure will live in the same jurisdiction. Since income is an important determinant of demand for local public services, this model predicts that people with similar incomes will live in the same jurisdiction. Obviously the explanatory power of this approach requires that there be many jurisdictions in the metropolitan area offering differing tax-expenditure packages. In many American metropolitan areas this is the case. It is less so in Canada; several metropolitan areas have only one government, and many others have local governments but also an area-wide second level of government that provides many important local public services. Nevertheless it is clear that households take account of public services and tax levels when choosing a house – for example houses near a good school command a premium – and there is evidence from the United States of Tiebout-type behaviour.[20]

SUGGESTIONS FOR FURTHER READING

Mills, E. S. (1972b) *Urban Economics* (Glenview, Illinois: Scott, Foresman). Chapter four.

Polinsky, A. M., and D. T. Ellwood (1979) "An Empirical Reconciliation of Micro and Grouped Estimates of the Demand for Housing,"

The Review of Economics and Statistics 61:199–205.

Quigley, J. (1979) "What Have We Learned About Urban Housing Markets?" in P. Mieszkowski and M. Straszheim, eds., *Current Issues in Urban Economics* (Baltimore: Johns Hopkins Press).

Rosen, S. (1974) "Hedonic Prices and Implicit Markets: Product Differentiation in Pure Competition," *Journal of Political Economy* 82:34–55.

3 | The Supply of Housing

The purpose of this chapter is to provide an economic analysis of the supply side of the housing market. As in the previous chapter we begin from the decision making of an individual economic agent. There the agent was the household, here there are two sorts of agents: those that produce housing services using housing stock and those that build housing stock. Again the choices of individual agents are analysed to yield supply functions, which can be aggregated to form a market supply function. In chapter four, the demand and supply functions are brought together in market models. Chapters two, three, and four have a parallel organization, first examining housing as a standard commodity, then modifying the analysis to deal with the heterogeneity, durability, and spatial fixity of housing.

Housing services are produced using housing stock (which is the building and the land), labour, and other inputs such as electricity and heating fuel. The producers of housing services are an extremely diverse group ranging from owner-occupiers who produce services using stock that they rent from themselves, to small landlords who live on the ground floor of a building and rent out the top floor, to companies owning a large number of rental buildings and whose shares are publicly traded on the stock exchange. These producers will obviously differ widely in their skills at combining inputs to produce services. It is remarkable that over half of the housing services consumed in our economy are produced by agents whose primary source of income is not the production of housing services. Homeowners become producers as part of an intertemporal consumption-savings decision; while landlords become producers because the rate of return is at least as high as alternative investments or uses of their time.

The producers of stock are an equally diverse group. Most attention is usually focused on the building industry. However it should also be remembered that owners of existing stock also make production decisions when they decide about repairs, maintenance, and renovation. Obviously, a building with no maintenance will deteriorate quite rapidly and so yield a diminishing flow of services over time. Alternatively a structure can yield an undiminished or even increasing flow of services over time with appropriate maintenance and renovation. The owners of housing stock (who are therefore producers of housing services) make decisions about the maintenance and therefore the production of stock. Homeowners and landlords are producers just as are the large building firms. In 1982 in Canada, the value of new dwelling units produced (excluding land cost) was $7,269 million; the value of major residential improvements was $1,955 million; and the value of repairs and maintenance was $3,451 million.[1] If these are taken as the sources of new housing stock each year, then 57 percent came from the construction of new dwellings and 43 percent from reinvestment in existing dwellings. Like any production, the level of output will depend upon the price of stock, the technology of production, and the prices of inputs.

Relatively little is known about the production of housing stock through the maintenance and renovation by homeowners and landlords, but a stylized picture can be provided. Some of the maintenance is done by homeowners or landlords themselves, other is contracted to small firms of plumbers, roofers, or painters; and major renovations are organized by a contractor who subcontracts with these small firms. Only rarely is all the labour employed within one renovation firm. The exemption of imputed income under the income tax law provides an incentive for homeowners to do their own maintenance and renovation, because the returns to their labour (the increased flow of housing services) is tax-free. The production function will be very difficult to discern, because the existing housing stock is so heterogeneous. Rational decision making and perfect capital markets would imply that owners would invest in maintenance until the last dollar spent just increased the value of the building by one dollar, or produced a service flow that the owner valued at one dollar.

Much more is known about the industry constructing new housing. The main inputs into the production process are land, building materials, and labour. For single-family houses, land costs, including improvements to the land, are roughly 29 percent of total costs, while materials are 27 percent.[2] The share of land has risen over the last ten years in response to changes in the relative prices of the inputs. The inputs into mutiple-unit housing are the same, but the share of land in total cost is lower because mutiple-unit housing is built using more materials per unit of land. There is considerable substitutability between land and materials in the production of housing stock, but rather less between labour and materials. Throughout the postwar period, construction labour costs have risen faster than materials costs, thus exerting pressure to substitute capital for labour. To some extent this has been achieved, but the growth of output per manhour has been much slower than in most other sectors of the economy. At one time it was felt that industrialized building techniques would permit substantial improvements in productivity. Rather than assembling all the materials on the site using high-cost, skilled labour, industrialized building techniques produce many components in a factory – such as pre-hung doors, staircases, and even entire rooms – where scale economies can be exploited. These large components are then assembled on site. It was hoped both factory and assembly would require less skilled labour. But many of the hoped-for savings failed to materialize. Consumers valued heterogeneity in housing. The factory-built components had higher transport costs than the costs of the parts shipped separately. The factory parts had to be machined to a fine tolerance which required skilled labour, and the assembly workers had to be able to make on-site marginal adjustments which also implied skilled labour. There is little factory building of entire rooms now, but almost all construction uses pre-hung doors and windows.

The process of producing housing stock is lengthy, involving a complex phasing of inputs and extensive interaction with government ministries and agencies. Consider the process of constructing a small subdivision. First the builder-developer must acquire the land. This often means buying from several different owners to assemble a parcel large enough for the subdivision. These purchases sometimes occur over a long time and must be disguised in order to prevent the last seller from extracting all the expected profit from the subdivision. Some firms assemble land for sale to builders, but the land market is not like a usual input market where a producer can come and acquire what it wishes. Most firms constructing a large number of dwelling units have integrated back into the land market to acquire new land and holds it as inventory. After the land has been assembled, the subdivision must be planned. The lots and streets must be surveyed, the specifications of the houses, roads, sidewalks, sewers, and so on drawn up, and the locations of houses on the lots, of schools and parks designated. These plans must be approved by the local government and in some cases the regional and provincial governments. There are no legal performance standards governing residential developments, and the approval process involves intensive interaction and negotiation between builder-developer and local governments. Scores of agencies or departments must approve or have the right to comment on a plan; and often public hearings must be held on the plans, and people have the right to appeal the decision of local government. The process of securing government approval usually takes from twelve to eighteen months and in many instances has taken several years.[3] As in the renovation sector, usually a contractor organizes production and employs other firms – bricklayers, plumbers, roofers, and so on – at different times in the process.

The purchasers of housing stock are the producers of housing services – owner-occupiers, landlords, or perhaps a division of the building company which will rent the new apartments. These purchases usually are financed with a mortgage loan with loan-to-value ratios as high as 0.8 and 0.9. Rather than having the builder arrange interim financing until the building is sold and the purchaser arrange his own mortgage loan, the usual procedure is for the builder to arrange a mortgage loan that the purchaser assumes. Advances are made on the mortgage loan as construction progresses. The supply of new housing stock is extremely sensitive to mortgage interest rates as a result, and is subject to great variations across the business cycle.

Traditionally, entry into the industry was relatively free. There were a large number of quite small firms suggesting there were few economies of scale. The industry has become more concentrated in recent years. In part, this was due to scale economies, especially at the level of securing approval and managing a project, and in part due to the larger and larger amounts of capital needed to enter the industry, because local governments imposed lot levies and required more and more services to be financed and installed by the developer.[4]

The production of new housing stock or the maintenance and renovation of existing stock is a complex process, but certainly no more complex than that to produce a car, airplane, or a movie. The task is to apply economic theory to explain the process; and as always, the theory abstracts from the complexity of reality, isolating the important elements to aid comprehension.

As a starting point let us set out a general framework while still assuming that there exists a homogeneous good called housing services. The production function for housing services is shown in equation 3.1, where q_s is the output of housing services, q_{st} is the quantity of housing stock, N is the quantity of labour, and $\mathbf{I}$ is a vector of other inputs such

$$q_s = f(q_{st}, N, \mathbf{I}) \tag{3.1}$$

as energy. Households demand housing services. The suppliers of housing services use housing stock as an input and so generate a derived demand for housing stock. The production function for new housing stock is shown in equation 3.2, where L is the quantity of land and M the quantity of materials. The production function for housing stock

$$q_{st}^n = g(L, N, M) \tag{3.2}$$

by augmenting an existing building is shown in equation 3.3, where q_{st}^* and L^* are the quantity of housing stock of given age and maintenance

$$q_{st}^e = h(N, M | q_{st}^*, L^*) \tag{3.3}$$

history, and land in the existing dwelling.

HOUSING AS A STANDARD COMMODITY: LONG-RUN SUPPLY

In long-run analysis, this framework is usually simplified. It is often assumed that housing stock is the only input in the production of housing services, and that one unit of housing stock produces one unit of housing service per time period. Further it assumed that new housing stock is produced using land and a composite input, non-land. In the long run, production using existing dwellings is irrelevant. The production function for housing services becomes that shown in equation 3.4, where K is the quantity of composite input, non-land. The dis-

$$q_s = f(L, K) \tag{3.4}$$

tinction between producing housing stock and housing services disappears. The distinction between producing new stock and augmenting old stock disappears. Again, housing may be analysed like the standard commodity of microeconomics.

The production function shown in equation 3.4 is that of a single firm. Assuming the technology has the usual properties, it may be represented as a series of convex to the origin isoquants as in figure 3.1. A profit-maximizing firm (or household) will produce each output level at minimum cost. For any output level the minimum cost will be where an isocost line is tangent to the isoquant. The output level and cost associated with the isocost line can be graphed on another set of axes as the total cost curve. If the production function exhibits constant returns to scale, the total cost curve will be a straight line through the origin. From a total cost curve such as that in figure 3.1, which exhibits first increasing, then constant, then decreasing returns to scale, can be derived the average and marginal cost curves of figure 3.2. If the firm is a price taker in the housing services market, the firm's supply curve is the marginal cost curve coincident with and above the average total cost curve.

The market supply curve of housing services is the horizontal addition of the individual supply curves subject to a number of important caveats. Since we are interested in the long-run supply curve we must consider the responses of all potential firms. If the price of housing services were p_2, the firm in figure 3.2 would supply an indeterminate amount but with a maximum q_3; however so could any number of potential firms, and therefore, assuming all of the further caveats below, the long-run supply curve is perfectly elastic. It is a horizontal line of height equal to the minimum point on the average total cost curve of the single firm. In much housing analysis the long-run supply curve has been assumed to be perfectly elastic. However for this to be the case, two further caveats must hold. All potential firms must be equally efficient; if firms differ in efficiency, the supply curve slopes upward,

FIGURE 3.1
The Production Technology and the Total Cost Curve

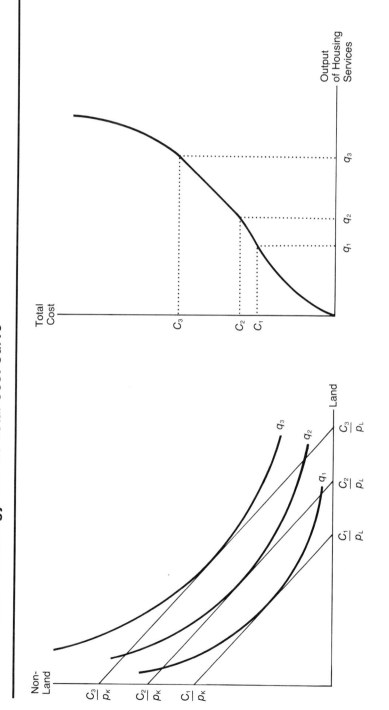

FIGURE 3.2
Average and Marginal Cost Curves

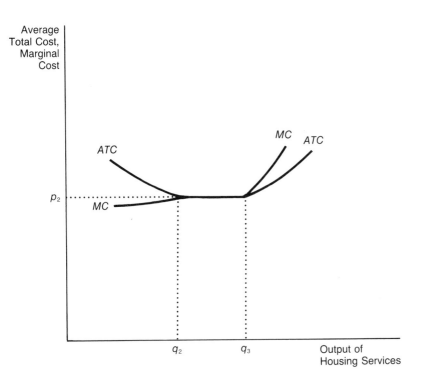

becoming more inelastic the greater the differences in efficiency. Furthermore the inputs must be perfectly elastically supplied not only to a single firm but also to the entire industry; if inputs rise in price as the industry expands, then the supply curve slopes upward. Suppose as the industry expands the price of land rises and the price of non-land also rises, but relatively less than the price of land. The elasticity of the supply curve depends on how much the relative price of land rises, and also on how easily non-land may be substituted for land. Firms will try to substitute away from land because it has become relatively more expensive. This ease of substitution is measured by the curvature of the isoquant. Flat isoquants indicate the inputs are easily substituted; a small change in relative input prices implies a large change in the input ratio, holding output constant. Sharply curved isoquants indicate difficulty in substitution; a small change in relative input prices implies a small change in the input ratio. This is just what the elasticity of substitution σ measures: as inputs are more easily substituted, the higher is the elasticity of substitution.

The industry supply curve will be less elastic, the less elastic are the supply curves of inputs, the smaller the elasticity of substitution and the smaller the share in total cost of payments to the more elastically supplied factor. Muth (1964) derived the expression 3.5 for the price elasticity of the supply curve assuming firms have a constant returns to scale production function, and all firms are equally efficient. The share of land and non-land are S_L and S_K, and the price elasticities of

$$\eta_p = \frac{\sigma(S_K e_K + S_L e_L) + e_K e_L}{\sigma + S_L e_K + S_K e_L} \tag{3.5}$$

their supply curves are e_L and e_K.

It is usually assumed that to any given housing market, non-land is perfectly elastically supplied, in which case it can be shown the price elasticity of the housing services supply curve becomes as shown in equation 3.6. In thinking further about this expression we are forced

$$\eta_p = \frac{S_K \sigma + e_L}{S_L} \tag{3.6}$$

to confront the spatial nature of a housing and land market. An increase in the supply of land to a housing market is not drawn from other uses throughout the economy as is the case for non-land, but rather is drawn away from other uses in the immediate area. The land is drawn away from non-residential uses within a city and away from agricultural uses at the periphery of the city. The supply of land will not be perfectly elastic, and may even be inelastic.

No direct estimates of this long-run price elasticity of the supply of housing services have been made, but a sense of its magnitude can be gained by substituting values into the expression 3.6. At the height of the housing boom in the mid-seventies in Canada, land was almost 30 percent of the cost of new NHA financed homes, but a long-run average is nearer 20 percent (Land Task Force, 1978)[5]. There is some range of estimates on the elasticity of substitution (see page 68), but a consensus estimate would put it slightly below 1; here it will be taken to be 0.8. If the elasticity of the supply of land is unity, the price elasticity of the supply of housing services would be 8.2. The long-run supply curve is likely very elastic.

THE INVESTMENT DECISION

It is useful to complement the framework set out above with a more intensive look at the decision by a single firm to build new housing stock. The principles developed could also be used to analyse the decision to add new stock to an existing dwelling. Whereas the previous framework emphasized the production function and choice of output level in a single period, here the choice from among several possible investments and the intertemporal nature of the problem are emphasized. The introduction of intertemporal choice leads naturally to consideration of uncertain outcomes.[6]

The firm is assumed to have a limited number of real investment opportunities, given the existing technology and the actions of other agents in the economy. For example, it might have the possibility of building a subdivision of large detached homes, or a subdivision of row houses, or of apartments, or some mixture of these housing types. At the outset let us assume that the initial costs, subsequent annual revenues, and annual costs associated with each investment opportunity are known to the firm. The start-up costs and subsequent net revenues define an essential characteristic of an investment: funds are not used for consumption today but are used to generate revenues for consumption in the future. The pattern of consumption postponed in return for consumption tomorrow will differ across investments. In order for the firm to decide which investments it should undertake, it must know its rate of time preference: how much consumption tomorrow will just compensate it for giving up a unit of consumption today. Finally, there exists a capital market, which for the moment will be assumed to be perfect, in which the firm can borrow or lend all it wishes at the market rate of interest. This presents another opportunity cost for funds, because funds can be lent in return for interest payments. As well, the capital market offers the possibility of rearranging through time the consumption implied by a given real investment. There are thus three basic ideas when analysing the investment decision – investment opportunities, time preference, and capital market.[7]

The firm's optimum is reached in two stages. The first selects what real investment to undertake: investment should be undertaken up to the point where the rate of return is equal to the market rate of interest. Or alternatively, all investments should be undertaken that have a positive present value; the present value of a project is the initial cost I_0 (a negative amount), plus the discounted value of all future revenues R_i (positive), and expenses E_i (negative). The general formula is 3.7. One can think of the sum to infinity, or think of the sum to a terminal date and add the disposal value of the investment to the present value calculation. This rule would be followed by firms that sought to maximize their equity value, for the equity value of a firm would increase by the present value of an investment project.[8]

$$PV = -I_0 + \frac{R_1 - E_1}{(1 + r_1)} + \frac{R_2 - E_2}{(1 + r_1)(1 + r_2)}$$
$$+ \frac{R_3 - E_3}{(1 + r_1)(1 + r_2)(1 + r_3)} + \dots \qquad (3.7)$$

The second stage determines the financing of this investment: consumption should be readjusted so that the rate of time preference is equal to the market rate of interest. At the optimum, three rates are equal – the rate of return on investment, the market rate of interest, and the rate of time preference.

The present value rule is a practical, operational procedure and it, or a close variant, is used by housing producers in deciding what investments to undertake. It can be used to consider maintenance and renovation decisions by owner-occupiers and landlords, or renovation decisions by firms engaged in that business. It can also be used to decide what sort of housing development to build on a given piece of land owned by a firm. A subdivision of large detached homes, townhouses, high-rise apartments, or a mixture will each have different start-up costs and patterns of revenues and expenditures over time. The land should be developed in the use that yields the largest present value. The rule can also dictate the timing of developments. If a project were delayed one year, the equation 3.7 would have a zero as the first term. The second term would be discounted construction costs, and so on. Construction costs might change if delayed a year. The beginning date for the project would be chosen such that the present value of a project starting then would be a maximum.

This capital theoretic framework for looking at the supply side of the housing market, emphasizing the selection of investment projects, the intertemporal flows of investment returns, and the market rate of interest, more explicitly and realistically describes the decision by firms to produce housing stock than the traditional production function approach. A great deal of real estate analysis and urban land economics is based on this framework.[9] It is particularly useful when considering the decision making of a single firm or an individual. The framework is consistent with the production function approach, and like it can be combined with a demand side in models of market equilibrium. The models of housing markets of chapter four use the production function framework.

The capital theoretic framework has been generalized in a number of ways.[10] The presentation above treated the firm's decision makers and the owners as synonymous. However, many real estate companies are publicly traded, and there is a separation between the management who actually make the investment decisions and the owners (shareholders). There is considerable debate about the significance of this separation for investment analysis. If management has different preferences than those of owners, the outcome will be different. The management cannot, clearly, act completely independently, and so the significance is likely one of degree. However, even when managers have the same preferences as owners, the firm and the individual shareholder may have different access to capital markets and face different tax rates; and this may modify the chosen investment level.

A very important generalization of the framework is to deal with risk. It was assumed that firms knew the start-up costs, future revenues, and expenditures with certainty; this clearly is not the case. A formal treatment of risk on the supply side is beyond the scope of the book.[11] The analysis of risk usually specifies the "riskiness" of the future and the attitude of decision makers to risk. Often it is assumed that there are a finite number of possible outcomes (for example, actual realisations of future revenues or expenditures), and that agents assign a subjective probability to each outcome. The mean and variance of the outcomes are assumed to be of interest to the agent. If two projects have the same expected outcome, the one with the larger variance is deemed to be more risky. The attitude to risk is represented in the utility function of agents. Agents are assumed to maximize expected utility (utility being a function of income) rather than maximizing expected income. Agents are usually assumed to be risk averse, that is, to prefer a certain income to an equal expected income but one that is risky. While one can be confident that modelling risk is an important part of supply analysis, there are few general results in the literature indicating how risk alters supply.[12]

Finally, the model has thus far assumed that investments are independent of one another. But, certain projects will tend to be influenced by the same exogenous factors, and so their returns will go up and down together. The covariance of the returns of projects within a firm's portfolio will also be of concern in investment decision making.

DURABLE HOUSING STOCK: SHORT- AND MEDIUM-RUN SUPPLY

Earlier in this chapter the extremely long-run supply curve – when all housing can be thought of as new housing – was analysed and found to be quite elastic. The extremely short-run supply curve deals with the case when all housing services must be produced using the existing capital stock, and that stock cannot be varied. Under the simple one-input production function for housing services, or a slightly more general fixed-coefficients production function, the short-run supply of housing services will be perfectly inelastic. These two extremes are illustrated in figure 3.3.

FIGURE 3.3
Supply Curves of Housing Services

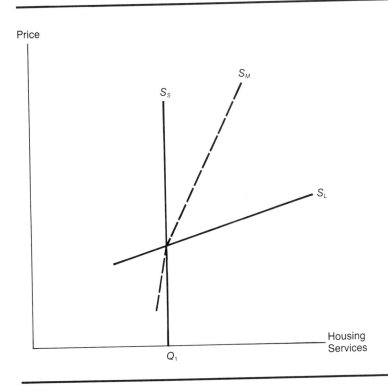

Between the two will be the medium-run supply curve whose elasticity will depend upon the length of the "medium" run. An example supply curve is the dashed line in figure 3.3. The supply of housing services in this case comes both from the construction of new houses and from the existing housing stock, recognizing that there can be changes in the stock embodied in existing dwellings.

The determinants of the supply elasticity in the long run have already been discussed, and only slight modification is required to deal with the medium-run supply of new construction. The production of new housing can take several years, so an increase in price of housing services may take a relatively long time to bring forth increased supply. It is helpful in thinking about these price changes to regard them as unanticipated changes (although expectations have not been formally introduced into the model). Furthermore the supply of land may be quite inelastic over the medium run, and even quantity constrained. Local governments exert considerable control over the flow of serviced land into the housing market, and have little incentive to increase the flow of serviced land in response to price signals.[13] Also the flow of mortgage credit may be constrained due to credit rationing. The supplies of other inputs such as construction labour, lumber, and concrete are likely to be much more inelastic in the medium run than the long run. All this suggests that the medium-run supply produced using newly constructed stock will be quite inelastic.

In the medium run, most of the housing services are produced using housing stock constructed in previous periods. To model this sensibly requires that the concept of durability be dealt with directly.[14] Let us retain the simplifying assumption that only housing stock is used in producing housing services, and that units of housing stock are homogeneous. Through the passage of time, housing stock depreciates; let us assume at a constant rate δ. However, the housing stock is maintainable; it can be renewed. In each period an owner of housing stock must decide how much to augment the stock. At one extreme, the owner could undertake no maintenance, and let the housing stock depreciate at the exogenous rate δ; at the other extreme, the owner could sustain a constant level of capital stock or even increase it. The important issue here is – how much new capital (maintenance) will be produced by the profit-maximizing owner of stock? The production function for capital added to an existing dwelling has been set out in general in equation 3.3. A total cost curve can be derived from it in the usual way. Assume that the cost of an additional unit of capital stock is independent of the levels of capital and land in the building, so that the cost function can be written as $C(A)$, where A is the units of stock added to a dwelling. This is often called the maintenance function. It is likely that costs increase with A, and that the marginal cost increases with A as well. A profit-maximizing landlord owning a building with K units of capital stock seeks to maximize the discounted profits from his building as in equation 3.8, assuming the price of housing services, the interest rate, and the maintenance function do not change over time. To maximize profits, the landlord chooses the maintenance level in the first period $A1$, in the second period $A2$, and so on. More complex price,

$$\pi = p_2 K + \frac{p_2 K(1 - \delta) + p_2 A1 - C(A1)}{1 + r}$$
$$+ \frac{p_2 [K(1 - \delta) + A1](1 - \delta) + p_2 A2 - C(A2)}{(1 + r)^2} + \dots \tag{3.8}$$

interest rate, and technology assumptions could easily be introduced. Since the discounted future returns are equal to the price of the dwelling, this problem can be seen as one of planning a maintenance path to maximize the value of the dwelling.

Two of the first order conditions for the problem are as shown in equations 3.9. In each time period, maintenance should be carried out until the marginal benefit of a unit of stock added is equal to the marg-

$$\frac{\partial \pi}{\partial A1} = \frac{p_2 - C'\,(A1)}{1 + r} + \frac{p_2(1 - \delta)}{(1 + r)^2} + \frac{p_2(1 - \delta)^2}{(1 + r)^3} + \ldots = 0$$

$$\frac{\partial \pi}{\partial A2} = \frac{p_2 - C'\,(A2)}{(1 + r)^2} + \frac{p_2(1 - \delta)}{(1 + r)^3} + \frac{p_2(1 - \delta)^2}{(1 + r)^4} + \ldots = 0$$

(3.9)

inal cost. The benefit is equal to the discounted value of the rents realised from renting the housing stock, recognizing that the additions to stock will also depreciate. Under the assumptions made here, all buildings will apply a constant amount of maintenance, A^*. Buildings with large amounts of capital stock ($\delta K > A^*$) will slowly yield fewer housing services per year despite maintenance until $\delta K = A^*$, after which time they will be maintained to yield a steady flow.

Very little is known about the production function (equation 3.3) or the maintenance function, and too much should not be made of the specific results above. However, there are several important points to remember. Owners of housing stock, whether owner-occupying households or landlords, are producers of housing services and through their maintenance and renovation decisions, alter the housing stock. In much housing analysis, especially that dealing with filtering (see chapter four), there is an implicit or explicit assumption that housing stock gradually deteriorates over time until it is demolished. However there is no a priori case that this is so. It is possible in an equilibrium that the existing stock will be maintained at a constant level.

Whatever the production and maintenance functions, one can be fairly certain that an increase in the price of housing services will lead to increased maintenance by homeowners and landlords. Therefore part of the supply response in the medium run comes from this source of housing stock. The supply curve is likely to be inelastic because the marginal cost of adding new units of capital likely rises quite quickly. If the price of housing services were to fall, maintenance would be reduced. Since the maximum rate of decline of stock is the depreciation rate δ, it is likely the medium-run supply curve is steeper below the original point than above as in figure 3.3.

The presentation above was deliberately stylized to draw out some fundamental points. A less stylized model would yield a richer and considerably more complex picture. The depreciation rate may not be constant over time, and the production function for adding capital stock through maintenance likely is different depending on the amount and age of stock and land already embodied in the building.[15] Landlords and owners do not have access to perfect capital markets as the above presentation implicitly assumes; and owners are not purely property-value maximizers because the creation of housing stock is a joint con-sumption-investment decision. Finally, the assumption of homogene-ous capital stock can be relaxed and a stock with both a quality and quantity dimension introduced. Depreciation and the maintenance function can differ across quality levels, and complex vintage effects arise. Rather than a single price of housing service there is a price function by quality level, and therefore in making maintenance deci-sions owners must consider the returns to stock at its current quality level and the returns if the stock were allowed to deteriorate to other quality levels.[16]

There has been little empirical analysis of the production of housing services from the existing housing stock. Moorehouse (1972) found some evidence of scale economies in the maintenance function, and also that the rate of depreciation varies with age. Leigh (1980) estimated the rate of depreciation (including losses due to fire, flood, and disaster) on the aggregate United States housing stock to be between 0.36 and 1.36 percent per year. Ingram and Oron (1977) estimated a constant elasticity of substitution (CES) production function for stock using existing buildings, and found that the elasticity of substitution was between 0.32 and 0.65 and surmised that the elasticity varied with building size. However, these estimates should be viewed as suggestive and a starting point for additional empirical work.

Supply in the medium-run also changes as a result of conversions or demolitions. As the price of housing services rises, and so the return to using a structure for residential purposes rises relative to the return to using it for commercial, industrial, or other purposes, some buildings will be converted to residential use. An entire building need not of course be converted. The upper floors of inner-city manufacturing buildings are often converted to loft apartments; a commercial floor of a mixed residential-commercial building may shift to residential use. As the price of housing services falls, housing stock will be converted to commercial or industrial uses, or demolished to make way for new non-residential structures. The conversion and demolition process is also obviously responsive to changes in the rate of return in industrial or commercial activity.

Thus in the medium run, the supply curve of housing services is the aggregate of production that uses newly constructed housing, of pro-duction that uses existing housing stock, and of production that occurs due to conversions or demolitions. Each of these supply curves is quite inelastic even over a period of several years.

De Leeuw and Ekanem (1971) estimated the price elasticity of what they termed the "long run supply curve" to be between 0.3 and 0.7 for different sorts of housing; and to be somewhere between these figures for the supply in aggregate. They emphasized the role of supply from existing dwellings, and so in the terms of this discussion estimated the elasticity of one component of medium-run supply. Grieson (1973) reinterpreted their results to estimate elasticities between 0.37 and 2.36. McDonald (1979) reinterprets them again to imply a zero elasticity, a result that he claims casts doubt on the plausibility of their study. Ozanne and Struyk (1978) estimated the elasticity of supply from the existing stock (over a ten-year period) to be about 0.3.

HETEROGENEOUS HOUSING SUPPLY

The supply of heterogeneous housing can be considered as the production of housing units that are described by a vector $(z_1, \ldots z_n)$ of measurable characteristics. Following Rosen (1974), assume that a firm produces only one type of housing stock. The firm's production function may be represented as in equation 3.10, where the quantity, q, of a certain type of housing $z_1 \ldots z_n$, is a function of land, labour, and materials inputs. This production function can be construed as a long-

$$(z_1, \ldots z_n, q) = f(L, N, M) \tag{3.10}$$

run function describing how housing services are produced from new stock or a medium-run function describing how services are produced from existing stock. Given input prices and assuming that the firm produces any output level of a given type at minimum cost, a total cost function $C(z_1, \ldots z_n, q)$ can be derived. It will be assumed that the marginal cost of an additional unit is positive and increasing, and that the marginal cost of one more unit of a characteristic is positive and increasing. The firm maximizes profit taking as given $p(z)$, the price per dwelling with characteristics z. At the profit maximum, the marginal revenue from adding a unit of a characteristic equals its mar-

$$q \frac{\partial p(z_1, \ldots z_n)}{\partial z_i} = \frac{\partial C(z_1, \ldots z_n, q)}{\partial z_i}$$

$$p(z_1, \ldots z_n) = \frac{\partial C(z_1, \ldots z_n, q)}{\partial q} \tag{3.11}$$

ginal cost, given an optimal output level, and the marginal revenue from another unit of output equals its marginal cost, given the optimally chosen vector of characteristics (equations 3.11).

For a firm at any given profit level, we can define an offer function (3.12) that indicates what price a firm is willing to accept for a dwelling of a certain type, when the output level has been optimally chosen. This offer function is analogous to the household's bid function of chapter two. Part of the offer function is shown in figure 3.4, repre-

FIGURE 3.4
Landlord Profit Maximum
Characteristic z_1

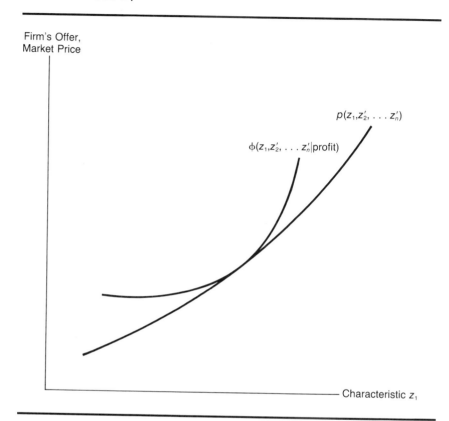

Firm's Offer,
Market Price

$p(z_1, z_2', \ldots z_n')$

$\phi(z_1, z_2', \ldots z_n' | \text{profit})$

Characteristic z_1

$$\phi(z_1, \ldots z_n | \text{profit}) \qquad\qquad (3.12)$$

senting an indifference curve or isoprofit curve. At a profit maximum the offer function will be tangent to the hedonic price function $p(\mathbf{z})$ as in figure 3.4. Figure 3.4 is analogous to figure 2.3 in the demand analysis.

In this world of heterogeneous services, builders and landlords behave as in standard micro theory, that is, they consider the production function, input prices and output prices in making their supply decision. The complication is that the producers must choose a vector of characteristics as well as an output level, and that the market price is revealed through a hedonic price function that shows the price per dwelling unit of a certain type. We cannot derive graphically the supply curve of a single firm because of the simultaneous choice of what type and how much of this housing to build, but it is important to recognize that the standard microeconomic tools can be applied to the analysis.

SUPPLY IN A SPATIAL HOUSING MARKET

When thinking about housing in a spatial model, one is considering where housing is produced and how it is produced at each location. Of most interest is the spatial housing market of a city or urban area. Let us assume that housing services are a homogeneous standard commodity produced using land and non-land as was done at the beginning of this chapter. Heterogeneity and durability are ignored, and the analysis is of very-long-run supply. The assumptions used in the analysis of demand for housing services in an urban area are retained – a homogeneous plane of land around an exogenously given employment point, and transportation equally easy in all directions, so that location need only be specified as distance from the centre of the city. The production function of a firm at location u is as in equation 3.13, where $q(u)$, $L(u)$, and $K(u)$ are output of housing services, land used and non-

$$q(u) = f[L(u), K(u)] \tag{3.13}$$

land used at location u. Assuming firms are price takers in the output and input markets, at any location firms will hire inputs until the value of the marginal product of the input is equal to the input price; as in equations 3.14, where $p_2(u)$, $R(u)$, and $r(u)$ are the prices of housing services, land, and non-land at distance u from the city centre. Since

$$p_2(u) \frac{\partial f[L(u), K(u)]}{\partial L(u)} = R(u)$$
$$\tag{3.14}$$
$$p_2(u) \frac{\partial f[L(u), K(u)]}{\partial K(u)} = r(u)$$

land and non-land are stocks whose flows of services are inputs into the production function, $R(u)$ and $r(u)$ are actually the rent per unit of land and the rent per unit of non-land. The essential aspect of the spatial model is that input and output prices vary across the city, and so profit-maximizing firms will have different output levels and input ratios across the city.

It is usually assumed that the price of non-land is the same everywhere – it is perfectly elastically supplied at each location. We have already seen in chapter two that for a spatial equilibrium of households the price of housing services must fall as distance from the centre of the city increases. Here the price of housing services is exogenous, but will be assumed to decline with distance. Assume also that the production function has constant returns to scale. For there to be a spatial equilibrium of producers, no producer can have an incentive to change location; in other words profits must be the same at each location. In long-run equilibrium with freedom of entry, there must be zero economic profits (just normal profits) at each location.

Given the price of housing services and these assumptions, land rent $R(u)$ is determined at each location. Profit-maximizing housing producers will bid against one another for a location, driving up the land rent until profits are zero. At this point, the firm's production decision satisfies equation 3.14, and total revenue is exactly equal to total factor payments. Therefore although the individual firm can be treated as a price taker (as in aspatial models), the addition of the concept of a spatial equilibrium has meant that the rent on land is endogenous. The firm's production decision in the spatial equilibrium is illustrated in figure 3.5. Since there are constant returns to scale, consider any arbitrary output level; and for ease of exposition consider one unit of housing service. The unit isoquant is illustrated. Total revenue is $p_2(u')$ at a location u'. The vertical intercept A of the firm's isocost line is $p_2(u')/r$, because we know total outlay will equal $p_2(u')$. At a profit maximum and a spatial equilibrium the isocost line will go through A and be tangent to the unit isoquant. From the horizontal intercept B of this line can be computed the rent per unit of land, $R(u)$. All firms located at distance u' will produce housing services using the input ratio (the non-land to land ratio) indicated. Now consider another location in the city, u'', further from the centre of the city. There, producers face a lower price of housing services and a lower rent per unit of land. They substitute land, whose relative price has fallen, for non-land, whose relative price has risen, and so produce housing services with a relatively lower non-land to land ratio. The non-land per unit of land gets lower as one moves away from the city centre. A rough proxy for non-land per unit of land is building height, and one does observe a decline in building height the farther one moves away from the city centre. High-rise apartments tend to be near the city centre, low rise apartments farther out, and single, detached dwellings still farther out. (This, of course, is an average with many exceptions.)

The analysis of supply in a spatial model thus takes as given, not a single price of housing services as in the aspatial model, but a function specifying price at each location and derives not a single output level but a function specifying output per unit of land at each location. The idea of the price elasticity of supply must be modified from its usage in an aspatial model. If the price function of housing services were to rise at all locations, the output of housing services would rise because more housing would be produced at each location and also because more land would be in residential use at the periphery. Most analysis of the price elasticity of supply in spatial models ignores this increase in supply coming from the increase in residential land, focusing instead on the increase in output at each location.

Suppose the price of housing services were to change at a location; how would the output per unit of land change? Firms are profit-maximizers, and there is zero profit, with land rents adjusting to absorb increased revenue per unit of land. The change in output per unit of land can be illustated using figure 3.5, by considering the rise in price from $p_2(u'')$ to $p_2 (u')$ not as a rise from changing location but as an increase in price at one location. As the price rises, there are a number of simultaneous changes: land rents rise, firms substitute non-land for land, so the non-land to land ratio rises, and the output per unit of land increases from $1/L(u'')$ to $1/L(u')$.

Muth (1969) showed the price elasticity of output per unit of land to be as shown in equation 3.15: the price elasticity is equal to the elasticity of substitution between land and non-land in production, multiplied by the ratio of the share of capital to the share of land. The

$$\eta = \sigma \frac{S_K}{S_L} \tag{3.15}$$

formula has intuitive appeal. The higher is the elasticity of substitution, the more easily non-land may be substituted for land. Therefore when the price of housing services rises (and land rents rise), the non-land to land ratio rises significantly, and so output per unit of land rises significantly. The supply elasticity thus critically depends upon the elasticity of substitution.

Empirical investigation of supply in spatial models has focused on estimating the elasticity of substitution in the production of housing services: two recent surveys of the literature are McDonald (1981) and Edelstein (1983). "At this time there is no consensus estimate of the elasticity of substitution . . . Indeed, there is good reason to suppose σ varies across metropolitan areas and within a metropolitan area" (McDonald 1981, 209). The evolution of research closely parallels that estimating demand elasticities: an initial group of estimates were produced that differed, and attempts to reconcile them emphasized a more careful specification of the underlying model and exploration of the econometric problems, given the data and functional forms used. To represent this exploration, problems of measurement error and aggregation bias will be discussed.

If it is assumed that the production function has a constant elasticity of substitution,[17] then it has the form as expressed by equation 3.16. The first order conditions for a profit maximum are as expressed in equations 3.17, which when expressed as a ratio become equation 3.18. Manipulating slightly and taking logarithms of both sides produces

$$q = A \left[\alpha L^{-\beta} + (1-\alpha)K^{-\beta} \right]^{-\frac{1}{\beta}}$$

$$\sigma = \frac{1}{1+\beta} \tag{3.16}$$

$$p_2(-\frac{1}{\beta})A[\alpha L^{-\beta} + (1-\alpha)K^{-\beta}]^{-\frac{(1+\beta)}{\beta}}(-\beta)\,\alpha\,L^{-\beta-1} = R$$

$$p_2(-\frac{1}{\beta})A[\alpha L^{-\beta} + (1-\alpha)K^{-\beta}]^{-\frac{(1+\beta)}{\beta}}(-\beta)(1-\alpha)K^{-\beta-1} = r$$

(3.17)

$$\frac{\alpha\,L^{-\beta-1}}{(1-\alpha)K^{-\beta-1}} = \frac{R}{r}$$

(3.18)

equation 3.19, which can be estimated using data on input ratios in housing production and input price ratios. The coefficients to be estimated are a and b; ϵ is the random error term. The coefficient on the input price ratio is minus the elasticity of substitution.

FIGURE 3.5
Spatial Equilibria of Producers

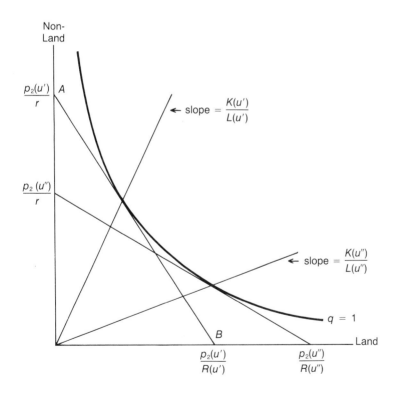

$$\ln\left(\frac{L}{K}\right) = \left(-\frac{1}{1+\beta}\right)\ln\left(\frac{1-\alpha}{\alpha}\right) - \frac{1}{1+\beta}\ln\left(\frac{R}{r}\right)$$

$$\ln\left(\frac{L}{K}\right) = a + b\ln\left(\frac{R}{r}\right) + \epsilon$$

(3.19)

The above equation and related variants were estimated by several researchers. One possible problem with the estimate of σ is errors in the measurement of R, the rent per unit of land. Of course all variables are subject to some measurement error, but measurement of R may be subject to large error because often researchers use data from tax assessors or real estate appraisors rather than observed market data. Suppose that the observed land rent $\overline{R}$ is related to the true land rent R as in equation 3.20, where δ is a normally distributed random variable with mean zero. The regression using equation 3.19 and observed rent becomes

$$\overline{R} = R\ e^{\delta}$$

(3.20)

equation 3.21. An ordinary least squares estimate of σ will be biased

$$\ln\left(\frac{L}{K}\right) = a + b\ln\left(\frac{\overline{R}}{r}\right) + \epsilon - b\ \delta$$

(3.21)

because there now is a correlation between the independent variable, $\ln \overline{R}/r$ and the error term $(\epsilon - b\delta)$. McDonald (1981) has shown that the estimate of the elasticity of substitution will be downwardly biased. Many of the early estimates of the elasticity of substitution were around 0.5 but were subject to this downward bias.

Another econometric problem relates to the aggregation of the data. Following Edelstein (1983), suppose that the production function has a constant elasticity of substitution as in equation 3.16, but that the production function is different at different locations, differing only in the β parameter. The elasticity of substitution will be different at different locations. Figure 3.6 plots data that hypothetically have been gathered on buildings at different locations across the city. For each building the non-land to land ratio and the factor price ratio are observed. If all the data were used together to estimate the elasticity of substitution, assuming the production function was the same at all locations, a regression line like AB in figure 3.6 would be fitted. The absolute value of the slope of the line is the estimated elasticity of substitution. If instead the data were disaggregated and separate regressions run on data from the suburbs, midtown, and city centre, lines such as CD, EF, and GH might be fitted. The misspecified aggregate model would, in this example, generate an estimate of the elasticity of substitution that was too low and be unable to detect the differences

FIGURE 3.6
Estimation of the Elasticity of Substitution

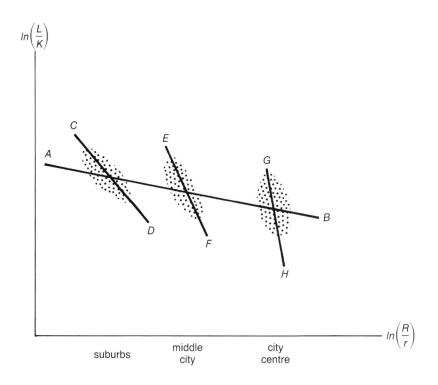

between locations. The variation in the estimates of the elasticity of substitution among researchers may in part be due to aggregation problems of this sort.

Most published estimates of the price elasticity of supply of housing services have actually estimated the elasticity of substitution and then used equation 3.15 and data on factor shares to compute a supply elasticity.[18] But as we have seen, there is no consensus about the magnitude of the elasticity of substitution. For illustrative purposes, let us assume it to be 0.8. If the share of non-land is 0.8, then the supply elasticity is 3.2. This supply elasticity will vary across the city because factor shares vary: in the city centre where the share of land is relatively high, the supply elasticity will be low compared to the suburbs where the share of land is relatively low.

SUGGESTIONS FOR FURTHER READING

Ingram G. K., and Y. Oron (1977) "The Production of Housing Services from Existing Dwelling Units," in G. K. Ingram, ed., *Residential Location and Urban Housing Markets* (Cambridge, Mass.: Ballinger, for the National Bureau of Economic Research).

McDonald, J. F. (1979) *Economic Analysis of An Urban Housing Market* (New York: Academic Press). Chapter four.

Muth, R. (1964) "The Derived Demand for a Productive Factor and the Industry Supply Curve," *Oxford Economic Papers* 16: 221–34.

Smith, B. (1976) "The Supply of Urban Housing," *Quarterly Journal of Economics* 90:389–405.

4 | Models of the Housing Market

The demand and supply sides of the housing market have now been discussed, and it remains in this chapter to bring them together. The exact definition of the "market" area will sometimes be rather vague – usually the notion will refer to the housing market of a city or region, but these models could be used in analysing a provincial or even a national market. A unifying feature in all usages is the explicit micro-foundations. Chapter five will discuss housing market models as they arise in a more macroeconomic context.

In a way, the previous chapters have provided background material, and we are now ready to analyse the operation of housing markets. Unfortunately, economists are not yet able to build tractable models of the housing market that incorporate at once all of the complexities of the commodity housing. For certain types of questions, the model will incorporate certain aspects of the complexity. The mark of good analysis is the retention of the essential features of a problem in the simplest possible framework.

Each model presented will be followed by an example of how it has been used. While not truly a case study, it is hoped to suggest how the analysis can be applied to address real-world issues. These models will be used again in chapter ten to analyse the effects of government housing policies.

HOUSING AS A STANDARD COMMODITY

Let us begin by treating housing as any other commodity in micro-economics. The model is obviously simple and "unrealistic," yet it is extraordinarily useful and yields insights that are often neglected in housing discussions. Retaining all the standard assumptions of previous chapters, there is no distinction between owning and renting housing. The market demand curve, DD, in figure 4.1 is the horizontal addition of the demand curves for housing services of individual households. All households are represented in this demand curve, both owners and renters. The long-run supply curve, $S_L S_L$, in figure 4.1 is based

FIGURE 4.1
Market Equilibria: Housing as a Standard Commodity

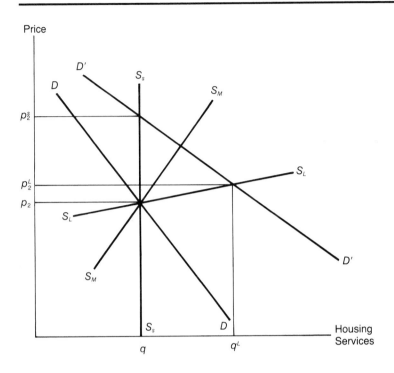

on individual firm supply curves recognizing the possibility of different efficiencies across firms and factor price changes as the industry expands. The long-run equilibrium price of housing services is p_2, and the quantity exchanged (produced/consumed) is q. These could be converted directly to the long-run price of housing stock and the quantity of housing stock. In long-run equilibrium, the short-run supply curve, S_sS_s, and the medium-run supply curve, S_MS_M, go through the point (q, p_2).

Suppose household incomes were to increase. The budget constraint of each household would shift out and, because the income elasticity of demand for housing services is positive, the individual demand curves shift out, and so the market demand curve shifts out to $D'D'$ in figure 4.1. The exact shift depends upon the amount of the increase in income and on the income elasticity of demand. If all households are identical and have a ten-percent increase in income, and the income elasticity of demand for housing services is 0.8, then at any given price the quantity demanded for housing services increases by eight percent. At low prices the absolute increase in quantity demanded is greater than at a high price. Such a shift is illustrated in figure 4.1. If households differ in the income elasticity of their housing demands, for example some researchers have found that the elasticity is higher for owners than for renters, then the shift in the market demand curve will depend upon the income changes of these two groups, their two income elasticities and the share of each in total housing consumption.

In the very short run, the market response to this increase in demand is a large increase in price to p_2^S. The quantity supplied does not increase at first in response to rising prices. Over time, the high price of housing services encourages new supply; the increase coming from existing buildings, new construction, and conversions. The housing market adjusts relatively slowly. The quantity supplied of housing services is greater than q, and the medium-run equilibrium price is lower than p_2^S.

The increase (and later fall) in the price of housing services is capitalized into the asset value of the housing stock. The shift in the demand function increases the wealth of the stock owner who can realize this wealth gain by selling the stock. The subsequent owner of stock and producer of housing services enjoys just normal profits and returns to stock ownership. It is important to recognize this capitalization effect in housing markets because buildings transact so frequently. The gainers or losers from a shift in demand are often not the current owners of houses or apartments.

Finally, and this can take many many years, the market fully adjusts to the shift in the demand curve. The new equilibrium is q^L, p_2^L. Through this point run a new short-run supply curve and a new medium-run supply curve. The long-run supply curve in figure 4.1 has been drawn as a less than perfectly elastic curve, so the new long-run equilibrium price is higher than before. If the curve slopes upward because land is not perfectly elastically supplied, then the annual rent and asset price of land have risen. Comparing the old and new long-run equilibria, households pay more per unit of housing service, producers of housing services still earn normal profits, and the original landowners have enjoyed a captial gain.

The size of the final price change depends upon the initial increase in income, the income elasticity of demand, the price elasticity of supply, and the price elasticity of demand. This can be illustrated with a simple algebraic model of the housing market. The market demand function is 4.1, which has a constant price elasticity, α, and a constant income elasticity, β. The supply curve is 4.2, which has a constant price elasticity θ. The market equilibrium condition is 4.3, and the

$$q_d = A\, p_2^\alpha\, y^\beta \qquad \alpha < 0, \beta > 0 \tag{4.1}$$

$$q_s = B\, p_2^\theta \qquad\qquad \theta > 0 \qquad\qquad (4.2)$$

$$q_d = q_s \qquad\qquad (4.3)$$

equilibrium price of housing services is 4.4. The percentage change in equilibrium price for a one-percent change in income is the ratio of the income elasticity to the difference between the price elasticity of supply and the price elasticity of demand, as in equation 4.5.

$$p_2 = \left[\frac{Ay^\beta}{B}\right]^{\frac{1}{\theta - \alpha}} \qquad\qquad (4.4)$$

$$\frac{dp_2}{p_2}\cdot\frac{y}{dy} = \frac{\beta}{\theta - \alpha} \qquad\qquad (4.5)$$

The price per unit of housing services has risen rapidly over the last fifteen years. For some households, and for some time periods in certain markets, prices rose faster than incomes. There was a widespread public perception that prices were rising faster than incomes for all people on average (although the data presented in chapter one do not support this). Furthermore, there was the belief that this could only occur if there were some "malfunction" of the housing market. Equation 4.5 shows that prices will rise faster than incomes if the income elasticity of demand is greater than the supply price elasticity plus the absolute value of the demand price elasticity. The available empirical evidence on these elasticities suggests this is very unlikely to occur. It might possibly occur during some short-run adjustment period after the demand increase, when the supply elasticity is very small.

The example above looked at the effect of income changes on the housing market. The model can be used in a similar fashion to explore a change in any exogenous variable on the demand side or the supply side – for example, to see the effect on prices and output of increases in the number of households in the market, or a fall in construction labour costs, and so on. The first step is to see the effect on the individual agents in the market – households or suppliers – and then convert this into a shift in the market curve. Then two equilibria can be compared. This method of studying the effect of a change in an exogenous variable by comparing two equilibria is called comparative statics analysis. The comparative statics approach can also be used to examine the effects of government policies on housing markets (see chapter ten).

The representation of the housing market in figure 4.1 made no distinction between ownership and rental tenure. Sometimes an identical model is used to analyse the ownership or rental markets alone. To do this one must assume that, for some reason, households can be partitioned into owners and renters, and no change in the relative cost of housing services through ownership or rental will alter this partitioning. Renters might be, for example, low income households who have not saved a down payment, and households who are going to move frequently. Under this assumption, the effects of an increase in renters' incomes on the rental price of housing services and the rental housing stock can be analysed exactly as above. However, this approach is really only suitable for short-run analysis. If the price of housing services under the two forms of tenure diverged for some time, households would shift from one form to another.

If the ownership and rental markets are to be separately articulated within the same model, the tenure choice decision must become endogenous, and there must be an equilibrium in and across markets. A reason why tenure will be relevant must be introduced into the model; for example income taxes that exempt imputed income (as in chapter two).

The treatment of housing services as a standard commodity (as in figure 4.1) left unstated exactly how the equilibrium price was reached. It was presumed that the price would be the equilibrium price, but there was no statement about the dynamics of market adjustment. Implicitly, it was presumed that the housing market operated "as if" there were a Walrasian auctioneer. Under such a process, the auctioneer announces prices and tabulates proposed demands and supplies until the price is discovered at which the quantity willingly demanded equals the quantity willingly supplied; and only then does exchange occur.

In recent years, economists have devoted much effort to explicitly modelling the process by which the market price is established; or stated another way, to modelling the market clearing process. There are cases that seem to operate "as if" there were a Walrasian auctioneer; for example, a commodity market. However for such markets to exist there must be no institutional barriers to price adjustment or exchange, and all agents must have complete information about available goods and prices. In housing markets it is obvious buyers do not have full information about the prices of sellers, and sellers do not have full information about the bids of buyers, or the prices of other sellers. When there is imperfect information, there may be a dispersion of prices rather than a single price; buyers will utilize resources in searching out different sellers to discover their prices; sellers will devote resources to announcing their prices and discovering the prices of other sellers; and firms may come into existence that gather and sell information about prices. In housing markets, real estate agents are such firms (see Yinger [1981a]). The lack and cost of information gives rise to the search problem: households do not know the true price of a house or apartment until they visit it because the characteristics must be discovered. What strategy should the consumer follow to gather information? In certain models it can be shown that households will adopt a reservation price, and the optimal strategy is to search until a house is found at less than or equal to the reservation price (Hey 1979). The reservation price falls and search increases as the costs of search decline and the dispersion of prices increases. As one thinks further, the question arises how dwelling unit owners establish their prices when demanders are following a search strategy. Certainly it makes no sense to think of owners as price takers when there is a dispersion of prices. The owners will establish a pricing strategy depending on how they believe demanders are behaving; and the search strategy of demanders will depend upon the pricing behaviour of owners. The elegant separation of demand side and supply side is no longer possible. The modelling of such a market will be extremely complex, and the idea of equilibrium will have to be rethought.

It is evident that rental markets do not clear as if there were a Walrasian auctioneer – there are almost always some vacant dwelling units that the landlord would be willing to rent at the market price. While we will not formally model the behaviour of buyers and sellers, and the market that would yield an outcome with vacancies, the explanation is obviously closely related to imperfect information and the resulting search behaviour of households and pricing strategies of landlords.[1]

If the market does not clear, how are we to determine the price and quantity that prevail in the rental market? They are no longer the intersection of the demand and supply curves.[2] The behaviour of the market can be represented by a clearing path, curve AB in figure 4.2. For any given rent level, the clearing path indicates the quantity of housing services exchanged. The horizontal distance between the clearing path and the supply curve indicates the unused housing services or vacancies. The model still does not tell us what the price and quantity will be; only what quantity will be given a price. And most such models are not complete in this sense, but rather postulate a rental ajdustment mechanism, usually that the rate of change of rents is a function of vacancies. But the relationship is not simply one of inverse proportionality. Vacancies are a normal result of turnover in a rental market with imperfect information. At some quantity of vacancies there will be no tendency for rents to change. The ratio of this quantity to total stock is referred to as the natural vacancy rate. In figure 4.2, amount GH is the natural level of vacancies, and if rent were R_1, this vacancy level would exist, and there would be no tendency for rent to change. If the vacancy level were IJ (rent would be R_2), there would be a tendency for rents to fall; while if vacancies were KL (rent would be R_3), there would be a tendency for rents to rise. Adjustments occur first through vacancy rates and then through rents.The rate of change of rents in this model is postulated to be a function of the deviation of the actual

FIGURE 4.2
Clearing Path in a Rental Market

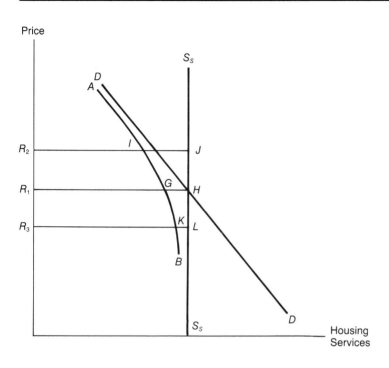

vacancy rate from the natural rate. Over time and between markets the natural vacancy rate can change. In spirit, such explicit models of the price-adjustment mechanism remain close to the Walrasian auctioneer, but permit exchange away from R_1, and admit of some vacancies even when rents are not changing.[3]

HOUSING AS A HETEROGENEOUS COMMODITY: HEDONIC PRICE EQUATIONS

Not surprisingly, the characterization of a housing market equilibrium and the use of comparative statics becomes much more complicated when housing is viewed as a heterogeneous commodity. The complexity arises because to find a market equilibrium one must find a $p(\mathbf{z})$ function such that the quantity supplied equals the quantity demanded at all relevant $\mathbf{z}$.[4] If for example the quantity demanded of houses of one particular type (a vector $\mathbf{z}$ of n observable characteristics) does not match the quantity supplied, $p(\mathbf{z})$ will need to change, and this affects not just houses of this type, but all types. The process of solving for an equilibrium cannot be dealt with here. However it is important to understand the nature of the equilibrium because of the extensive use of hedonic price functions in housing analysis.

The equilibrium can be characterized by bringing together figure 2.3 of chapter two and figure 3.4 of chapter three in figure 4.3. Suppose there are many producers, and they face different input prices, or differ in efficiency, or have different production functions; and suppose there are many households, and they have different bid functions for some reason, for example they differ in tastes or incomes. In equilibrium, all producers' offer functions and all households' bid functions will be tangent to $p(\mathbf{z})$, as in figure 4.3.

If there were only one sort of household in the market, then the producers' offer functions would be tangent to the single household bid function, and the observed $p(\mathbf{z})$ in equilibrium would be the bid

FIGURE 4.3
Market Equilibrium of Heterogeneous Housing Characteristic z_1

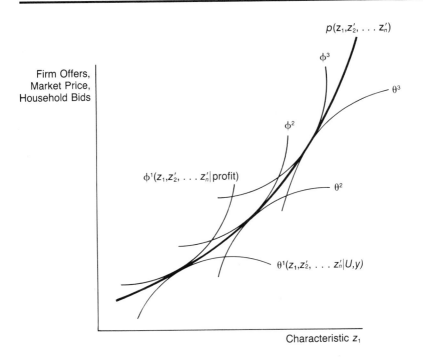

function. The $p(z)$ function would tell us about the nature of demand for the characteristics. If there were only one sort of producer in the market, then the households' bid functions would be tangent along the single firm's offer function, and the equilibrium $p(z)$ would be the offer function and would tell us about cost. In general however there are different sorts of firms and different sorts of households, and $p(z)$ tells us neither about underlying demand nor cost.

A large number of studies have estimated empirically the hedonic price function $p(z)$, regressing either rent or house price on the characteristics of a dwelling unit. These characteristics include not only such things as the number of bedrooms and lot size, but also accessibility to job locations and the characteristics of the neighbourhood. The most commonly estimated functional forms have been the linear (equation 4.6) and the semilog (equation 4.7). The partial derivatives of these functions with respect to a characteristic are the prices – the

$$p(z) = \beta_0 + \beta_1 z_1 + \beta_2 z_2 + \ldots + \beta_n z_n \qquad (4.6)$$

$$p(z) = e^{\beta_0 + \beta_1 z_1 + \beta_2 z_2 + \ldots + \beta_n z_n} \qquad (4.7)$$

hedonic prices – of a marginal unit of a characteristic at a particular market equilibrium.[5]

These hedonic prices have numerous uses in housing analysis. They are used to create a price index in comparing the cost of housing in different cities. Hedonic prices are estimated for the two markets, and the index is the ratio of average price in market one to the average price in market two – these averages being computed using the building characteristics of one of the markets as weights. The procedure is analogous to that used to compare food prices in two cities. Hedonic prices are used in a similar sort of way to correct for quality changes in creating a housing price index for time series analysis. Real estate assessors sometimes use hedonic prices to estimate the market value of a dwelling when no recent sale of exactly that sort of dwelling has occurred. Some researchers have focused on the estimated coefficient of the variable that measures distance from the centre of the city: if the coefficient is negative, this is taken as support for the standard spatial model of a housing market. Still others have used the coefficients to analyse consumer demand for characteristics.

Hedonic prices can also be used in demand analysis. Consider the case where all producers are identical, but households differ.[6] The hedonic function reveals cost conditions but nothing directly about demand. Demand functions can however be estimated with some additional data. Let us suppose that households differ in incomes, and we have data on income. Also, we can observe how much of each housing characteristic each household consumes. Thus, there are data for each household on quantity consumed, and incomes; it only remains to gather data on the prices faced by each household. This can be done by estimating a hedonic price function. The price faced by a household for a characteristic is the partial derivative of the hedonic function evaluated at that bundle of characteristics consumed by the household. The data set is now complete, and a demand function can be estimated.

In recent years numerous demand functions have been estimated using this two-step procedure. These demand functions have been especially useful when estimated for urban amenities such as clean air, because there is no explicit market trading in air quality, yet it is important to know how people value air quality when evaluating a pollution control investment.[7]

FILTERING IN HOUSING MARKETS

There exists a large housing literature dealing with what has been called filtering, but perhaps which should be seen more broadly as the dynamics of housing markets. Suppose an urban housing market were in equilibrium, and then the relatively high income households enjoyed an increase in income. And further suppose that the high income households had a high income elasticity of demand for newness, and moved into newly constructed housing. The houses that they vacated would fall in value, allowing a household of lower income to move in, and so on through the housing market until the lowest income households moved out of the lowest quality housing, and that housing was abandoned. Roughly speaking this is what is meant by the housing filtering process.

Unfortunately, much of the writing on housing filtering has not developed formal analytical models, and there remains ambiguity about the precise meaning of the term. Rather than attempt a new or consensus definition of filtering, it is perhaps more fruitful to set out some of the essential features involved in any notion of filtering. Housing is recognized as a heterogeneous commodity, but in a very simple way – housing units differ in quality. Over time housing depreciates, which means that it declines in quality (rather than depreciating by using up units of one quality level). Through maintenance and renovation this depreciation can be slowed and even reversed. Households demand housing, and the various quality levels are substitutes for one another. Households have different incomes, but all share the same ranking of the quality levels. The housing market establishes the price of each quality level, allocates the different income groups to quality levels, and determines rates of new construction, maintenance, and demolition. Sometimes exchange in a quality level is referred to as a housing submarket. Over time exogenous variables change – incomes change, the number and composition of households change, tastes change, construction and maintenance technologies change, prices of inputs into construction and maintenance change – which cause changes in the endogenous variables. The prices of quality levels change, the allocation of income groups to quality levels changes, and rates of maintenance and construction change. All these ideas are part of housing filtering.[8]

The idea of filtering has always played an important part in public policy debates. It is obvious that the poor will not be able to live in newly constructed housing, but will subsidies to new construction improve the living conditions of the poor because better quality housing will "filter down" to them? Sweeney (1974) was able to show that there exists a system of subsidies to construction at certain quality levels that reduces prices at all quality levels. But any arbitrary construction subsidy will not do this. It is even possible that a construction subsidy will lower prices at high-quality levels and increase prices at lower-quality levels – thus benefitting the rich and not the poor.

A SPATIAL HOUSING MARKET

The purpose of this section is to show the spatial equilibrium of households and suppliers around the central point. The analysis must solve not just for a single equilibrium price of housing services but the price at each distance away from the centre, $p_2(u)$; and it must also solve not just for the total quantity supplied or demanded but the quantities at each distance from the central point. Once an equilibrium solution is derived, then the method of comparative statics can be applied to see how changes in exogenous variables influence the equilibrium configuration.

Consumers maximize a utility function subject to a budget constraint, and a household demand function for housing services at each distance from the centre $x_2(u)$ can be derived. Demand is a function of the price of the composite good p_1 which is the same everywhere, the price of housing services $p_2(u)$, income y, the cost of commuting one unit of distance t, and tastes (equation 4.8). Let us assume that all consumers

$$x_2(u) = f(p_1, p_2(u), y, t) \qquad \text{(4.8)}$$

are identical. It has already been shown that for consumers to be in equilibrium, equation 4.9 must hold. One can think of the de-

$$\frac{dp_2(u)}{du} = -\frac{t}{x_2(u)} \qquad \text{(4.9)}$$

mand side therefore as dictating the rate of change of the price of housing with distance, but not the precise $p_2(u)$ function. If $p_2(u)$ were to be represented graphically, the demand side dictates the curvature of the $p_2(u)$ at each u, but not its height above the horizontal u axis.

On the supply side, profit-maximizing producers, faced with given non-land and housing services prices, bid against one another for locations until profits are exhausted. This determines the rent per unit of land, the non-land per unit of land, and the output to land ratio at each distance from the city centre.

When the two sides are brought together the usual sorts of equilibrium conditions apply as well as spatial equilibrium conditions. The quantity supplied of housing services at each location must equal the quantity demanded. No household or producer can have an incentive to change location. However, more information is needed to close the model. There are an infinite number of $p_2(u)$ functions that satisy the conditions set out so far.

There are two approaches to closing the model. The first approach is to assume a closed city or closed housing market; that is to assume that the total population of housheolds to be housed is exogenous. Once it is known how many households live in the city, the model can select the $p_2(u)$ function consistent with utility functions, production functions, and the equilibrium conditions. The level of household utility is established endogenously. The closed-city model is appropriate for analysing large cities in advanced industrial societies. It is reasonable to assume that there is no alternative to living in the large city, and so when the level of welfare is established within the city there will not be large flows of people either into or out of the city.

The second approach is to assume an open city; that is to assume that the utility level of households is exogenous. The city housing market is a small part of a much larger system where this utility level is established. If the utility level in the city fell below this exogenous level, people would leave, housing prices would fall, and utility levels would rise. The out-migration would stop when the utility level had risen to its level in the larger system. Conversely, if the city utility level were above that in the larger system, people would in-migrate, raising housing prices, until equal utilities were established once again. This approach to analysing a spatial housing market is appropriate for small cities in advanced industrial societies, and for cities in developing nations where the level of utility is established in the rural areas.

The final bit of information to close the model relates to other users of land. In both the closed-city and open-city approaches, the producers of housing services bid for land. This land has an opportunity cost equal to the bid of agricultural users of land, $\overline{R}$. At every location agricultural users will bid $\overline{R}$ per unit of land. Locations will be used to produce housing services if $R(u) > \overline{R}$. Thus the distance to the edge of the housing market will be established where $R(\overline{u}) = \overline{R}$.

Wheaton (1974) worked out a full set of comparative static results for a simplified closed city, on which the exposition below is based.[9]

Of most interest is to examine how changes in the population to be housed, N, changes in the marginal cost of commuting, t, and changes in household income, y, affect the equilibrium configuration of the spatial housing market: especially the utility level realised by the representative household, the price of housing services at each location, and the supply of housing services at each location. Wheaton's results are summarized in table 4.1.

If the total population to be housed in a city increases, the utility level of each household falls, housing prices rise at every location, the housing consumption of households at each location falls, and the distance to the edge of the city increases. Population density, which is the inverse of housing consumption per person, rises everywhere. Thus the effect of increasing the number of households in the market on prices and consumption are what one would expect (having done comparative statics analysis on an aspatial housing market).

If the cost of transportation falls in a closed city, utilities rise, housing prices at the city centre, $p_2(0)$, fall, housing consumption at the city centre $x_2(0)$ rises, and the distance to the edge of the city increases. These results imply a rather more complex pattern of housing price changes. Central prices have fallen, but $\bar{u}$ has increased; this implies that as you move out from the centre of the city the price of housing services is at first lower and then at some point becomes higher (figure 4.4). The consumption of housing services per household increases at the city centre, hence population density decreases there.

If the incomes of consumers were to rise, their utility level would increase, the price of housing services at the city centre would fall, the

TABLE 4.1
Comparative Statics Results in a Spatial Housing Market (closed city)

variation in city population:

$$\frac{\partial U}{\partial N} < 0 \qquad \frac{\partial p_2(u)}{\partial N} > 0 \qquad \frac{\partial x_2(u)}{\partial N} < 0 \qquad \frac{\partial \bar{u}}{\partial N} > 0$$

variation in transportation cost:

$$\frac{\partial U}{\partial t} < 0 \qquad \frac{\partial p_2(0)}{\partial t} > 0 \qquad \frac{\partial x_2(0)}{\partial t} < 0 \qquad \frac{\partial \bar{u}}{\partial t} < 0$$

variation in household income:

$$\frac{\partial U}{\partial y} > 0 \qquad \frac{\partial p_2(0)}{\partial y} < 0 \qquad \frac{\partial x_2(0)}{\partial y} > 0 \qquad \frac{\partial \bar{u}}{\partial y} > 0$$

SOURCE: Based on Wheaton (1974)

FIGURE 4.4
Housing Price Changes as Transport Costs Fall
(closed city)

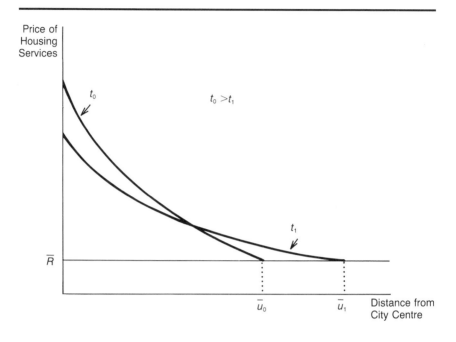

consumption of housing services at the centre would increase, and the city would become larger. The results are qualitatively the same as those following a decline in marginal commuting cost and would be depicted similarly to figure 4.4. The results of a rise in income are therefore somewhat different from what one might expect having studied the aspatial partial equilibrium model. Again, utility and housing consumption have risen, but some households have faced a rise in housing prices, while others have enjoyed a decline in prices (although all have enjoyed the same increase in utility).

The comparative static results for an open city are somewhat different. The solution process can be illustrated graphically. Consider for example the case of an increase in the incomes of households in one city, as in figure 4.5. The utility level remains at U^*, thus at any given location, housing prices rise and housing consumption falls. The distance to the edge of the city increases, density increases everywhere, and so the total population in the city increases. In sharp contrast to the standard or closed-city models, a rise in income causes a fall in housing consumption.

FIGURE 4.5
Consumption and Housing Price Changes as Incomes Increase (open city)

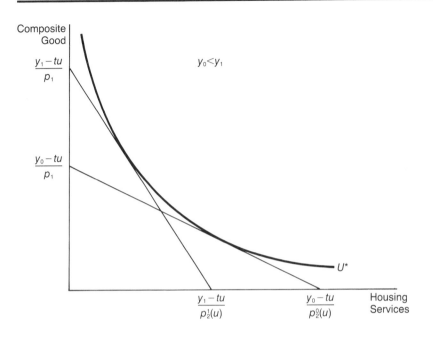

These spatial models of the housing market form the centre of what is often referred to as the "new" urban economics. The analysis has been extended in a number of directions from the simple framework here. Major innovations have been to make commuting costs endogenous because of congestion on an existing road system, and to relax the assumption of perfectly malleable housing stock.[10]

No one disputes the unreality of the assumptions that underlie these models or the rigour with which analysis is conducted using them. However there is some controversy about their "usefulness" for analysing all but the most long-run phenomena.[11] Implicitly, when comparative statics analyses are undertaken, new housing is built at each location in response to the parameter change, allowing any alteration in non-land to land ratios (with the exception of the vintage models alluded to above). The past has no impact on the present. But we know that housing is very durable, that past decisions strongly influence the present, and that housing markets take a long time to adjust.

However, controversy about the realism of spatial models should not be allowed to obscure the fact that they represent a formal analytical treatment of the relationships between location and housing prices; while most of the more "realistic" alternative analysis becomes *ad hoc* and unable to predict the effect of parameter changes. Studies that focus on a long-run phenomenon avoid some of this controversy, because the assumptions of the spatial model are more appropriate. A good example is the study of the suburbanization of cities. Indeed, much of the early work on spatial models was done in attempts to explain the suburbanization process.

One summary measure of an urban housing market that has been extensively studied is the population density function $D(u)$; the number of persons per unit of land, living at distance u from the city centre. Population density can be decomposed into three components as in equation 4.10: density is the product of the number of persons per household at distance u, $h(u)$; the inverse of housing consumption per

$$D(u) = h(u) \cdot \frac{1}{x_2(u)} \cdot \frac{q(u)}{L(u)} \tag{4.10}$$

household; and the output of housing services per unit of land. Changes in any of these components alter population density. Most empirical estimates of the population density function have assumed that it was a negative exponential function (equation 4.11), where D_0 is density at the centre of the city and α is the constant percentage change in density with a unit change in distance. One definition of suburbanization or de-

$$D(u) = D_0 e^{-\alpha u} \tag{4.11}$$

centralization is a fall in D_0 and α over time. The housing market has become flatter, more spread out. In order to make comparisons between cities of different sizes, suburbanization is usually more narrowly defined as a decline in the α parameter. The D_0 may be higher or lower, but the lower α implies a flatter – more suburbanized – city. This has been documented in not just North American cities but also western European and Asian cities. Although often associated with the building of new suburbs after the Second World War, the process began much earlier, and it appears, in the United States at least, to have been going on since the late nineteenth century (see Mills [1972a]).

There are numerous contributing factors to the suburbanization of cities. Employment locations have decentralized, and people have moved out to be near their jobs (the causation is not direct, rather a simultaneous relationship exists because jobs move out to be near the suburbanizing people). Increases in population have tended to be accommodated by building new housing at the periphery rather than by increasing density across the city because of the durability of housing stock. Neither of these factors can be represented in the simple models of this chapter. However the two primary causal factors can be represented in the simple models: falling real commuting costs and rising real incomes. The comparative static analyses above give a flavour for how changes in the parameters can be analysed. Consider the closed-city model. A fall in commuting cost and a rise in income work in the same direction. Housing consumption per household increases everywhere and so decreases population density but without necessarily making the city more or less suburbanized. However the price of housing function has become flatter, so the variations in output per unit of land become less across the city, and therefore both declining transport costs and increasing incomes tend to suburbanize the city (see equation 4.9). In an open-city model, increases in income or declines in transport cost raise the price of housing services everywhere and so increase output per unit of land everywhere. Recalling equation 3.15 of chapter three, the price elasticity of the output per unit of land is equal to the elasticity of substitution times the ratio of non-land's share to land's share. Because the share of land is much higher near the centre of the city than near the periphery, the increase in housing prices will increase output per unit of land a larger percentage in the suburbs than near the centre. The open-city model therefore also implies suburbanization in response to declining transport costs and rising incomes.

It is interesting to speculate whether the long trend of suburbanization will continue in the decades to come. Certainly changes in employment location and new communications technologies will have effects. It may be however that the trend of declining commuting costs will be reversed, and certainly many forecast a much slower growth in real incomes than in the past. The spatial housing models, with extensions to deal with congestion and the durability of housing stock, are probably the most appropriate framework for analysis of these long-run trends.

This chapter has presented a number of models of the housing market. None of the models was able to include all of the complexities of the commodity housing. Attempts to include them all would have produced analytically intractable formulations. A strategy to create more realistic models is to use computer simulation. These are capable of handling spatial fixity, heterogeneity, durability, a local public sector, and multiple employment locations in the initial specification. On the basis of the realism of the assumptions, the models appear very promising. However this has been achieved at the cost of economic, analytic content. The richer the models, the less they have incorporated an explicit market process. Some versions have no role for prices in shaping consumer or producer behaviour. Often resource allocation follows *ad hoc* assignment procedures. Often the equations of the simulation model have not been estimated. Parameters are given values so that the simulation outcomes conform with actual outcomes.

The unrealistic, analytic model and the realistic simulation model thus have their advantages and disadvantages. A survey of the former approach by Wheaton (1979) and of the latter by Ingram (1979) very clearly draw out the trade-offs between them. As in all analyses, the choice of framework will depend largely on the sorts of questions one is trying to answer.

SUGGESTIONS FOR FURTHER READING

Blomquist, G., and L. Worley (1981) "Hedonic Prices, Demands for Urban Housing Amenities, and Benefit Estimates," *Journal of Urban Economics* 9: 212–21.

Mills, E. S. (1972a) *Studies in the Structure of the Urban Economy* (Baltimore: The Johns Hopkins Press for Resources for the Future, Inc.). Chapter three.

Sweeney, J. L. (1974) "A Commodity Hierarchy Model of the Rental Housing Market," *Journal of Urban Economics* 1: 288–323.

Wheaton, W. C. (1974) "A Comparative Static Analysis of Urban Spatial Structure," *Journal of Economic Theory* 9: 223–37.

5 | Housing and Mortgage Markets in the National Economy

The previous three chapters have explored housing markets, emphasizing the theory of consumer behaviour, the theory of the firm, and the theory of market equilibrium. These chapters have had a microeconomic orientation; the models were used to analyse independent regional or local housing markets. For many purposes, local housing markets can be considered as independent of one another. For example, an increase in immigration to Vancouver will have little effect on the demand for housing in Halifax. Of course the housing markets are not completely independent of one another because households move between cities partially in response to differences in real wages, and the local price of housing services is an important determinant of the real wage in a city. Thus an increase in immigration to Vancouver may raise the price of housing services and reduce the real wage there, and hence reduce the migration from other cities to Vancouver, and so keep the price of housing services higher in these cities than it would have been. However in most housing analyses this interdependence can be ignored unless the issue of interest is intercity migration. People are not very mobile, and it takes a long time for migration to equilibrate a system of housing markets.[1]

For certain purposes it is useful to think of one national housing market as part of the national economy. The construction of new housing is an important component of national income and of gross investment, and a source of employment for thousands. The study of national income and employment leads naturally to the study of major sectors such as housing. The level of new construction is subject to wide fluctuations, and so again a concern with the fluctuation and stabilization of the national economy leads naturally to the study of the fluctuation and stabilization of the housing sector. The purpose of this chapter is to examine the national housing and mortgage markets. It is macroeconomic in orientation, focusing more on aggregate measure such as the level of housing starts or the mortgage interest rate and less on the decision making of individual agents than the previous three chapters. There is an enormous literature in this tradition to which one chapter cannot do justice, but the text and notes supply many references.

HOUSING STARTS AND FLUCTUATIONS

It is vital in approaching the literature dealing with housing in a national context to understand the primary motivation for the research. The interest was in modelling housing and mortgage markets as part of the construction of econometric models of the national economy. These national models were to be used to predict the levels of national income, employment, and prices and to be used in the design of macroeconomic policies to stabilize fluctuations in these levels. The desire was prediction as a prelude to stabilization. Reflecting a belief that fine-tuning was possible, most of the models used quarterly data and some even monthly data. As a result, the emphasis was on estimating equations that "worked," that is fitted the data well and were able to predict output levels, especially turning points. The theory underlying the estimated equations was often not formally set out, and it was unclear whether the estimated equation was a demand function, supply function, or reduced form equation (or some *ad hoc* combination).[2] There is now beginning more work on the microfoundations of national markets drawing on the sorts of analysis outlined in the previous chapters.

Given the interest in short-run changes in national income, the macro literature concerns itself mainly with the level of new housing starts or with the value of new construction. New construction is a volatile sector in the short run; recall figure 1.2 showing the deviation of starts from their long-run trend. The production of services from the existing stock and the creation of new stock using existing buildings are given less attention because these are relatively inelastic in the short run.

The stylized model of the housing market underlying the econometric work (often implicitly) is set out graphically in figure 5.1.[3] Households demand *dwelling units*, and the national market demand curve for dwelling units is *DD*. The supply of dwelling units in the short run is completely inelastic, *SS*; the existing stock is supplied regardless of price. This market for existing dwelling units establishes the equilibrium price per dwelling unit: where *DD* intersects *SS* at P_1. This price is assumed by builders to prevail during the month or quarter under consideration because the volume of new construction is such a small fraction of the total number of dwelling units. The level of housing construction is established by the intersection of the *CC* curve and the price line. Such models are often called stock-flow models: demand and existing stock determine the price of stock; the price and the new stock supply curve determine the flow of new stock. The new units constructed, C_1, are added to the stock at the end of the first period. The short-run supply curve of dwelling units in the next period is *S'S'*, which represents the net effect of the depreciation of the old stock and the addition of C_1 new units. A new price per dwelling unit is established, P_2, and the resulting level of new construction is C_2. This process continues until in equilibrium new construction just equals depreciation: there is no tendency for price, stock, or construction levels to change.

This model of the housing market is really not very different from the model of housing as a standard commodity presented at the beginning of chapter four. This treatment separates for special emphasis the volume of new construction; the phenomenon depicted however is implicit in the supply curve of the previous model. Here the analysis is in terms of dwelling units, while there it was in terms of housing services; but implicit in figure 5.1 is the assumption that all dwelling units are identical and yield the same quantity of housing services. Both approaches ignore the heterogeneity of housing and any spatial features of housing markets. The national model assumes that separate local markets can be aggregated, and the housing sector behaves "as if" it were one single market.

Figure 5.1 is often used to study the level of all types of housing starts in aggregate, and sometimes used to represent separately the markets for single detached houses (which households purchase) and multiple-unit housing (which households rent), although tenure choice is not modelled explicitly. The single and multiple starts are separated because households and builders respond somewhat differently in the two markets, and it is felt more accurate forecasts of total starts can be achieved with disaggregated predictions.

The factors influencing the housing markets for both single and multiple dwellings are familiar. On the demand side, the influences are mediated through changes in the number of households because, by definition, one household occupies one dwelling unit. Increases in permanent income increase the demand for dwelling units because more households are formed – the young leave home sooner; individuals, couples, and families no longer double up; the elderly remain in their own homes longer. Also there is a positive income elasticity of demand for new units. Demographic factors have a strong influence on household formation; not only the numbers of people but also the age and sex composition, average family size, and so on. Household formation is also a function of the price of housing services (see Smith [1984]). If the ownership and rental markets are disaggregated, the price of a dwelling unit in one market affects the demand curve in the other market. The "price" of a dwelling unit in the ownership market is not the price of purchasing a dwelling unit but rather the user cost, which is extremely sensitive to changes in the mortgage rate of interest. Any changes in the other terms of the mortgage also influence the user cost. The income tax treatment of housing also shapes demand because the nom-

FIGURE 5.1
Stock-Flow Model Emphasizing New Construction

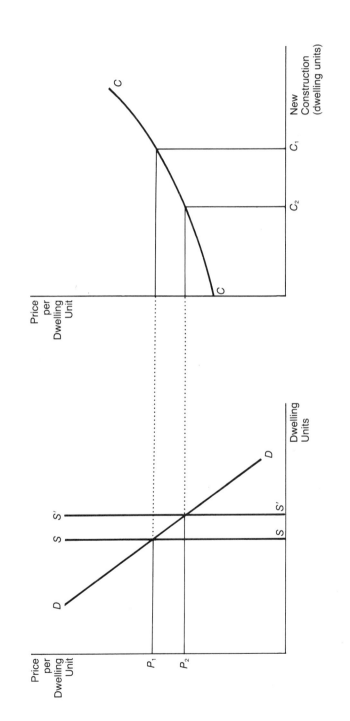

inal price will differ from the after-tax price. In a dynamic model, expectations about incomes, prices, mortgage rates of interest, mortgage terms, and capital gains become relevant variables.

The usual variables influence the CC function. Dwelling units are produced using land, labour, and materials; the production function (importantly the elasticity of substitution between inputs), the factor prices, the share of each factor in total outlay, and the price elasticity of factor supply as the industry expands all shape the new construction supply curve. As well, the industrial structure is important – in Canada the building industry is quite competitive, with many different sized firms. If supplies of single and multiple units are separated, the multiple supply curve is influenced further by expected vacancies, operating costs, and property taxes, and most importantly by the mortgage rates of interest and the terms of mortgage credit. Multiple unit construction is financed primarily through a mortgage, with loan-to-value ratios as high as ninety and ninety-five percent. Builders of single detached houses for sale are also concerned with the mortgage rate of interest, but analytically this should be recognized as a demand side influence: the supply curve indicates how much will be constructed at a given price; construction takes a long time, and so builders must make decisions on the basis of expected future prices, and the mortgage rate of interest (like all demand side factors) influences a builder's expectations about the future prices of single detached houses.

Examination of the exogenous factors to the markets in figure 5.1 reveals that most are not very changeable in the short run. Demographic factors, permanent income, and the production function all change relatively slowly. They would be useful in explaining long-run alterations in the housing market.[4] There is however at least one very changeable factor – mortgage credit. Explanations of the short-run fluctuation in housing starts have focused on this.

The level of new construction is very sensitive to the mortgage rate of interest (and of course other variables, especially the change in expected prices). Multiple-unit dwellings have high loan-to-value ratios, and variations in the mortgage rate of interest substantially affect the profitability of a project. Similarly households finance the purchase of a home usually with a mortgage for well over half the purchase price, so variations in the mortgage rate of interest substantially affect the owner-perceived price (assuming these are not offset by perceived increases in capital gains). Thus variations in the mortgage rate of interest lead to substantial variations in the level of housing starts.

The interest rate however does not capture all of the effect of the mortgage market on housing starts. A mortgage is a contract with many terms besides the interest rate: the amortization period, the term, the loan-to-value ratio of mortgages can also change. Variations in these terms affect the comprehensively measured profit to a developer or comprehensively measured price to a household, and so also affect the level of housing starts.

And the effects do not end with the mortgage rate of interest and the terms of mortgage loans. Many economists believe that mortgage markets do not equilibrate, in the sense that the quantity demanded of loans equals the quantity supplied at the announced market interest rate and loan terms. The rate and terms do not adjust to choke off demand, and credit is rationed. Some borrowers receive smaller loans than they desire, and the requests of some borrowers are turned down despite the fact that similar borrowers received loans. Thus it is felt the availability of credit, as well as the mortgage interest rate and mortgage terms, affect the level of housing starts. There is, however, considerable controversy about whether such rationing occurs.[5]

While the theoretical framework of the stock-flow model of figure 5.1 and the list of variables that influence single- and multiple-housing starts (with the exception of credit availability) are widely accepted, there is no agreed upon specification of the equation to be estimated. This is because most of the specifications are *ad hoc*, not derived from an explicit stock-flow model. As a result there are no consensus estimates of the elasticity of starts to changes in variables. Some flavour for the work can be gained by considering an example of an estimated equation. Equation 5.1 was reported in Smith (1974).

$$HS = 14.85 - 21.65Q1 + 7.22Q2 + 6.39Q3 + 8.88WW$$
$$+ 104.58(PH/CLC) - 10.75RM_{t-1} + 6.07\,(RM - RB)_{t-1} \quad \text{(5.1)}$$
$$+ 1.87\,(CMHC/PH)_t + 6.07\,(CMHC/PH)_{t-1}$$

$$R^2 = 0.94$$

The equation seeks to explain quarterly housing starts. Housing starts (in thousands of units) are a function of the price of dwelling units, PH, relative to construction and land costs, CLC, the mortgage rate of interest in the previous period, RM_{t-1}, and the availability of credit measured as the difference between the mortgage interest rate and the yield on long-term bonds in the previous period, $(RM - RB)_{t-1}$. The cost and availability of credit variables were lagged one-quarter because financing is usually arranged some months prior to the actual start of construction. These usual variables are augmented to deal with seasonal factors and public sector mortgage lending.

Regardless of the overall level, starts follow a regular pattern across the year because of the weather in Canada. They are low in the first quarter (January, February, March), high in the second and third quarter and low again in the fourth quarter (October, November, December). This is dealt with by adding three seasonal dummy variables: Q1, Q2, and Q3. Variable Q1 takes the value one if the observations relate to the first quarter and zero otherwise; variable Q2 takes the value one if the observations relate to the second quarter and zero otherwise, and so on. If all three dummies have the value zero, the observations relate to the fourth quarter. The estimated equation reveals the expected pattern. Suppose all the independent variables (except the seasonal dummies) were constant across the year – housing starts would not be constant. They would be 21,650 units lower than fourth-quarter starts in the first quarter; 7,220 units higher than fourth-quarter starts in the second quarter; and 6,390 units higher than fourth-quarter starts in the third quarter.

The equation must also be modified to deal with public sector lending. In the 1950s and 1960s, the period from which the data used to estimate this equation were taken, only the federal government was a significant mortgage lender (since then the provincial governments have loaned large amounts). A dummy variable, WW, is added to represent a winter works program that provided a $500 subsidy per dwelling in buildings of one to four units; the dummy takes the value one in the fourth quarter of 1963 to 1965 inclusive, and zero elsewhere. Two variables – the current-quarter mortgage lending (in hundreds of millions of dollars) and the previous-quarter mortgage lending by Canada Mortgage and Housing Corporation, deflated by 1957 dwelling unit prices – are added to represent public sector lending.

All of the variables have the expected signs. The winter works program increased fourth-quarter starts. Increases in house prices, private credit availability, and public lending increase starts; while increases in construction costs or the mortgage interest rate reduce housing starts. At first glance it might appear that one million 1957 dollars of public sector lending would generate an additional 79.4 housing starts, but this would not correctly measure the result of public sector lending. Public loans must be financed, either by reducing expenditures, increasing taxes, or increasing public sector borrowing. The borrowing may be from the private sector or from the central bank. The offsetting effects of the financing must be balanced against the lending to establish the net effect of increased public mortgage lending. If, as is likely, the financing raises interest rates, there will be substantial offsets in reduced privately financed housing starts.

HOUSING FLUCTUATIONS AND MACROECONOMIC FLUCTUATIONS

As already noted, housing starts are a particularly volatile component of national income and have been singled out for special study in the context of analysing fluctuations in the national economy. Housing starts fluctuations were explained largely by variations in the cost and availability of credit, with some secondary influence from the variations in construction and land costs. The influence of public sector mortgage lending was also strong; although it is not clear whether overall it smoothed or widened the fluctuations. A central concern of this work was whether the fluctuations in housing moved in phase with fluctuations in the national economy or were countercyclical.

During the 1950s and 1960s, it was widely believed that housing starts were roughly countercyclical; turning down well before the peak in the national cycle and turning up well before the trough in the national cycle. The explanation, developed mainly by Guttentag (1961), was that mortgage credit was a residual. The total credit available was constant over the business cycle. Financial intermediaries made both loans to businesses for investment and mortgage loans, but serviced the business loans first. During an upturn in the national economy, the demand for business loans and mortgages rose, but because business loans were serviced first, mortgage lending was squeezed and housing starts fell after the economy had expanded for a time. The reverse held true in a downturn. This argument for a countercyclical housing cycle was based on a pure availability of credit effect, but there was no explicit modelling of the loan and mortgage markets or explanation of why lending of this sort was in the interests of intermediaries.

An alternative mechanism that can imply a countercyclical housing sector, relies on the cost rather than availability of credit. As the economy expands, the demand for credit increases, raising interest rates. The housing starts sector is more interest sensitive than the remainder of the economy, especially business investment, and so as the economy expands housing starts fall (and the business sector gains a larger share of total credit). As the economy goes into recession, the reverse occurs and starts rise. The effect of changes in credit costs dominate the effects of income changes, which would tend to make housing procyclical.

Both explanations rely on mortgage credit moving in a regular way, with the expansions and contractions of the national economy. In times of stagflation – falling output and rising inflation – this regular relationship can break down. A recession may be accompanied by high mortgage interest rates, and so housing starts and the national economy will be in phase.

The analysis thus far has said nothing about the behaviour of government macroeconomic policy during business fluctuations. A more complex analysis would make monetary and fiscal policy endogenous and then consider whether the housing sector is pro- or countercyclical. If fiscal and, especially, monetary policy tighten to reduce the peak, and relax to raise the trough of the national business cycle, again housing will be countercyclical. However if a recession is accompanied by high inflationary expectations and monetary policy is tightened as a result, housing can follow the national economy.

The available evidence suggests that in the 1950s and early 1960s, in both Canada and the United States, housing starts were counter-cyclical. In recent years this pattern has broken down (recall figure 1.2). Housing starts have tended to move more with the national economy, but also have had fluctuations not seen in the national economy.[6] This of course does not deny the importance of mortgage interest rates (and perhaps) availability in determining housing starts and their fluctuations; it merely points out that the relationship between the mortgage market and the national economy has become more irregular than in the past.

HOUSING IN A GENERAL EQUILIBRIUM MODEL

There is an alternative way to consider the operation of the housing market in the national economy that is microeconomic rather than macroeconomic in orientation. It considers the national economy as a series of separate but interrelated markets – both markets for goods and services, and markets for factors of production. These markets are per-fectly competitive and in equilibrium simultaneously – hence the name, general equilibrium analysis. The effects of changes in variables on the economy are studied using the comparative statics technique. This ap-proach to the economy is in sharp contrast to the macroeconomic models that emphasize disequilibrium of the system and adjustment over time. Economists are now attempting a synthesis, but it is by no means complete.

The general equilibrium approach is therefore not very useful in analysing the level of housing starts and its fluctuations, or similar short-run phenomena. However it is central to understanding the operation of the housing market in the national economy in a longer-run perspective. The microeconomic models of a single-housing market in chapter four were unable to show the relationships between the housing market and other commodity markets or the factor markets. They dealt with the equilibrium in only one market – and hence the analysis is called partial equilibrium analysis. Suppose the housing production function were to change, and the supply curve of housing services shifted down and to the right; partial equilibrium analysis predicts that the price of housing would fall, and the quantity ex-changed would increase. This implies that consumers have allocated their incomes differently. How does this reallocation affect demand and prices in other commodity markets? And if other commodity prices change, how does this affect the demand curve for housing services? The partial equilibrium demand curves were drawn assuming other prices were fixed, but the expansion of output of the housing sector may change relative factor prices. How does this affect other commodity markets? It is toward answering these sorts of questions that general equilibrium analysis is directed. General equilibrium analysis is especially useful in examining relative commodity prices and relative factor prices, and therefore in examining changes in the distribution of income.

The simplest general equilibrium model contains two goods markets and two factor markets. While obviously an abstraction, the two-good, two-factor model is very powerful and of assistance in developing one's intuition about the operation of a multimarket economy.[7]

Suppose the two goods in the economy are housing and a composite good, both produced using the two factors: capital and labour. Assume, as it is realistic to do, that the production of housing services is more capital intensive than the production of the composite good – that is, at any factor price ratio the capital to labour ratio in housing will be higher than the capital to labour ratio in the composite sector. In a competitive economy factors will earn the same return in all sectors, or they would leave the low-paying sector for the high-paying sector. The factor price ratio will be the same in all sectors. Also, all consumers pay the same price for the two final goods, and all producers receive the same price.

The technique of comparative statics can be used to show the effect of a change in an exogenous factor on the general equilibrium. Suppose household preferences shifted in favour of housing. The economy would produce more housing and less of the composite good, and the relative price of housing would rise. As the output of housing rises the relative price of capital rises. This is intuitively appealing, because housing is capital intensive. As the housing sector expands, inputs – capital and labour – must be drawn from the composite goods sector. But these inputs are released from the composite goods sector in a lower capital-labour ratio than exists in the housing sector. Therefore the relative price of capital is bid up to restore factor market equilibrium. The extent of the relative factor price change depends upon the differences in the factor intensities of the two sectors, and the elasticities of substitution of their production functions.

These relative price changes have effects on the distribution of household income. On the uses side of the household budget, all would be affected by the change in relative product prices. On the sources side of the budget, those whose incomes came from capital would gain, while those whose incomes came from labour would lose. Neither partial equilibrium analysis nor macroeconomic analysis is able to explore these relative product and factor price changes. To answer questions where these price changes are central – for example, to answer how a change in labour supply or a large government housing program will alter the distribution of income – the general equilibrium framework is appropriate.

THE MORTGAGE MARKET

Like the work on housing starts, most research into mortgage markets has been undertaken in the context of large econometric models of the national economy. And again the emphasis has been on estimating equations "that worked." The microfoundations of the equations have not been spelled out, and it is not clear whether the estimated equations are demand, supply, or reduced form functions. This can in part be explained because the verbal descriptions of the operation of mortgage markets place much emphasis on disequilibrium and adjustment, but micro modelling of these phenomena is in its infancy.

The starting point in thinking about the mortgage market is to see it situated in a larger system of credit markets, which in turn is part of the entire economic system. Regardless of whether one is monetarist or Keynesian, macroeconomic theory offers an explanation of the determinants of the rate of interest (and price level, the level of national income, and the rate of unemployment). The interest rate and national income are jointly determined by equilibrium in the goods market (aggregate demand equals aggregate supply) and the assets market (the demand for money equals the supply of money). Therefore both real and monetary sides of the national economy are determinants of the rate of interest. This theory also emphasizes the role of government, through both monetary and fiscal policy, as a determinant of the rate of interest.[8]

The next step is to consider the mortgage market separately, although in the context of the nationally set aggregate interest rate. If the mortgage market is perfectly integrated into the aggregate market, and only a small part of it, there will be a perfectly elastic supply of mortgage loans at the aggregate rate of interest. The demand curve for mortgage loans – the aggregation of the demands of builders of apartments, of buyers of new detached houses, and of those buying or refinancing existing housing – has the usual downward slope: as the mortgage rate of interest falls, the demand for mortgage loans increases. In this model, the demand for mortgage loans determines the volume of mortgage lending, and the national economy determines the mortgage rate. If monetary policy for example raises interest rates, the supply curve shifts up, interest rates rise, and the volume of mortgage lending declines.

A slightly different model assumes the supply curve of mortgage funds is slightly upward sloping after some volume of lending. To secure a larger flow of mortgage credit the mortgage rate must rise to encourage financial intermediaries to place a larger fraction of their portfolios in mortgages, and to encourage savers to place more funds in those financial intermediaries that specialize in mortgage lending. The gap between the mortgage rate and the bond rate must be widened.

This is illustrated in figure 5.2, where *SMSM* is the supply curve of mortgage funds and *DMDM* the demand curve. Now both the national economy and the demand for mortgage loans establish the mortgage interest rate. If the demand for mortgage loans increases (and the causal factor had no significant influence on the national economy), the *DMDM* curve shifts up and to the right to *DM'DM'*; mortgage interest rates rise, the gap between mortgage rates and the national rate widens, and the volume of mortgage lending increases.

The two above models assume that the mortgage market equilibrates or clears (demand equals supply), and the issue of availability does not arise. However as noted earlier in this chapter, many economists argue that the mortgage market does not clear, especially in response to shifts in the macroeconomic economy. This view is represented in figure 5.3. There is an initial equilibrium at r_m and L_m; monetary policy becomes more restrictive, and the supply curve shifts to *SM'SM'*. The market however does not clear. The old interest rate prevails, r_m, and the quantity

FIGURE 5.2
Mortgage Market: Less Than Elastic Supply

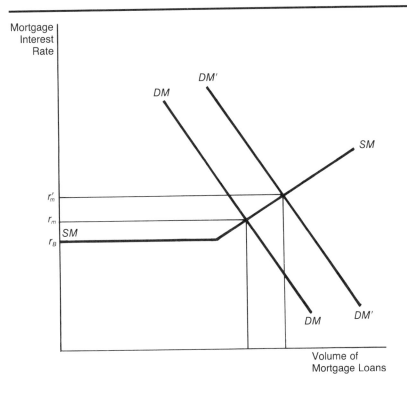

FIGURE 5.3
Mortgage Market: Credit Rationing

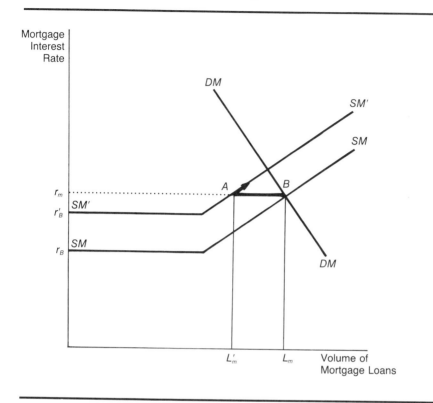

exchanged is determined by the intersection of a horizontal line through r_m and the supply curve. Only L'_m is loaned. There is excess demand for funds equal to the distance AB, and there is credit rationing. Availability becomes an issue as well as the interest rate in describing credit conditions. The rate of change of the mortgage rate is a function of excess supply or demand: in this case there is upward pressure on rates. In this model the mortgage rate adjusts with a lag. Exogenous factors increase the bond rate, but the mortgage rate does not follow immediately, so the gap between the rates narrows, causing intermediaries to adjust their portfolios and savers to place fewer funds in mortgage institutions. Gradually however the mortgage rate does adjust.

Now let us look more closely at the demand and supply sides of the mortgage market. There is very little writing on the demand for mortgage credit – most writers treat it simply as proportional to the demand for housing services or stock. This of course is not true. Loan-to-value ratios can vary for a number of reasons. For example, in the credit rationing model, some of the rationing is achieved by lowering loan-to-value ratios. Loan-to-value ratios change over the housing cycle. The demand for mortgage credit depends on portfolio considerations of owner-occupiers and landlords. The tax treatment of each, their desire for liquidity, their attitudes to risk all influence the demand for credit and the resulting loan-to-value ratio.

At the outset let us retain this assumption of proportionality. Demand for mortgage credit arises from the owners of housing stock, the credit being a means to finance the purchase. In the rental market, the owner of the stock is the landlord; in the ownership market the owner of the stock is the occupant, in his capacity as landlord renting to himself. Let us abstract for the moment from the problem of housing tenure and return to the world of housing as a standard commodity. Equilibrium in that market for housing services in the medium run was depicted in figure 4.1, reproduced here as the top diagram in figure 5.4. The demand curve for housing services was derived assuming that the mortgage rate of interest was given; as the price of housing services falls, the quantity demanded of housing services increases, given the mortgage rate. However as the quantity demanded of housing services increases, the demand for mortgage credit increases, and so implicit in figure 4.1 was the assumption that the supply of mortgage credit was perfectly elastic. Suppose however that mortgage credit is not perfectly elastically supplied, then the housing and mortgage markets cannot be separated but must be solved simultaneously. This is illustrated in figure 5.4. Each demand curve DD, $D'D'$, and $D''D''$ has been derived in the usual way assuming mortgage credit is perfectly elastically supplied at a different mortgage rate of interest r_m, r'_m and r''_m ($r''_m < r'_m < r_m$). Assume that the quantity demanded of mortgage credit is strictly proportional to the quantity demanded of housing services. The "demand curve" for mortgage credit can be derived from the top diagram of figure 5.4; it represents the pairs of mortgage interest rate and mortgage lending (proportional to housing services) that are consistent with equilibrium in the housing services market.[9] This is curve $DMDM$ in figure 5.4. If the supply of mortgage credit $SMSM$ is added, the simultaneous determination of the two markets is complete. The equilibrium interest rate is r^*_m, the quantity of lending is L^*_m. The "demand" for mortgage credit thus depends not only on those variables that influence the demand for housing services, but also on those variables that influence the supply of services. For example, suppose incomes rose; the demand for housing services would increase, each DD curve would shift right, and the $DMDM$ curve would shift right (the extent of the shift depending upon how much the DD curves shift and the shape of the SS curve). The mortgage rate of interest would rise, but the increase would be muted by the fact that the price of housing services rose as well.

FIGURE 5.4
Housing and Mortgage Markets: Both Clear

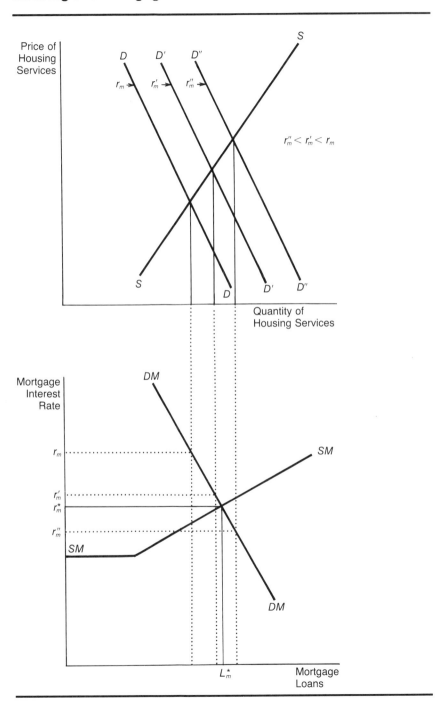

On the supply side, mortgage loans are provided by many agents with different objectives.[10] They fall into three groups: private financial institutions such as banks and insurance companies; governments; and a composite group made up of estates, co-operatives, and individuals.

For the first group, the making of mortgage loans is part of their business of financial intermediation. They are profit-making enterprises – gathering savings from the public in return for obligations, and then investing these assembled funds. The obligations that intermediaries issue to attract savings are many and varied – banks and trust companies offer chequing accounts, savings accounts, and certificates under which funds are deposited for established time-periods (30 days, 90 days, one year, five years, and so on); insurance companies offer insurance policies. An institution's success in attracting savings will depend on the supply function of savings and the obligations offered by competing institutions. The alternative investments available to intermediaries are similarly varied – ranging from goverment and corporate bonds, to personal loans and short-term financing loans for businesses, and of course mortgages. Each of these investments has different characteristics. They differ in return, risk of loss, probability of early repayment, length of time over which the funds are committed, and liquidity. The allocation of the intermediary's investment portfolio into these investments depends upon their relative characteristics. In general, if all characteristics remain the same except that the return on one investment increases, a larger share of the portfolio will be allocated to that investment. Hence if the difference between the mortgage rate of interest and the government bond rate declines (for example as the economy expands), intermediaries will place a higher fraction of new investment funds into bonds.

The relationship between the obligations and investments of intermediaries determines profitability. Obviously the return on the latter must exceed the cost of the former. In periods of volatile and unpredictable interest rates, such as the last fifteen years, the relationship between the term of investments and obligations becomes critical. Suppose savings were being secured using savings deposits on which interest rates were set weekly , and the deposited funds were being invested in mortgages with a twenty-five-year term ("borrowing short and lending long"). If interest rates in the economy were different than expected, the payments to savings account holders would change, but the returns from mortgage investments would remain the same. An unexpected decrease in interest rates would cause unexpected profits (assuming mortgage borrowers do not pay the prepayment penalties and refinance at the lower interest rate); an unexpected increase in interest rates would cause unexpected losses and even insolvency. As inflation rates became more volatile in the last fifteen years, savers lent their funds on shorter terms, and mortgage terms became shorter and shorter. The terms of investments were shortened and matched to those of obliga-tions; and the interest rate risk was shifted to the mortgage borrower.[11]

The behaviour of the other two groups of mortgage lenders is some-what different. The government sector responds to conditions in the economy – such as rising mortgage interest rates, low housing con-sumption by the poor, or falling housing starts – but its decisions are the outcome of a complex interaction of voters, politicians, media, civil servants, and interest groups. Almost all housing analysis treats the government sector as exogenous and does not provide positive analysis that would explain the government's decisions. The third group has some members such as co-operatives whose behaviour is relatively close to that of a standard intermediary, and other members such as individuals lending higher risk second mortgages, and corporations lending as part of their employee compensation package. As a whole this group is less responsive to changes in relative characteristics of obligations and investments, and therefore has attracted less attention in the research connected with macroeconomic models.

The sort of econometric work that has been done related to mortgage markets can be best illustrated by an example; the equations below are taken from Smith (1974). The analysis sought to explain the conven-tional mortgage interest rate, as opposed to the NHA rate. The supply of conventional mortgage approvals came from three types of lending institutions – life insurance companies, trust companies, and mortgage loan companies – and was a function of certain variables as in equation 5.2; where $CRMA$ is conventional residential mortgage approvals,

$$CRMA = g(RC - RB, RC - RNHA, A, M_{t-1}) \qquad (5.2)$$

$RC - RB$ is the difference between the conventional mortgage interest rate and the average yield on long-term Government of Canada bonds, $RC - RNHA$ the difference between the conventional and NHA mortgage interest rates, A is the total assets of a financial institution, and M_{t-1} is the stock of mortgages of the institution lagged one period. The specification is based on a stock-adjustment model of institutional be-haviour with desired mortgage holdings depending on the yield on conventional mortgages relative to alternative investments and on the institution's assets. The total supply of conventional approvals was the sum of approvals by each institution. The demand for approvals was taken to be related to the demand for new residential construction, and therefore primarily influenced by the relationship between the demand for housing and the existing stock of dwellings as in equation 5.3; where DCM is the demand for conventional approvals, YD/FAM is perma-

$$DCM = f(YD/FAM, SH/FAM, RC, RNHA, RB) \qquad (5.3)$$

nent real family disposable income, and SH/FAM is per family stock of dwelling units. RB is included as the opportunity cost of funds.

Supply and demand equations were equated and solved for RC. The results of the ordinary least squares estimation of the equation are 5.4.

$$RC = 17.33 - 16.85 \, (SH/FAM)_{t-1} + 3.11 \, (YD/FAM)$$

$$- \, 0.0036 \sum_i A^i + 0.0057 \sum_i M^i_{t-1} \qquad (5.4)$$

$$+ \, 0.24 \, RNHA_{t-1} + 0.54 \, RB_{t-1}$$

$$R^2 = 0.96$$

The coefficients are all significant and have the expected signs. The conventional rate falls as the previous period housing stock rises (the demand for new construction will be less, *ceteris paribus*); rises with family income; falls with increases in total institutional assets (the flow of credit would be larger); rises with the lagged stock of mortgage debt (for a given desired stock of mortgages, the larger previous stock, the lower will be current approvals and hence the higher current rates); and rises with the rates of return on competing investments. While not precise, the link with the previous graphical models and discussions is clear.

Thus far, a mortgage loan has been analysed as a homogeneous commodity exchanged between a borrower and a lender – the demand side and the supply side interact to determine an interest rate, and the volume of loans exchanged. This, however, is an extreme theoretical abstraction; the actual market is much more complex than this standard market model. Most importantly, the commodity exchanged cannot be described simply by the dollar amount; there are many other terms to the loan. The amortization period, the term, the payment schedule and prepayment privileges are also aspects of the contract. These have varied significantly in the postwar period. Amortization periods lengthened during the 1950s with an accompanying extension of the term; then in the late 1960s and 1970s, mortgage terms were reduced from 25 to 30 years to a period as short as one year. In the past, mortgages were almost always paid back with a constant monthly payment over the amortization period; now graduated payment mortgages are available. Sometimes the rate adjusts automatically with credit conditions. Any complete mortgage market model would have to make these aspects of the contract endogenous; the outcome of the interaction between borrower and lender.

Even these loan terms do not fully describe the commodity exchanged. A loan is not a once-and-for-all exchange between the demand agent and the supply agent. Rather, a loan is a commitment by the demand agent to repay the money advanced by the supply agent over a period of time. The security that the demander can provide that the repayment obligation will be met in the manner specified is an important characteristic of the commodity exchanged. Under a mortgage, the borrower contracts to repay, and if he does not, the lender can take ownership of the house. The ultimate security on the loan is the value of the house or apartment. One sort of risk to the lender is that the value of the property will fall below the principal outstanding on the mortgage. This risk is dealt with by only lending a portion of the value of the property. The greater the probability of a decline in property values, the lower the loan-to-value ratio must be to maintain the same probability of capital loss.

And finally, the borrower is part of a full description of a mortgage. The borrower has agreed to follow a certain payment schedule, with provisions for penalties if payments are missed, and provisions for more rapid repayment. Usually an individual has the right to repay an NHA mortgage after three years or on any anniversary date thereafter, and a conventional mortgage after five years, subject to a penalty of three months' interest. A complete description of the commodity exchanged would describe the possible repayment patterns, and the probability of each occurring. Borrowers can deviate from the expected repayment schedule for a number of reasons. They may miss payments because of unexpected decreases in income, or increases in other expenditures. If these unexpected changes prove permanent, the owners may feel they can no longer carry the house, and so decide to sell the house and use the proceeds to pay off the mortgage. When the monthly payment becomes too burdensome, it is in the owner's interest to sell the house and repay the mortgage rather than default on the mortgage, assuming that the house value is greater than the mortgage principal outstanding. A good – though not perfect – proxy measure for the probability of periodic delinquency or repayment due to falling income is the ratio of the annual mortgage payments to the annual income of the borrower. The higher this gross-debt-service ratio the greater the probability of delinquency or forced sale and repayment. This ratio is important in describing the commodity exchanged for it helps to indicate what sort of payment patterns are likely to occur. Advance payment can also occur if the borrower decides to move; decides to prepay some of the mortgage because of an unanticipated increase in income or decrease in other expenditures; decides to have a larger mortgage in order to raise money for other expenditures; or if mortgage interest rates fall so far that even with the prepayment penality the borrower is better off with a new mortgage at the lower interest rate. (Note that lenders cannot call in mortgage loans if interest rates rise.) Advance payment due to most of these causes is hard to predict and presumably does not vary in any systematic way across borrowers.[12]

The possibility of prepayment, for whatever the reason, is of considerable importance to a lender. There are significant costs, which are not fully compensated for by the prepayment penalty, to relending the funds. Therefore, prepayment reduces the rate of return on a given pool of funds. Furthermore, if the prepaid mortgage can only be reinvested at a lower interest rate, the rate of return on a given pool of funds with a given pattern of obligations will be reduced. Falling interest rates can severely squeeze the profits of intermediaries if prepayments occur and obligations are fixed at the old higher interest rates. Of course, during periods of rising interest rates, prepayments can raise the rate of return on a portfolio.

Thus the commodity exchanged in the mortgage market is extremely complex. The characteristics of the loan are not only the interest rate, and the other terms of the mortgage contract, but also the characteristics of the property, the characteristics of the borrower, and the general economic environment. Lenders differ in their evaluation of these characteristics according to their attitudes to risk, their costs of reinvestment, and the nature of their obligations. It is not surprising that there is only a very small secondary market in mortgages, except those insured under the National Housing Act. Every mortgage has special characteristics, and it is very costly to assess a portfolio of mortgages offered for sale.

One often reads in popular writing that mortgage lenders set the loan-to-value ratio, or that mortgage lenders set the gross-debt-service ratio. In a certain mechanical sense these conditions are set by the lender, just as in a mechanical sense the lender sets the mortgage rate. However, it should be understood that the loan-to-value ratio and the gross-debt-service ratio are market outcomes and subject to the influence of both the demand side and the supply side – just as the mortgage interest rate.[13]

HOUSING, MORTGAGE MARKETS, AND INFLATION

During the 1970s and 1980s in Canada, the rate of inflation has been high, variable, and unpredictable. This has meant considerable turbulence in housing and mortgage markets. The evolution of housing policy over this period is the evolution of our understanding of and response to the effects of inflation on the housing and mortgage markets. A look at these effects offers the opportunity to expand on some of the themes developed in this and previous chapters – the relationship between the mortgage market and the national economy, the market determination of the terms of the mortgage contract, and the relationship between housing demand and the mortgage market.

High inflation rates create a so-called tilt problem with the standard level payment mortgage (LPM). Consider first a world with no inflation and a real rate of interest of 5 percent – so the nominal interest rate is 5 percent. A $50,000 mortgage implies annual monthly payments of $3,490, assuming a twenty-five-year amortization period. The real value of the annual payment is the same at the beginning of the mortgage and at the end of the amortization period, because the rate of inflation is zero. If the household had an annual income of $25,000 which grew at 2 percent per year in real terms, the annual mortgage payments would be about 14 percent of income in the first year, and 9 percent in the twenty-fifth year (see table 5.1). Now consider a world with a 10-percent inflation rate – a fully anticipated inflation rate. The nominal interest rate would be 15 percent; as the sum of the real interest rate and the anticipated inflation rate. The annual payments using an LPM would become $7,685. However, the real value of these constant payments would decline substantially over the life of the mortgage because inflation is 10 percent. The real value of the annual payments in the twenty-fifth year is only $780, in initial dollars. Nominal annual payments would be 31 percent of household income in the first year, and only 2 percent in the final year, assuming household income grew at a rate 2 points above the inflation rate (see table 5.1). An increase in the fully anticipated rate of inflation affects interest rates and mortgage payments immediately, but only affects household income over time. The present value of mortgage payments in both the zero inflation and

TABLE 5.1
Level Payment Mortgages and Graduated Payment Mortgages

	Annual Payment ($)	Borrower Income ($)	Annual Payment-to-Income Ratio
I LEVEL PAYMENT MORTGAGE			
(i) zero inflation, 5-percent real interest: 5-percent nominal interest.			
year 1	3,490	25,000	.1396
10	3,490	29,877	.1168
25	3,490	40,211	.0870
(ii) 10-percent inflation, 5-percent real interest: 15-percent nominal interest.			
year 1	7,685	25,000	.3074
10	7,685	69,327	.1109
25	7,685	379,466	.0203
II GRADUATED PAYMENT MORTGAGE			
(ii) 10-percent inflation, 5-percent real interest: 15-percent nominal interest.			
year 1	3,490	25,000	.1396
10	8,483	69,327	.1224
25	42,551	379,466	.1120

SOURCE: Carr and Smith (1983). Reprinted with permission from Goldberg and Gau's *North American Housing Markets Into the Twenty-First Century*, copyright 1983, Ballinger Publishing Company.

10-percent inflation worlds is the same and equal to the principal – however the timing of the real payments has been changed. Under an LPM the real payments are tilted forward into the early years of the mortgage – hence, the "tilt" problem. The higher are inflation rates, the more the real payments are tilted forward.[14]

Another way to view this problem is through the user cost concept. Let us suppose that a $100,000 house is purchased using $50,000 in savings and a $50,000 mortgage. The user cost of acquiring housing services for one year through ownership is foregone interest on equity, mortgage interest, less capital gains (plus other costs of operation that are ignored here). In the zero inflation world, the user cost is $5,000, and constant over time. For simplicity the actual payment schedule of an LPM has not been used (which includes both principal and interest payments), and pure mortgage interest cost is used (see table 5.2). In the 10-percent inflation world, the user cost measure remains at $5,000 in the first year, and rises at 10 percent per year. This is as one would expect: inflation does not alter the true cost of housing services in the beginning, but over time the cost of services rises at the rate of inflation. However owners face a cash flow problem with inflation – nominal mortgage interest payments rise which are offset by capital gains, but mortgage payments must be made now while capital gains are accrued but unrealised. Over time the cash-flow problem diminishes as the real value of current mortgage payments declines.

It is essential in thinking about the effect of the tilt problem on housing demand to recognize the intertemporal nature of the choice problem. If the expected inflation rate were to increase and households are forced to use an LPM, the price of housing services would rise in the early periods of the mortgage – and this has often been recognized. However what is often forgotten is that the real cost of consuming a

TABLE 5.2
User Cost of Ownership

	Foregone Interest on Equity	Mortgage Interest	Capital Gains	Total
(i) zero inflation, 5-percent real interest: 5-percent nominal interest.				
year 1	50,000 × .05	50,000 × .05	100,000 − 100,000	
	= 2,500	= 2,500	= 0	5,000
year 2	50,000 × .05	50,000 × .05	100,000 − 100,000	
	= 2,500	= 2,500	= 0	5,000
(ii) 10-percent inflation, 5-percent real interest: 15-percent nominal interest.				
year 1	50,000 × .15	50,000 × .15	110,000 − 100,000	
	= 7,500	= 7,500	= 10,000	5,000
year 2	60,000 × .15	50,000 × .15	121,000 − 110,000	
	= 9,000	= 7,500	= 11,000	5,500

given stream of housing services is reduced in the later years of the mortgage. It is the income and substitution effects of these two price changes that determine the impact on housing demand. They will depend on the household's willingness to postpone the consumption of other goods into the future. The decrease in current demand for housing as expected inflation rises is, therefore, much less than one first might anticipate when looking at the rise in the constant monthly payment. The tax system further mitigates the decline in demand. The imputed income from owning a house is not taxed, and capital gains realised on sale of a principal residence are not taxed, so the relative attractiveness of housing as an investment increases in times of inflation. On balance, an increase in expected inflation likely reduces current demand mildly, when borrowers use an LPM.[15]

An increase in fully anticipated inflation does not alter the present value of payments with an LPM, only the timing of real payments; and an accommodating adjustment in the mortgage market should be possible in order that the time pattern of real payments would be the same as the zero inflation world. This is just what occurs through what are called graduated payment mortgages (GPM). Under a GPM, nominal mortgage payments rise over time and may be designed so that the real payments are constant.

A number of other adjustments to the mortgage contract are also possible to deal with high inflation, such as a price level adjusted mortgage (PLAM), or a shared appreciation mortgage (SAM). Under a PLAM, the borrower and the lender agree on a real mortgage rate of interest to be used in computing monthly payments; the outstanding principal on the mortgage is periodically re-evaluated according to some agreed upon price index. Suppose the real rate of interest were 5 percent and the inflation rate were 10 percent over the duration of the mortgage; then a PLAM would generate the same flow of mortgage payments as the GPM of table 5.1. However if the inflation rate were to fall below 10 percent over the amortization period of the mortgage, the payments under a PLAM would fall below those of the GPM; whereas PLAM payments would be higher if inflation rose above 10 percent. Under a SAM, the lender agrees to a lower rate of interest in return for a share of the capital gains when they are realised.

Despite the disruptions caused by inflation over the years, these new mortgage contracts that adjust for inflation are not widely used. Certainly institutional and household "inertia" are part of the reason why, but a proper economic explanation requires a model of the mortgage market with the mortgage contract endogenous. One must look at the effects of LPMs, GPMs, PLAMs, and SAMs on both the borrower and the lender. For example, each mortgage instrument implies a pattern of payments and also a pattern of real saving over time. This savings stream may or may not correspond to the optimal lifetime savings path emerging from the household's intertemporal decision. If the effect of inflation on households is to increase current savings, the LPM with its tilt effect may be better suited to the desired savings plan than the GPM. On the other side of the market, lenders find initial payments lower under a GPM than an LPM, to such an extent that the loan-to-value ratio rises in the early years of the mortgage. The default risk in the early years is therefore greater under the GPM.[16]

So far the analysis of this section has emphasized the impact of high rates of inflation, but equally and perhaps more important in recent years has been the variability and unpredictability of inflation rates. With unpredictable inflation rates, people become unwilling to enter long-term contracts. Depositors commit their funds to financial intermediaries for a shorter time, and so the terms of mortgages get shorter. Mortgage terms dropped from twenty-five to thirty years in the late 1950s to one year in the early 1980s – mortgages became virtually variable rate mortgages (VRM) adjusting to current financial conditions. Such mortgages shift all the risk of unexpected changes in the inflation rate onto the borrowers, because lenders obtain a very close match between their short-term mortgage loans and their short-term obligations to depositors. In the past, home buyers knew what their monthly payments would be over the entire mortgage – now with LPMs with short terms they face considerable uncertainty. In contrast, under the GPM the lender faces the risk of unexpected changes in the rate of inflation. Under a PLAM the buyer bears the risk.

This variability and unpredictability extend also to house prices and household incomes; and they may become less correlated with the inflation and mortgage rate. This causes greater risk to a homeowner of losing his home, and greater risk to a lender of capital loss. Again, the nature of these risks will differ under the various mortgage instruments. For example under an LPM after a few years, an unexpected drop in income or property values is unlikely to cause a default because the loan-to-value ratio and gross-debt-service ratio have been falling. This is not the case for a GPM; a drop in income growth or property value below the rate of inflation can cause serious problems for the borrower and lender.

The high and unpredictable inflation rates of the last fifteen years led to innovations in the mortgage contract, but no single form emerged dominant. As with any heterogeneous commodity, differences in producers and buyers ensured diversity in the market outcome. Even as inflation rates fall in the mid-1980s it is likely that the new mortgage contracts that were developed will remain.

SUGGESTIONS FOR FURTHER READING

Fair, R. C. (1973) "Monthly Housing Starts," in R. B. Ricks, ed., *National Housing Models* (Lexington, Mass.: Lexington Books).

Lessard, D., and F. Modigliani (1975) "Inflation and the Housing Market: Problems and Potential Solutions," in *New Mortgage Designs for Stable Housing in an Inflationary Environment* (Boston: Federal Reserve Bank of Boston).

Schwab, R. M. (1982) "Inflation Expectations and the Demand for Housing," *American Economic Review* 72: 143–53.

Smith, L. B. (1974) *The Postwar Canadian Housing and Residential Mortgage Markets and the Role of Goverment* (Toronto: University of Toronto Press). Chapters three, four, six, and seven.

6 | The Economic Rationale for Housing Policy

The remaining chapters of the book are devoted to the economic analysis of housing policy.

Should society subsidize the construction of new dwellings? Are shelter allowances a better way of assisting households than public housing? Ought the housing sector be protected from high interest rates that are caused by restrictive monetary policy? It is on how to answer these sorts of questions that chapters six, seven, and eight concentrate.

Chapters nine and ten approach policy in a different way. Instead of exploring what housing policy should be, they explore the actual housing programs in Canada and the effects of these programs.

In order to propose a role for government in housing matters, a different approach is required than was presented in previous chapters. Notice how each question above contains words like "should," "ought," or "a better way." Clearly, criteria are going to be required that permit one to judge whether something "should" be done. Previous chapters did not require any such criteria. There the questions dealt with measurement or explanation: What is the price elasticity of housing supply? What determines the equilibrium price of housing services in a rental market? Answering these sorts of questions is called positive analysis. In contrast to the measurement and explanation of positive analysis, normative analysis explores what ought to be. It explores a possible role for government to bring about a more desirable allocation of resources.

Normative analysis is also often called welfare economics. This is not the economics of welfare assistance to the poor, but of how to decide whether a resource reallocation leads to an improvement in society's welfare or well-being. This chapter and the next two can be thought of as the application of welfare economics to housing.[1]

THE SOCIAL WELFARE FUNCTION
The criteria or values used in welfare economics are often represented in a social welfare function (equation 6.1) that ranks all possible alter-

native situations or "social states" as they are often called. Mishan (1981, 114) defines social states "in their most general form as comprising alternative sets of outputs of private and collective goods, along with alternative factor supplies and with alternative ways of dividing the outputs among the different individuals that make up society." With the most commonly used functions, social welfare depends only on the

$$W = W[U_1(x_{11}, x_{12}, ... x_{1m}), U_2(x_{21}, x_{22}, ... x_{2m}),$$
$$... U_n(x_{n1}, x_{n2}, ... x_{nm})] \tag{6.1}$$

utility levels of the n persons in society; the utility level of the ith person is determined by their utility function, U_i (   ); and their utility depends upon their own consumption $(x_{i1}, . . . x_{im})$ of the m goods and services including leisure in the economy. The specification in equation 6.1 is general, and does not reveal the specific criterion for interpersonal utility comparisons. It is usually, though not always, assumed the social welfare function is Paretian, that is if the utility level of one individual rises and all other utility levels stay constant, the level of social welfare increases.

The way in which such a social welfare function ranks various states of the world, and how different standards of justice make interpersonal comparisons, can be illustrated graphically. Consider a simple world with only two people whose utility functions are known and assumed to be the same.[2] In figure 6.1, the horizontal axis measures the utility of individual two, and the vertical axis the utility of individual one. The points in this quadrant represent all possible pairs of utility levels that the two individuals could achieve. The social welfare function assigns a value to each pair, and therefore can rank the pairs. If two pairs receive the same value, society would be indifferent between them; and the joining of all pairs of equal value would trace out a social indifference curve. Figure 6.1 shows social indifference curves for several widely discussed social welfare functions.

Curve AA represents a utilitarian social welfare function: the sum of individual utilities measures social well-being. Curves such as BB favour equality more; the more L-shaped are the curves the greater is the value placed on equality. The curve CC is L-shaped and implies that if the two individuals begin equal, an increase in one individual's utility has no social value. This is the maxi-min principle advanced by Rawls (1971): social welfare is measued by the utility of the person with the lowest utility. Curve DD represents a non-Paretian social welfare function that is concerned with relative utility levels rather than absolute levels. An increase in utility of the person with the higher utility reduces society's welfare.

These social welfare functions, while differing in their concepts of justice and how they value alterations in the utility levels of the various

FIGURE 6.1
Social Indifference Curves of Alternative Social Welfare Functions

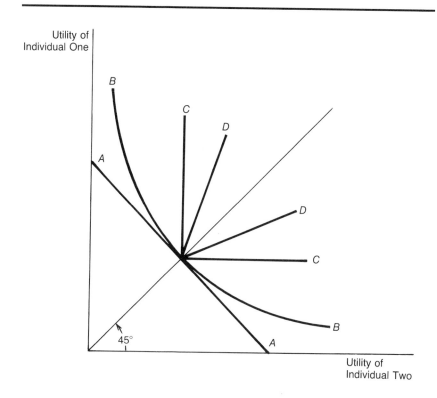

members of society, all perform the same function: they rank all possible social states, and therefore can be used as a guide to whether government intervention is justified, and which program is best. Stated very simply, the problem of housing policy is to intervene in housing matters in order to achieve the highest possible level of social welfare, as indicated by the social welfare function. This statement, of course, applies to any area of government policy, from income redistribution to stabilization.

A direct representation of the policy problem and of the importance of the social welfare function is presented in figure 6.2. Curve XY is the utility possibility frontier and represents the outer boundary of the feasible pairs of utility levels of individuals one and two, given society's resource endowments, technology, and the policy instruments available to government. Suppose the social state of an economy with no government intervention produced the pair of utilities corresponding to

FIGURE 6.2
Choice of the Optimal Social State

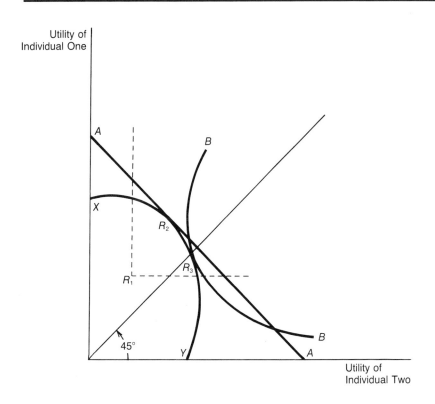

R_1. Then the government should intervene to reallocate resources and produce the utility pair R_2 if it followed a utilitarian social welfare function, or to produce pair R_3 if it followed the social welfare function represented by curve BB. In each case, the government chooses the resource allocation from the feasible set to maximize social welfare. Different social welfare functions, however, imply different outcomes and implicitly different interventions in the economy.

It is important to remember what determines the shape of the utility possibility frontier. The attainable set of utility pairs is shaped by several factors. It is shaped by the total initial endowments of factors of production – land, natural resources, time, labour, human and physical capital, and so on. It is shaped by the available technology of production, the behaviour of producers, the utility functions of consumers and their behaviour. Also, the feasible set is shaped by the instruments available to the government to be used to alter resource allocation. Economists usually summarize the available instruments into three categories – taxes, expenditures, and regulations – although these must be defined broadly to include such things as the creation of a central bank or a public enterprise.

Embodied in the shape of the utility possibility frontier, therefore, is both what instruments are available to government, and the response of consumers and suppliers to any intervention of government. Returning to the simple two-individual world of figure 6.2, the utility possibility frontier would be a straight line of slope -1 if available technology and endowments meant that only one output level was possible (the size of the "pie" was fixed), if household utility functions exhibited constant marginal utility, and government could redistribute income costlessly with lump-sum taxes and transfers that did not affect output levels. More usual assumptions about technology and utility functions imply a frontier that is concave to the origin. Suppose further that the instruments available to governments for income redistribution have incentive effects, and that policies to promote income (or utility) equality will reduce total output, then the utility possibility frontier might curl at the axes as shown in figure 6.2.

Figure 6.2 may seem an austere and abstract way of talking about housing policy, and indeed it is. However it should be remembered that the purpose of these chapters is not to analyse and describe the real world process of policy development, but to set out what is the optimal policy according to some criterion. It is to explore how changing ideas of how the economy functions, or changing the objective function leads to changes in the recommended policy. It is to set out "the grammar of arguments about policy" (Hahn 1973, 106).

Thus far the social welfare functions discussed have ranked the social states using a function whose arguments are the utility levels of members of society. This does not however exhaust the possibilities. Reading the analysis of housing policy by non-economists and listening to public discussion of housing problems makes it obvious that people judge the well-being of society not simply by utility levels. Society cares not only about the general distribution of people's well-being, but also about the consumption levels of certain commodities – housing, medical care, education, and so on. Society has a collective view that people are entitled to adequate housing. This idea will be referred to here as housing being a merit good. The term merit good has been used in several different ways by economists, but the definition below will make clear its usage here.[3]

A merit good is a commodity about whose consumption society has collective views. Society collectively believes that its consumption is meritorious. More formally, housing is a merit good if the housing consumption levels of people are arguments in the social welfare function; the consumption of housing contributes to social welfare beyond the utility it yields to the person consuming it; for example as in equation 6.2, where housing is good 2. Perhaps a restriction should be added, equation 6.3, to indicate that only when the housing consumption of an individual is below some basic minimum, call it $\bar{x}_2$, is it an independent argument in the social welfare function. Any increases in housing consumption beyond this level do not have merit good characteristics.

$$W = W[U_1, U_2, \dots U_n, x_{12}, x_{22}, \dots x_{n2}]$$

$$U_i = U_i(x_{i1}, x_{i2}, \dots x_{im}) \tag{6.2}$$

$$\frac{\partial W}{\partial x_{i2}} > \frac{\partial W}{\partial U_i} \cdot \frac{\partial U_i}{\partial x_{i2}}$$

$$\frac{\partial W}{\partial x_{i2}} > \frac{\partial W}{\partial U_i} \cdot \frac{\partial U_i}{\partial x_{i2}} \qquad x_{i2} < \bar{x}_2$$

$$\tag{6.3}$$

$$\frac{\partial W}{\partial x_{i2}} = \frac{\partial W}{\partial U_i} \cdot \frac{\partial U_i}{\partial x_{i2}} \qquad x_{i2} \geq \bar{x}_2$$

To emphasize the similar normative basis of merit goods and income distribution, merit goods can be thought of as part of a broad conception of equity – a broader conception than most economists use. Some writers on housing issues broaden it still further, and regard home ownership as a merit good, or assert that security of tenure is a value, and so the security of tenants and homeowners should be assessed in any ranking of the social states.

PARETO EFFICIENCY

Economists have always struggled to minimize the role of ethical norms in their analysis, although of course they cannot be removed entirely in normative analysis. Many economists consider the approach discussed above, of explicitly assuming a social welfare function, to be too controversial because they fear that there can be no consensus about what is the appropriate social welfare function. Instead they propose an alternative criterion to rank social states: Pareto efficiency. A social state is Pareto efficient if there is no other state in which someone is better off, and no one else is worse off. A Pareto improvement is a change from one social state to another by which at least one person is made better off, and no one is made worse off. To make a policy recommendation on the basis of the Pareto efficiency criterion is to recommend a Pareto improvement. In figure 6.2, if R_1 were the utility pair that existed with no government intervention, the Pareto criterion would conclude all pairs to the northeast of R_1, indicated by the dashed lines, are preferred to R_1. To judge the social states according to the Pareto criterion involves assuming a value just as much as judging using a social welfare function. However it is felt by many that the Pareto criterion is less controversial. Assuming that people care only about their absolute, not relative, well-being, a Pareto improvement would be unanimously approved.

Almost any conceivable intervention in the economy will make some better off and others worse off. There are few pure Pareto improvements possible. However there are likely many interventions after which those who are better off could compensate those who are worse off and still remain better off. The combination of the intervention and subsequent redistribution is a Pareto improvement, but the intervention is only a potential Pareto improvement. In the real world, almost all policies recommended by economists are potential Pareto improvements, not actual Pareto improvements.[4]

There are however a number of problems with the Pareto efficiency approach, especially in applying it to some aspects of housing policy. The Pareto criterion does not yield a unique ranking; there are an infinite number of Pareto efficient social states (in figure 6.2 all the points along the XY locus within the dashed quadrant are Pareto efficient). It is quite evident that society does not believe all of these are equally desirable. The final choice of the optimal social state requires an additional criterion beyond the Pareto criterion; which takes us back to the social welfare function.

The proponents of Pareto efficiency however argue that the best approach for economists is to separate efficiency and equity issues. Economists should recommend Pareto improvements to secure a Pareto efficient social state, and then the government can use a system of taxes and transfers to secure the most preferred state; but economists should have relatively little to do with the latter activity (except to indicate how a given desired redistribution can best be achieved[5]). Unfortunately this separation is not possible on theoretical grounds. The argument requires that redistribution occur using costless lump-sum taxes and transfers. However, redistribution is not costless, but uses real resources. And the instruments of redistribution are not, in a practical situation, lump-sum taxes and transfers, that is, taxes and transfers based on the intrinsic characteristics of people. In fact taxes and transfers are based on the behaviour of people, and have welfare costs.

Finally when applying the Pareto criterion by evaluating whether someone is better off, or how much someone would have to be compensated to be indifferent to a change, analysts use current prices. But these prices are a function of the current distribution of income. In a sense the economist is "accepting" the current distribution of income in deciding on which interventions are potential Pareto improvements;

but the "acceptance" of any distribution of income is precisely what economists are trying to avoid.

Therefore using either the social welfare function or the Pareto criterion to rank the social states, or as a guide to policy development, has significant difficulties. There are proponents of both. Perhaps the best that can be offered are rough, admittedly *ad hoc*, rules of thumb. If the essence of the government involvement in the economy relates to income distribution or merit goods, or if the intervention is large and likely to involve a substantial redistribution of income, then the social welfare function must be a central part of the analysis. Much of government involvement in housing matters does relate to income distribution and merit goods. On the other hand if the intervention is not essentially related to income redistribution or merit goods, and if the redistribution as a result of the intervention is not large (or, perhaps more precisely, not a significant movement away from an equitable distribution), then the Pareto criterion or the potential Pareto criterion can be used.

THE ROLE FOR GOVERNMENT

Having set out criteria that will be used to rank the social states, several questions follow next. Is there any need for government intervention in the economy to achieve the most desirable social state? It seems fairly likely that some intervention will be needed, but when precisely will government intervention lead to a more desirable social state, and how should policies be designed to ensure that the most desirable social state is achieved?

The literature of welfare economics contains theorems[6] that demonstrate that if a number of very restrictive conditions hold, a market economy will be Pareto efficient. Government would only be needed to establish and enforce laws of contract, and to define property rights. These theorems are the formal statement of Adam Smith's theorem of the "invisible hand." The conditions are, however, highly restrictive. In order for the private market to generate Pareto efficiency (i) markets much be perfectly competitive; (ii) there must be no externalities; (iii) there must be no public goods; (iv) there must be no uncertainty, and (v) there must be no macroeconomic problems of inflation, unemployment, or growth.[7]

If one or more of these conditions do not hold, then the laissez faire economy cannot be shown to generate a Pareto efficient social state, and the intervention of government *may* lead to a Pareto improvement. The list of conditions can thus be thought of as a list of rationales for possible government intervention in the economy. Each item is a reason why the private market might fail to achieve the optimum, and is therefore a possible justification for intervention. Furthermore, and perhaps most important, a Pareto efficient world will not necessarily have a distribution of income that is fair (somehow defined), or ensure that all consumers have adequate (somehow defined) amounts of merit goods. Government intervention is further justified to (vi) redistribute income or (vii) deal with merit goods, when the criterion of the social welfare function is used.

These seven items provide a checklist from which to begin the normative analysis of housing policy. In order to establish whether government ought to intervene in housing matters, it must be determined whether any of these seven items are relevant. Is the distribution of income fair in the absence of government? If the answer is yes, this cannot provide a reason for government policy. If the answer is no, then there exists the potential for collective action to increase social welfare. Are housing markets perfectly competitive? If they are not competitive, an intervention might improve welfare. Each condition on the list must be considered and an empirical analysis undertaken to determine whether it holds true. This exercise will produce a list of reasons why government might intervene in housing matters. Chapter seven deals with items (vi) and (vii), while chapter eight deals with items (i) to (v).

However while the fact that one of the conditions does not hold is a necessary condition for government intervention to improve social welfare, it is not a sufficient condition. It may be the case that no intervention can improve social welfare or achieve a Pareto improvement. There are a number of reasons why this might be so. For example, there may be positive externalities from home renovation, but because there are only a small number of persons involved, negotiation costs are small and income redistribution is not significant, the private market makes adjustment for the externality. This result is an application of the famous Coase (1960) theorem. Or the mortgage market may face uncertainty about lending to a certain class of borrowers because information is expensive to obtain. However , the public sector faces the same information costs, and so may not be able to improve on the private allocation of mortgage credit. Or housing construction may fluctuate over time,which increases long-run average costs, and so it would appear that to stabilize these fluctuations would improve social welfare. However, it may prove that, given recognition lags, legislative lags, and execution lags, attempts to stabilize housing construction are actually destabilizing.

If an intervention is considered, the government has many instruments at its disposal. For example, if there is a desire to redistribute income, there are many ways to achieve this. Redistribution can occur through tax-financed cash transfers, or transfers in-kind, or subsidies to education. Or it can be done through regulations such as minimum-wage laws or rent controls. Each instrument must be calibrated to achieve the maximum possible social welfare – the tax-transfer system designed, the form and level of education subsidy set, and so on. Then the instrument is chosen that achieves the maximum possible social welfare. The best of the best is chosen. Of course it may be that no instrument improves things, and the best of the best is no intervention.

In summary, the normative approach to housing policy is to choose the policy that leads to the maximum possible social welfare (or the largest possible Pareto improvement). The choice involves three steps. The first is to set out the value system that will govern the choice, and to develop the theorems that prove that the laissez faire market will achieve the best possible state of the world if a list of conditions hold. The second step is to verify which of these conditions does not hold, and so to develop a list of rationales for government intervention. The final step is to choose and design the policy instrument that will yield the best possible social state according to the assumed value system.

This discussion of normative housing policy has made no reference to what level of government ought to carry out the policies. In Canada, this is a critical issue. The federal and provincial governments have overlapping jurisdiction in housing matters, and the responsibilities delegated to municipalities by the provinces also deal with housing. A complete normative treatment of housing policy would set out a system of optimal government that prescribed what levels of government should exist, the spatial boundaries of their jurisdictions, their responsibilities, and the policy instruments at their disposal. However, it is beyond the scope of this book to provide such analysis.[8]

PUBLIC CHOICE ANALYSIS

It has been pointed out that the purpose of these chapters on normative policy analysis is to explore how a certain objective function, given the way households and firms operate in the economy, leads to a certain policy recommendation. The purpose is not to describe how governments actually make decisions about policy. Just exactly how the sorts of policies that are discussed here would be implemented, or whether any system of government would have an incentive to implement such policies, is left unspecified.

During the last ten or fifteen years economists have begun to apply their methods of analysis to the study of how governments make decisions, of how society makes collective choices.[9] This is sometimes referred to as public choice analysis or the economics of politics. It is not normative in orientation – seeking to determine what governments ought to do; but rather positive in orientation – seeking to explain why we have certain policies. In a sense the research seeks to make the operation of government endogenous within the model of the economy.

Public choices are made within a given constitutional framework that sets out powers of governments, voting rules, and so on (some research seeks to make even the choice of a constitutional framework endogenous). All agents are assumed to be rational: to act in their self-interest subject to constraints. Voters make choices in favour of the proposals that yield them the net benefits (benefits less taxes paid) consistent with maximum utility. Politicians offer proposals that maximize the probability of election. Civil servants generally have more information about the operation of their departments than legislators, and the interaction between them is in some ways similar to that between managers and shareholders of private firms. Essential to the analysis are the ideas that individuals are different, and that information is scarce and costly to acquire. Public choice analysis is the study of how conflicting views are mediated in the political process, of how collective decisions are reached, given diverse interests. Politicians do not have full information about the preferences of voters, voters do not have full information about the implications of proposed policies, legislators do not have full information about the operation and outputs of their departments. This shapes the nature of interactions that occur in the system of public choice. Political parties emerge in part as a method of interest aggregation and in part as suppliers of information to voters and politicians. Interest groups in part function to supply information to politicians and civil servants.

We are a long way from a complete positive theory of public choice. Voting models, analysing the voter-politician interaction, bureaucratic models analysing civil servant-politician interaction, and interest group models analysing why interest groups are formed, are in themselves quite developed, but a full integration is a long way off. The empirical research has focused mainly on aggregate public choices such as the level of public expenditure, rather than specific choices in one policy area, such as why we have rent controls. Nevertheless, the insights being developed by public choice analysis, are considerable, and students of housing policy should be aware of them.

In the public choice literature there are no general theorems that show those constitutional arrangements that would result in governments acting to secure either Pareto optimality or the maximum of a social welfare function; indeed the suggestion is more that such constitutional arrangements may be impossible. But this is at a formal theoretical level. At a rough intuitive level, it seems clear that legislators in the Canadian political system have some incentive to adopt Pareto improvements (because some voters are better off, and none worse off), and even potential Pareto improvements; or likewise to adopt policies that improve the level of social welfare according to the social welfare function that is the consensus of the Canadian society.

SUGGESTIONS FOR FURTHER READING

Atkinson, A. B., and J. E. Stiglitz (1980) *Lectures on Public Economics* (Maidenhead, England: McGraw-Hill). Lectures one and eleven.

Stigler, G. (1975) *The Citizen and the State* (Chicago: University of Chicago Press).

Tobin, J. (1970) "On Limiting the Domain of Inequality," *Journal of Law and Economics* 13:263–77.

Walker, B. (1981) *Welfare Economics and Urban Problems* (London: Hutchinson). Chapters one to four.

7 | Policies to Achieve Equity

The previous chapter outlined the general approach of welfare economics to deciding what the government's role in housing matters should be. The purpose of this and the following chapter is to apply this approach to the Canadian situation. Having established the criteria that will govern choice, and discussed the conditions under which a laissez faire economy will achieve the most desirable outcome, the next step is to go down the list of possible rationales for intervention to see which might justify a housing program. Two rationales – income redistribution and merit goods – arise through specification of a social welfare function, and may be thought of as being concerned with equity, broadly defined. These are taken up in this chapter. The exploration of these two rationales and the optimal responses correspond to the debate between policy analysts about the difference between an "income problem" and a "housing problem," which is one of the central issues in the debate about housing policy.

INCOME DISTRIBUTION

The first question to pose is whether the distribution of income that would prevail in the absence of government would be fair.

This is hard to answer because of the difficulty of establishing what the distribution of income would be in the absence of current government programs. Even the best analysis of what the distribution of income would be is filled with gaps, extreme simplifications, and arbitrary assumptions. Nevertheless, most analysts would agree that the net effect of government in Canada has been to raise significantly the incomes of the very least well-off. For the middle- and upper-income groups, the net effect has been to reduce income, with all income levels experiencing roughly the same proportional reduction. This proportional reduction is rather slight. Middle- and upper-income families pay high taxes but also receive many benefits.[1]

It is probably safe to say that the true redistributive effect of government is much less than the public perception, and therefore that the public perception of what the distribution of income would be in the absence of government is characterized by greater inequality than would actually be the case. The least well-off however would be extremely poor in a world without government. There can be little doubt that the Canadian social welfare function would call for some redistribution.

The next step is to design and choose the optimal instrument of intervention. A fully general analysis would also solve for the total amount of redistribution that should occur. In principle, there are two ways to raise the utility of households. One is to alter their income: by a cash grant or by changing their endowments of factors of production, or by changing the prices that the factors of production they own command in the market. The other is to alter their consumption choices by changing the prices they must pay for goods and services, and even reducing the price to zero by giving them amounts of goods and services.

Traditionally in economics, the two basic ways to distribute income have been summarized as a lump-sum cash transfer and an in-kind transfer that reduces the price of a single commodity to a household, permitting the household to buy as much as it wishes at the reduced price. Then an analysis is conducted to see which is the better instrument to distribute income, that is to raise the utility of the recipient.

The analysis is most easily presented graphically. Consider the household in figure 7.1, with preferences represented by indifference curves U_1, U_2, and U_3, and with fixed income y. All income is to be spent in the period on a composite good with price p_1 and housing services with price p_2. The locus of pairs of the two goods that the household can consume is the budget line AB, with equation 7.1, where x_1 and x_2 are

$$p_1x_1 + p_2x_2 = y \qquad (7.1)$$

the amounts of composite good and housing consumed. The utility-maximizing household will choose point C^1, representing the pair (x_1^1, x_2^1). Suppose the government offered the household an in-kind subsidy on housing that reduced its price to $\bar{p}_2$. The budget line would rotate about point A to a position such as AC, with equation 7.2. The house-

$$p_1x_1 + \bar{p}_2x_2 = y \qquad (7.2)$$

hold will choose point C^2, representing pair (x_1^2, x_2^2). If the price elasticity of demand for housing is negative, the household will buy more housing. It may buy more of the composite good as in figure 7.1, or it may buy less. With the housing subsidy, the household has enjoyed an increase in utility from U_1 to U_2. The cost to the government of providing this housing subsidy is $(p_2 - \bar{p}_2)x_2^2$.

FIGURE 7.1

A Lump-Sum Transfer and an Equal-Cost Housing Subsidy

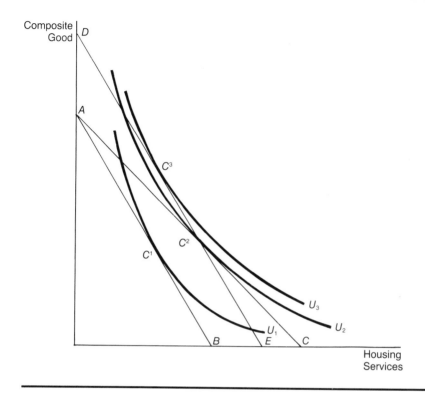

Suppose now that the government were to substitute an *equal-cost*, lump-sum cash grant for the housing subsidy. The household would now have to face the original market prices but would have an increase in income. Graphically (figure 7.1), the new consumption choices facing the household are represented by the straight line *DE*, parallel to the original budget line *AB*, and through the point C^2. Line *DE* has equation 7.3. Because C^2 is a point of tangency between indifference curve U_2 and

$$p_1x_1 + p_2x_2 = y + (p_2 - \overline{p}_2)x_2^2 \qquad (7.3)$$

line *AC*, and because the indifference curves are convex to the origin, budget line *DE* must have points above indifference curve U_2. Therefore the household reaches a higher level of utility under a lump-sum grant than under an *equal-cost*, in-kind housing subsidy. The conclusion may also be stated in an alternative way. The household may be raised to any level of utility more cheaply using a lump-sum cash grant than using an in-kind subsidy.[2]

It is worth noting here, for future reference, that a lump-sum grant (that is, non-wage income) is equivalent to an equiproportional in-kind subsidy on all commodities. This can be seen by dividing both sides of the budget constraint by $1 + b$ as in equation 7.4, where T is the amount of the lump-sum transfer, and b is the ratio of transfer payment to original exogenous income. The prices of both goods would be reduced to $100/(1 + b)$ percent of their original level.

$$p_1x_1 + p_2x_2 = y + T \tag{7.4}$$

$$\left(\frac{1}{1 + b}\right) p_1x_1 + \left(\frac{1}{1 + b}\right) p_2x_2 = y$$

The graphical argument of figure 7.1 is logically correct, although general policy recommendations do not follow from it so easily as is often supposed. Figure 7.1 deals with the case of one household, with given income, choosing between two commodities. However the actual situation faced by government is considerably different. There is not one household but many. And these households choose not only between two commodities but also between work and leisure, so that their incomes are not exogenous. Labour supply can be varied in the short run by varying effort, by working overtime, or by taking a second job, and in the long run by choosing between different firms, forms of the labour contract, and between occupations. Finally, the households are not identical and summarizable as a single "representative" household but are heterogeneous. They have different wage rates, in part because of different original endowments and in part because of different decisions about training.

In thinking about redistribution, one must recognize that the government is dealing with a group of heterogeneous households. A lump-sum, cash grant, in the sense of giving everyone the same amount, is obviously inappropriate because the purpose of the redistribution is to treat people differently and so create greater equality. Actual cash transfers are usually designed to vary with household income. Thus the more relevant comparison between cash and in-kind transfers is to compare a cash transfer which is a function of income with an in-kind transfer which reduces the price of a commodity or prices of several commodities.

Consider the household that maximizes the utility function 7.5, subject to the budget constraint (equation 7.6), where x_3 is leisure, and p_3

$$U(x_1, x_2, x_3) \tag{7.5}$$

$$p_1x_1 + p_2x_2 = (24 - x_3)p_3 \tag{7.6}$$

is the wage rate. It is assumed for simplicity that the household could work twenty-four hours per day. The budget constraint can be restated as in equation 7.7, and the household can be thought of as "buying" composite goods, housing, and leisure at unit prices p_1, p_2, and p_3, using "full income," $24p_3$. As before, a true lump-sum transfer, T, would

$$p_1x_1 + p_2x_2 + p_3x_3 = 24p_3 \tag{7.7}$$

be an addition to non-wage income, and independent of choices; and could be represented as an equiproportional subsidy on all commodities, including leisure as in equation 7.8, where b is the ratio of transfer payment to full income.

$$p_1x_1 + p_2x_2 + p_3x_3 = 24p_3 + T \tag{7.8}$$

$$\left(\frac{1}{1+b}\right)p_1x_1 + \left(\frac{1}{1+b}\right)p_2x_2 + \left(\frac{1}{1+b}\right)p_3x_3 = 24p_3$$

A simple actual transfer in cash may be represented as a linear function of income as in equation 7.9 – the payment to households declines

$$T = c - d(24 - x_3)p_3 \tag{7.9}$$

as income rises. Adding this transfer payment to the right-hand side of the household budget constraint and rearranging, yields equation 7.10. The cash transfer is a combination of lump-sum payment and reduction

$$p_1x_1 + p_2x_2 + (1 - d)p_3x_3 = 24(1 - d)p_3 + c \tag{7.10}$$

in the price of leisure. It is not equivalent to a true lump-sum grant as a comparison with equation 7.8 makes clear.

A transfer in-kind, represented as a $t_2 \times 100$ percent reduction in

$$p_1x_1 + (1 - t_2)p_2x_2 + p_3x_3 = 24p_3 \tag{7.11}$$

the price of housing services (equation 7.11), is obviously also different from a true lump-sum transfer.

The true lump-sum transfer is not affected by any choices of the household, and is equivalent to an equiproportional reduction in all prices faced by the household, including the price of leisure (the wage rate) with no change in full income. Actual transfer systems, whether in cash or in kind, depend upon the choices of households and are representable as a combination of lump-sum grant and price changes on a subset of all commodities purchased by the household. When seen as price changes on a subset of commodities, it is evident that all transfer systems have efficiency costs. No general statement can be made about which system has lower costs. Therefore housing subsidies cannot be ruled out as instruments for income redistribution.

So far nothing has been said about how the levels of the parameters c and d of the linear cash transfer, and t_2 of the housing subsidy should be established (recall that in figure 7.1 the comparison was between an equal-cost transfer in cash and transfer in kind). When studying the effects of each, it must be on a comparable basis. These parameters of each transfer system should be established to maximize the social welfare function, given the amount of money the government has available for redistribution – they would be the parameters of the optimally designed instrument. Then the two optimally designed instruments would be compared to see which yielded the higher level of social welfare. Unfortunately, the solutions to these problems are quite complex and still very much the subject of current research. No general solution emerges, and work focuses on solving cases with restrictions on the functional form of the social welfare function and utility functions. Nevertheless the layout of the problem above highlights certain important points. The design of policies for redistribution must use the social welfare function criterion rather than the Pareto optimality criterion. All relevant transfer systems will influence the prices of some subset of commodities, and so will have an efficiency cost compared to a lump-sum grant. The optimal design of a transfer system and the choice between alternative optimally designed systems will involve both efficiency and equity concerns as combined in the social welfare function.[3]

The problem of the optimal transfer system is analogous to the optimal tax problem which has been extensively studied in the public economics literature.[4] This literature has few general results but does suggest that the burden of proof should be on those who wish to use housing subsidies as an instrument of income distribution. Pending further theoretical and empirical work there is not a strong case for the use of housing subsidies to redistribute income.

MERIT GOODS

Despite the preference among economists for transfers in cash as opposed to transfers in kind, this has not been the preference of our political system. It seems most people would rather provide assistance to the poor to buy housing, clothing or food; and actual government policies reflect this. There are many, many programs that reduce the price of housing services to the household and seem intended to increase housing consumption.[5] It is likely that the Canadian social welfare function considers housing as a merit good up to some threshold.

For the concept of a merit good to be of relevance, there must be households that consume less housing than the threshold after the optimal income transfer system has been put in place; that is, when the income distribution is as fair as we desire it to be. Economists often remark that, when the poor do not have adequate housing, this is an "income problem" not a "housing problem." In the terminology developed here, they are saying that when the income distribution is fair, everyone will consume adequate housing. If however when the income distribution is fair, the poor still do not have adequate housing, then there is indeed a housing problem. It is a merit goods issue.

If the distribution of income were fair in Canada, would some households still consume less housing than the threshold? The answer depends of course on the social welfare function; but a strong case can be made for the allegation that Canadians accept considerable inequality provided that the poor have adequate housing and education, health care and so on. Even if one disagrees with this, it is interesting analytically to explore what is the optimal response to merit goods concerns.

A rigorous approach to the problem would begin by specifying a social welfare funtion that included housing as a merit good. The general form of such a function was set out in equations 6.2 and 6.3 of the previous chapter. Then all of the possible policy instruments that could be used to increase housing consumption would be considered; each would be optimally designed, given the available money; and that instrument would be selected that yielded the highest social welfare. This does not imply that resources should be devoted to housing until everyone consumes $\bar{x}_2$. When resources leave other sectors, the production of other goods declines, and utilities decline. This decline must be traded off against the social welfare gains from increased housing consumption.

There are many alternative policy instruments to increase housing consumption. A price reduction will increase housing consumption assuming a negative price elasticity. A cash transfer will also increase housing consumption, assuming a positive income elasticity. Usually price and income transfers contain no constraints on consumption choice, but either can be made contingent on the recipient consuming a certain amount of housing. A third approach is to require by law that a certain level of housing consumption be maintained. This does not seem acceptable in our society (although for example we do accept compulsory consumption of education).[6] Here we cannot compare these instruments in the rigorous fashion outlined above, but understanding of some of the issues at work can be gained by examining the effects of various instruments on the housing consumption of a single household.

Compare first the unconstrained income and price transfers. Using figure 7.1, it can be shown that a housing price reduction increases housing consumption more than an equal-cost, lump-sum cash grant.

The housing price reduction moves the household from C^1 to C^2, and the equal-cost grant from C^1 to C^3. It is obvious that C^3 lies to the left of C^2, and implies less housing consumption.

Alternatively it can be shown that any increase in housing consumption can be achieved more cheaply by using a price reduction. Let the desired increase in consumption be from x_2^1 to x_2^2. The points with x_2^2 housing consumption lie on the vertical line through C^2. The price reduction to achieve this change in housing consumption is represented by budget line AC. Assuming that the income elasticity of demand for housing is everywhere positive, the income consumption path at original market prices through C^1 goes through C^3, and only intersects the vertical line through x_2^2 to the right of C^3. Therefore the income transfer that would cause housing consumption to increase to x_2^2 will cost more than the price reduction program.

If the objective were to maximize the increase in housing consumption subject to a given level of assistance, a price reduction is preferable to a cash grant.

But a price reduction does not dominate all possible instruments. Let us suppose that the government has $X to distribute, and the *sole* purpose is to maximize the increase in housing consumption. The solution would be to coerce the household to a point *I* on the horizontal axis as in figure 7.2. The household would be compelled to spend all of its own income and the $X transfer to acquire housing; the distance BI being equal to X/p_2. One's initial reaction is, of course, to say such a policy of coercion would never be adopted because the household would be forced to a very low level of utility. The reaction is understandable but reveals an important point: the objective of intervention would never be to maximize the increase in housing consumption. At the very least, the objective would be to maximize the increase, subject to the household willingly participating in the program; that is, subject to the household realizing a utility greater than the original level, U_1.

The solution to the problem of how to distribute $X to maximize the increase in housing consumption subject to the utility constraint will not be a price-reduction policy. The solution will be a program that offers the household the single choice of consuming bundle C^4 (x_1^4, x_2^4). The bundle C^4 is assumed to lie infinitesimally above the indifference curve U_1, and the length C^4G is equal to X/p_1. The household might be offered a cash grant of $X provided that x_2^4 of housing is consumed; or the household might be offered x_2^4 of housing and only have to pay a price per unit of housing service corresponding to the price reflected in line AJ. The latter sort of program is essentially what is involved in public housing. Households are offered a single choice of government-owned housing on which a certain aggregate rent is due, with an implicit price per unit of housing service below the market price.

Of course the objective of government in dealing with merit goods

FIGURE 7.2
Transfer with a Housing Consumption Constraint

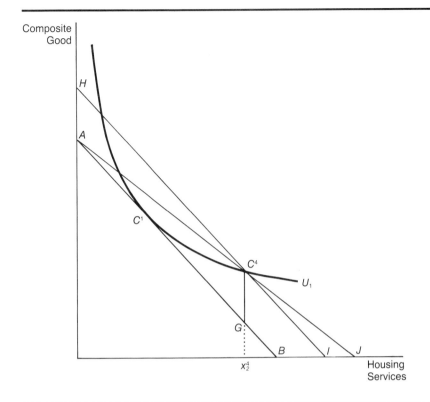

is not to maximize the increase in housing consumption subject to a utility constraint. The point of providing these examples is to show the relationship between government objectives and government policies, and the importance of defining what policies are available in determining the best policy. The literature provides little formal treatment of the general merit goods problem,[7] but does suggest the optimal policy will not be a reduction in p_2 to those consuming less than $\bar{x}_2$, as is often suggested.[8] Indeed the best policy may be something like public housing (now much criticized for many reasons), precisely because it interferes with consumer choices.

DIRECT CONSUMPTION EXTERNALITIES (DONOR PREFERENCES)

The concept of donor preferences is closely related to the concept of merit goods. The discussion of donor preferences is included in this chapter on policies to achieve equity, although donor preferences are properly an efficiency-based rationale for intervention.

A direct consumption externality exists if the housing consumption of one household appears as an argument in the utility function of another household; for example as in expressions 7.12, where the utility of individual i depends on their own consumption of the composite good, housing, leisure, and on the housing consumption of the other n households in the economy. The housing consumption of the kth household is x_{k2}. If externalities exist, and there are so many agents affected that negotiation between them cannot occur, then private decision makers in a laissez faire world will not take account of these external effects, and a Pareto efficient allocation of resources will not be attained. It is normally assumed that this is a positive externality,

$$U_i = U_i(x_{i1}, x_{i2}, x_{i3}, x_{12}, x_{22}, \ldots x_{i-1\,2}, x_{i+1\,2} \ldots x_{n2})$$

$$\frac{\partial U_i}{\partial x_{k2}} \begin{cases} > 0 & \text{if } x_{k2} < \bar{x}_2 \\ = 0 & \text{if } x_{k2} \geq \bar{x}_2 \end{cases} \qquad (7.12)$$

so that the utility of the ith household increases if the housing consumption to the kth household increases. In other words, the ith household cares about the housing consumption of others. The ith household will be willing to pay to see the housing consumption of others increase. This willingness to pay will depend upon the utility derived from seeing others' housing consumption increased compared to the utility derived by keeping the money and increasing their own consumption. It is plausible to assert that this externality ceases once housing consumption has reached some level, $\bar{x}_2$. If this is the case, and there is a positive income elasticity of demand for housing services, then the rich will care about the housing consumption of the poor, and be willing to pay to see it increase, while the poor will not care about the housing consumption of the rich. This form of externality is sometimes called donor preferences, for obvious reasons. The rich would be willing to pay taxes to finance a transfer to the poor that would increase the housing consumption of the poor. The rich care about the housing consumption, not the utility level, of the poor.

It is very difficult to prove the existence of direct consumption externalities. We do hear people say that they are willing to support transfer programs, provided the money is spent on housing. Also, governments assist some low-income households through housing assistance, and private charities seem to prefer to provide assistance in kind, very often through subsidized housing.[9] But the careful econometric work necessary to prove the existence of the externalities and to estimate the willingness to pay remains to be done.

Let us suppose for the moment that donor preference externalities exist, and that private negotiation has not led the rich to subsidize the housing consumption of the poor. What would be the government's optimal instrument to achieve a Pareto efficient allocation? The problem is very complicated for the case of many heterogeneous donors and recipients, but study of a simple, two-person world, diagrammatically, is useful for it illustrates the fundamental points at issue. This presentation is based on Browning and Browning (1979).

Assume that there are two groups in the society, the rich and the poor, each made up of identical households. There exists the direct consumption externality of the sort outlined in expressions 7.12. The poor consume well below the threshold level $\bar{x}_2$, and the rich consume well above it. Thus, there is a situation of donor preferences. To simplify as in equation 7.13, the utility of the poor is assumed to depend upon their own consumption housing, x_{p2}, and of the composite good, measured in dollars, x_{p1}. The utility of the rich depends upon their consumption of *all* goods measured in dollars, x_{r1}, and upon the consumption of housing by the poor x_{p2}.

$$U_p = U_p (x_{p1}, x_{p2})$$
$$U_r = U_r (x_{r1}, x_{p2})$$

(7.13)

Figure 7.3 measures x_{p1} along the vertical axis and x_{p2} along the horizontal axis. In this quadrant can be drawn the budget constraint of a poor household, AB, with given income, and facing a given price of housing services, assumed to be \$1, and given prices of other things. As well, the indifference curves of a poor household can be drawn, for example PU_1 and PU_2. On another set of axes the regular indifference curves of the rich, relating x_{r1} and x_{p2}, might be drawn. However in order to capture the idea of donor preferences, another sort of indifference curve – what Browning and Browning (1979) have called the adjusted indifference curve – can be drawn on the set of axes of figure 7.3. Consider any point C^1 on the poor household's budget line, with the poor paying for their own housing and other goods. For a given income of the rich, the utility level of the rich is determined. Suppose that the housing consumption of the poor were to increase, and that the rich were to finance a transfer to the poor in order to sustain this higher level of housing consumption. The utility of the rich is affected in two opposite ways: it rises because the housing consumption of the poor rises, and it falls because income is being transferred from them to the poor. The original utility function of the rich relates income levels and housing consumption by the poor. The information contained there can be redrawn as the adjusted indifference curves of figure 7.3. Suppose the poor were to increase their housing consumption by \$4 (by four units, since the price of housing has been assumed to be

FIGURE 7.3
Housing Consumption Externalities
and Pareto Improvements

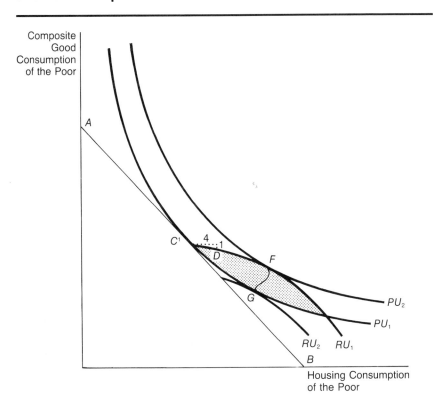

Housing Consumption
of the Poor

$1), and the rich could pay $3 and be as well-off as before. Then D is a point on the adjusted indifference curve of the rich. The poor have reduced other consumption $1 to pay the remainder of the cost of the increased housing. For a further $4 increase in housing consumption, the preferences of the rich are likely, such that they would be willing to contribute less than $3 and still be as well-off. The curves are concave from below, for example, RU_1. From each point on the budget line of the poor, an adjusted indifference curve of the rich can be drawn. If the point on the budget line corresponds to higher housing consumption by the poor, the adjusted indifference curve is a higher utility level for the rich ($RU_2 > RU_1$).

Let us assume that the appropriate amount of income redistribution according to the social welfare function (ignoring the direct consumption externality) has been carried out. The poor choose C^1 and enjoy utility PU_1, and the rich have utility level RU_1. However there exists the lens-shaped shaded area in which the points are above curve PU_1 and below curve RU_1 – both the poor and the rich would be better off to end up in this area. Private decisions did not achieve Pareto efficiency, and the poor have underconsumed housing (because all points in the lens-shaped area lie to the right of C^1). There exists the possibility that government intervention can achieve Pareto efficiency (assuming that private negotiation did not deal with the externality). Pareto efficiency exists where an adjusted indifference curve and a regular indifference curve are tangent. The locus of Pareto efficient points, given C^1, is FG. A policy to achieve a point along FG will likely require a combination of an income transfer and price reduction on housing for the poor, financed by a lump-sum tax on the rich. It is unlikely that the poor will voluntarily choose any specific point on FG in response to a simple price reduction on housing.

Obviously merit goods and donor preferences are related concepts. Both can lead to "underconsumption" of housing, and can provide a rationale for government intervention, perhaps in the form of a housing subsidy. Although distinct concepts, they can be viewed as alternative ways of theorizing about the same thing. Similarly there are two ways of theorizing about income redistribution: one is based on the social welfare function already discussed, and the other is based on interdependent utility functions. The utility of a household depends upon their own consumption of goods and leisure, and the utility levels of other households (see Hochman and Rogers [1969]). If a threshold exists where the utility interdependence ceases, there can be a one-way interdependence where the rich would have a willingness to pay to raise the utility of the poor, but the poor do not wish to raise the utility of the rich. One can speak of income redistribution justified by Pareto efficiency, not by the social welfare function. The problems of these two approaches have already been discussed in chapter six, but a point can be reiterated. If one were to handle income distribution or housing consumption issues purely through Pareto efficiency considerations, one is forced to consider only Pareto improvements from the existing situation. This still leaves the final solution indeterminate. The approach recommended in this book is to assume several social welfare functions, however arbitrary, and explore the policy recommendations that follow from them.

OTHER EQUITY ISSUES

There are several other issues in housing policy that can be considered as equity concerns when fitted into the framework of welfare economics. These will not be explored in detail, but four issues warrant particular comment because they are widely referred to in public discussion: security of tenure, rent gouging, homeownership as a merit good, and affordable housing. In each case there is value used to judge the social state, which has been used as a justification when calling for government intervention in the housing market. The point of this section is not to agree or disagree that these are further values to justify housing policy. Rather it is to define these values in a manner that facilitates policy analysis and to point out considerations that should shape an intervention based on these values.

Calls for government intervention to increase the security of tenure of households, and particularly of tenants, have been heard frequently over the last decade; however no definition sufficiently precise to permit determining who does and who does not have security of tenure has been provided. Let us explore the concept. Absolute security of tenure would imply that a household could remain in a dwelling unit as long as they choose to do so. But the meaning of the word "choose" must be clear. Suppose the income of a tenant were to fall. The tenant might choose to move to a smaller apartment. This is how economists use the word choose; yet some commentators would argue that the tenant had been forced to move, and so did not have security of tenure. For tenants, absolute security of tenure implies there are no conditions under which a landlord could evict them; even eviction for non-payment of rent would be forbidden. Thus absolute security of tenure, for tenants or homeowners, would exist if occupants had full ownership rights of their dwelling units, and there were no costs to exercising these rights. It is obvious households in a laissez faire world would not have absolute security of tenure. Tenants would face insecurity from rising rents, a fall in income, changes in other prices, and the decision of a landlord to evict; perhaps for frivolous reasons, or perhaps because the landlord wishes to renovate the unit, or because the rent is not paid. Homeowners would face insecurity from an increase in any of the costs of homeownership, such as increases in property taxes, mortgage interest rates, or insecurity from a fall in income, or increases in other non-housing prices. Both tenants and owners face insecurity arising from the possibility of expropriation. It also seems obvious that society would not want households to have absolute security of tenure. The policy issue is how much security would households have in the absence of government, how much would society desire that they have, and what are the best programs to secure the increased security.

Until recently, homeowners were reasonably secure at least against increases in the costs of ownership. Mortgages were for a twenty- or twenty-five-year term with a constant monthly payment. The homeowners knew exactly what their mortgage costs would be until the mortgage was paid off. During the 1970s, however, high and unpredictable inflation rates meant that mortgages had much shorter terms, even as short as one year, so homeowners faced considerable uncertainty. In 1981, it was widely predicted that many households, forced to renew their mortgages at interest rates of more than twenty percent, were going to lose their homes. The policy options discussed were to compel mortgage lenders to extend the mortgages at the old rates (placing the burden of the policy on owners of lending institutions and savers); to offer households special loans while they rearrange their expenditure patterns to cope with the higher mortgage payments (placing most of the burden on homeowners); and to publicly subsidize the interest rates of the renewed mortgages (placing the burden on taxpayers). Both of the last two options were used in Canada. But the assistance was little used, because it proved homeowners had already rearranged their finances in anticipation, and had had sufficient increases in income to carry the new mortgage.

The case of tenants is somewhat more complicated, because the landlord owns the dwelling unit. And it is a widely held belief in Canada that people have the right to the enjoyment of private property. In the market, the tenant and landlord enter into a contract, explicit or implicit, under which the landlord gives the tenant certain of his property rights (the right to use and enjoy the unit) in exchange for the rental payment. Government intervention is justified if there is a belief that tenants ought to have more security of tenure, that is, acquire more of the landlord's property rights under the contract, than would arise through unregulated contracts. In most jurisdictions, landlords cannot evict (or refuse to rent) for malicious, frivolous, or discriminatory reasons; but can evict with proper notice if the tenant is disruptive, has not paid the rent, or if the landlord wishes to renovate, demolish, or live in the unit. It has been suggested that rent control be used to increase the security of tenure of tenants. While control would increase security of tenure by reducing rents, most analysts believe the opportunity costs of the intervention are too great.

In the popular debate, it is heard that there should be no rent gouging, or that there ought to be no unconscionable rent increases. The popular debate does not give much guidance about what constitutes "rent gouging," but in economic terms it can perhaps be thought of as rents that are above the costs of production, including a normal rate of return. This redistribution from tenant to landlord, it is argued, ought to be prevented. These above-normal profits could occur for several reasons. If because of monopoly the standard analysis of welfare economics applies; but monopoly or even oligopoly in rental markets is extremely rare. Above-normal profits can also accrue to existing landlords as the market adjusts from one equilibrium to another. If a redistribution of these profits is regarded as desirable, consideration of a policy must recognize the likely efficiency costs of weakening the signal (profit) that draws resources into the housing market. Finally one single landlord may secure above-normal profit if their tenant faces extremely high transactions cost to move. Rents could be raised until the discounted difference between market and actual rent was just less than the transactions cost. This is a case of non-competitive (non-price taking) behaviour with implications more for distribution than efficiency. Presumably a policy response would be targeted at specific cases.

It is sometimes alleged, at least implicitly, that homeownership is a merit good; and certainly there are many actual housing subsidies to homeowners that cannot be justified as attempts to equalize the distribution of income. The design of a merit-goods-based policy must clearly separate income distribution from merit-goods concerns, must recognize that even if ownership is meritorious there is an opportunity cost to increasing ownership, and should target those households that would not have been owners in the absence of government intervention, rather than offering a general subsidy to owners.

The fourth value to consider is that there ought to be affordable housing. Perhaps of all values discussed in this section, this is the most widely mentioned. Many housing analysts distinguish between problems of housing adequacy (already dealt with in a previous section under the heading of merit goods), and problems of housing affordability. A household is said to have an affordability problem if it spends more than some percentage – usually twenty-five or thirty percent – of its income on housing. Affordability problems are said to increase if rents or ownership costs rise faster than income, because to acquire the same housing would require a larger percentage of income. But why is it a social problem if someone spends more than twenty-five percent of their income on housing? The percentage distribution of expenditure is certainly not part of our value system, and surely it is not a social problem if high-income households choose to spend more than 25 percent of their income on housing. The implicit logic of the affordability concept is set out in the following sentence. If a low-income household spends more than 25 percent of its income on housing, *then it will not have enough money left over to buy adequate food, clothing, transportation, medical care, education, and so on;* therefore there is a social problem, *because society holds the value that all people are entitled to the necessities listed above.* The italicized portions of the sentence are omitted in much writing on housing. The housing affordability concept is a proxy. It is a proxy for the values that food, clothing, and so on are merit goods. But the affordability concept – the 25-percent rule – is a poor proxy for several reasons. The percentage should fall with income. The rule should change as relative prices change. It should recognize that people's preferences differ, that in urban areas the percentage of income spent will vary depending on how people trade off commuting costs and housing consumption, and that over the lifecycle the percentage will vary. Use of the 25-percent rule shows none of these variations. Most important of all, it is a poor proxy because it treats the problems of a group of merit goods as a housing problem; and housing policies are a poor way to ensure the adequate consumption of all merit goods.

This chapter has sought to explore a broader definition of equity than is usual in welfare economics. Ideas such as adequate housing, rent gouging, or security of tenure reflect valid public concerns. Housing economists should not dismiss them, as they often do, because the values do not fit into traditional welfare economics; but, should struggle to see how the values can be defined, what policies might be used to achieve them, and what are the opportunity costs of the policies. Of course there is the danger that every policy can become "justifiable," because a value can be concocted to rationalize it. Obviously care and balance are required.

SUGGESTIONS FOR FURTHER READING

Aaron, H., and G. von Furstenberg (1971) "The Inefficiency of Transfers in Kind: The Case of Housing Assistance," *Western Economic Journal* 9:184–91.

Atkinson, A. B. (1977) "Housing Allowances, Income Maintenance, and Income Taxation," in M. S. Feldstein and R. P. Inman, eds., *The Economics of Public Services* (London: Macmillan).

Hillman, A. (1980) "Notions of Merit Want," *Public Finance/Finances Publiques* 35:213–25.

Sandmo, A. (1976) "Optimal Taxation – an Introduction to the Literature," *Journal of Public Economics* 6:37–54.

8 | Policies to Achieve Pareto Efficiency[1]

Chapter seven grouped together a number of rationales for government intervention in housing markets under the general heading of equity. This chapter deals with another group under the heading of Pareto efficiency. The fundamental theorems of welfare economics show that if four conditions hold – all markets are competitive, there are no externalities,[2] there is no uncertainty, and there is no stabilization problem – then a laissez faire economy will generate a Pareto efficient allocation of resources.

These four conditions are considered below. For each, there is a brief exploration of why Pareto efficiency may not exist if the condition does not hold; then evidence from the Canadian economy is sought to establish whether the condition holds. For example, it will be asked whether housing markets in Canada are competitive. If the evidence shows the necessary condition does not hold, then the optimal instrument of intervention will be explored. As each condition is studied it will be assumed that all other conditions hold; most importantly, that the distribution of income is appropriate, and there is no underconsumption of housing arising from merit goods concerns (or direct consumption externalities).[3]

COMPETITIVE MARKETS

When a market is competitive, all agents in the market, whether buyers or a sellers, behave as price takers. They accept the price as given, and assume their behaviour will not alter the price. The definition sometimes also includes the assumptions that there is full information (no uncertainty) and no transactions costs. It is usually assumed that if there are a large number of buyers and a large number of sellers, and none of them have a significant share of the market, then the market will be competitive. If a market is competitive, price will equal marginal cost, and resources will be Pareto efficiently allocated. When markets are not competitive, price may not equal marginal cost, and a Pareto improvement may be possible.

A lack of competition can be associated with a small number of agents, either on the demand side or the supply side of a market. The supply side will be discussed here because in the housing and housing-related markets, non-competitiveness arises on the supply side. Recent work in industrial organization (see Baumol [1982] for a survey and references) suggests that a market with few agents on the supply side may have price and output levels consistent with Pareto efficiency if the market is contestable. In essence a contestable market is one in which potential entrants have full information about a market, have the same cost and production conditions as existing producers, and for whom entry and exit is costless. Any above-normal profits are vulnerable to a hit-and-run entrant. Even a single supplier may behave as a perfect competitor in a perfectly contestable market.

How then does one establish whether markets are allocating resources Pareto efficiently? Obviously the first step is to see how many suppliers there are. But even if there is only one or a few sellers, this is not sufficient proof that government intervention should be considered. The market must be examined to see if it is contestable. Where there are several suppliers, collusive behaviour is often difficult to prove, and rather *ad hoc* tests are applied instead. Often the market is examined to see whether there are barriers to the entry of new firms; for only if there are barriers to entry can existing firms push profits above the competitive level in the long run. There are many possible barriers to entry. One of importance is economies of scale relative to the market demand. Others are, a patent on a production process, and government regulation restricting entry to an industry. A final piece of evidence that is sometimes used to show non-competitive markets is the rate of return to investment in the market. If the long-run rate of return, adjusted for risk, is higher than in other sectors, then there is an inefficient allocation of resources.

In analysing whether a government housing program is required to deal with non-competitive markets, the general approach above must be applied not only to the output market – the market for housing services – but also those for inputs into housing production, such as land and related markets, such as those for mortgage finance and mortgage insurance.[4]

Consider first the output market. Here the analysis can depend upon how the market is defined. If one is analysing the market for housing services demanded by all households, whether owners or renters, and supplied by owners of existing and newly built owner-occupied and rental stock, then the market is obviously competitive. There are many agents on both sides of the market. If one is considering the rental or ownership market separately, again there are many suppliers. It is sometimes popularly asserted that a few companies own a large fraction of the rental stock. This is simply untrue – the rental stock is widely held in Canadian cities. Another popular assertion is that the development and building industry is concentrated, thus resulting in a restriction of new supply and housing prices above those consistent with Pareto efficiency. There is some evidence of concentration in the building and development industry. In some metropolitan areas, over fifty percent of new supply is provided by the four largest firms (for Toronto data, see Muller [1978]). The concentration ratio is sensitive to the chosen geographical boundaries of the market area. A single municipality in a large metropolitan area can show a very high ratio; but the relevant market area is that where dwelling units are close substitutes and will likely extend beyond a single municipality in a large metropolitan area.

How does concentration in the supply of new units affect the price and output of housing? For the sake of analysis, let us assume that the supply of new housing is a monopoly, that the rental and ownership markets are independent, and consider a monopoly supplier of new rental housing. Assume that newly produced housing stock yields identical housing services to that derived from the existing stock. A useful framework for analysis is the stock-flow model to illustrate a series of short-run equilibria (as before, one unit of stock yields one unit of service, so the terms may be interchanged). Figure 8.1 illustrates an initial equilibrium. Curve DD represents the market demand for rental housing services, curve SS is the market supply derived from the existing stock, $\bar{Q}$, the equilibrium rent is R_1, and MC and AC are the marginal and average cost curves of the monopolist builder. There is no incentive for new supply in equilibrium (depreciation is assumed to be zero on the existing stock). Suppose there was an unanticipated shift in the market demand curve to $D'D'$. In the very short run, the rent would rise to R_2. The monopolist faces segment AD' of the market demand curve, which has been redrawn on the axes on the right-hand side of figure 8.1. If the monopolist maximizes profits in that period, it will choose output level q_1 (where $MR = MC$). This shifts the market supply curve to $S'S'$, and the market rent falls to R_3. In the next period the monopolist faces section BD' of the market demand curve, and the process repeats itself. Eventually in this model the supply expands until the rent returns to R_1, because the cost curves have been assumed constant over periods. If the supply of new units were competitive, and we assume that the competitive supply curve would be MC, then competitive supply would be q_2 in the first period, and the rent correspondingly lower. In the long run, competition would also return the rent to R_1. Thus a monopoly restricts the new supply and causes increased rents as the adjustment to a new equilibrium is made, but does not alter the long-run stock level or rent. This model still implies a Pareto improvement could be made; but only over the adjustment period.

The monopolist in the above model has been very short-sighted, not taking into account how its production in one period influences the

FIGURE 8.1
New Construction Monopoly

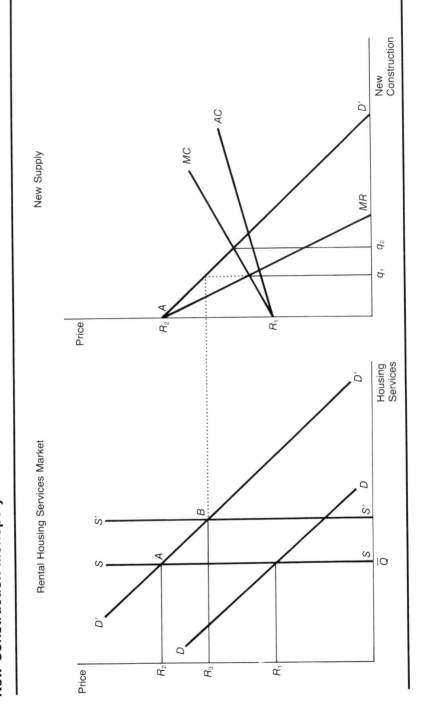

Rental Housing Services Market

New Supply

demand curve it faces in the next period. A more far-sighted monopolist would maximize not current-period profits but the present value of current and future profits. If the monopolist were to cut back production from q_1, profits in the first period would fall (by $MR - MC$ for a small change in q), but would be higher in future periods. Depending on the cost curves, demand curves, and interest rate, the monopolist may select a lower output level than q_1. In this intertemporal framework, the efficiency costs of monopoly could be higher.

Although there are relatively few suppliers of new rental housing or new owner-occupied housing in Canadian housing markets, there is little evidence of resource misallocation. There are few economies of scale in residential construction and few barriers to entry. The market in any one area is likely very contestable, with above-normal profits attracting builders from other cities. Canadian developers and builders have proven mobile between cities. The Land Task Force (1978) also reached the conclusion that no Pareto improvement was possible, but cautioned there exists the potential for substantially increased concentration that should be monitored.

Besides the output markets, there are a number of related markets to be examined in thinking about a government housing policy, in particular the land, mortgage, and mortgage insurance markets. It is sometimes asserted that the ownership of developable land is concentrated. Landowners withhold land, thus raising prices, raising new housing costs, and causing a suboptimal stock of housing. However neither economic theory nor the data support the conclusion that concentrated ownership has distorted resource allocation. Markusen and Scheffman (1977) showed that not even monopoly ownership of vacant land on a city's periphery will necessarily result in a slower rate of development than widely diversified land ownership. A monopolist may even sell a given inventory of land more rapidly when it is recognized that a low current rate of development (and so higher current prices) implies that the returns on some of its inventory must be postponed until a future period when sales will be higher and so prices will be lower. The Land Task Force (1978) examined the ownership of land that could be potentially developed over about five years in thirteen metropolitan areas. The data identified both nominal owners and effective owners, established by pooling together linked companies. In all but four cities, the four largest landowners held less than 50 percent of the developable land. In the four exceptions, the high concentration ratios were produced because the public sector held large amounts of land; the four largest private owners held less than 50 percent of the land. There seem to be enough agents to have a fairly competitive market.

The land market is rather unique because supply is constrained by the actions of municipalities. Local governments through their planning and zoning activities designate certain land for development, and through the development approvals process regulate the flow of raw land into the housing industry. There may be a barrier to entry, but it is established by the public sector. Redress, if any is needed, can come through changes in the approval process. Any inefficiency caused by slow approvals must be weighed against any gains from better planned developments.

Rates of return to land ownership have clearly been very high. The Land Task Force (1978) found returns on equity to be between 30 and 40 percent. While this can be evidence of market power, it can also be a result of other things. In the case of land around Canadian cities, it is a result of a large unanticipated increase in demand for housing, and of an unanticipated increase in the rate of inflation (see Scheffman [1978]). As anticipated demand for housing matched actual demand, and inflation moderated in the late 1970s, land prices rose less rapidly and rates of return fell.

Turning now to the mortgage market, there is little evidence of concentration in the intermediation of Canadian mortgage markets. Mortgages are suplied by banks, trust companies, mortgage loan companies, credit unions, caisses populaires, and life insurance companies. No single lender or even type of lender dominates the mortgage market (CMHC 1982, tables 37 and 38). As well, much mortgage lending is done directly between individuals or intermediated by real estate agents or lawyers (Rowe 1981). There are few barriers to entry into the field, although there are significant regulatory barriers to entering banking (Economic Council of Canada 1976). There has been no evidence presented that mortgage lending yielded higher returns than other activities, although at certain times banks have enjoyed higher after-tax returns to shareholders' equity than other sectors (Economic Council of Canada 1976, 40). Thus there seems no reason to conclude that mortgage lending is concentrated, a conclusion supported by the Royal Commission on Corporate Concentration (Canada 1978). Nor are there significant government regulations constraining the market allocation of mortgage credit. Since 1950 there has been a gradual removal of regulations which has facilitated the integration of the mortgage market with other credit markets.

It is sometimes argued that, although not concentrated, Canadian mortgage markets do not have all the characteristics of perfectly competitive markets. It is said that mortgage markets do not equilibrate "properly" because mortgage interest rates lag the adjustment of other security yields, and mortgage lending is a residual, squeezed when the demand for loanable funds increases. Public mortgage lending to deal with this lagged adjustment is then often recommended. There are a number of problems with this reasoning. The mortgage rate of interest is the most important component in the "price" of mortgage credit, but there are other components as well. The loan-to-value ratio, term, and amortization period all vary and influence the cash flow of the mortgage and the risk. Other fees are also often paid on initiation of a mortgage. Only by considering all components could the price of mortgage credit be established and then compared with the adjustments in the yields of other standardized securities. Furthermore the efficient adjustment of all terms of a mortgage to changing credit market conditions would have to be established before it could be proven that the existing pattern of adjustment was evidence of market failure. In a similar vein, some of the lag is due to the special institutional arrangements surrounding mortgage lending, such as forward commitment which may be efficient. Certainly the mortgage market did not equilibrate when there were ceilings on the mortgage rate charged on NHA insured loans, but these were lifted in 1969, and now the rate is market determined.

The other allegation of non-competitive behaviour sometimes heard is that mortgage lenders discriminate against such groups as women, immigrants, households with several income earners, owners of inner-city housing, and owners of older housing not conforming to current zoning laws and building standards. This is exceedingly difficult to prove because a rejected loan application at current mortgage terms is not proof of discrimination. It is likely these classes of borrowers are riskier, and it is more expensive to acquire information about their credit worthiness because few of this class have borrowed previously. It is quite possible that at an interest rate reflecting costs and risks, the loan demand would disappear. However, substantial evidence to confirm or deny the existence of discrimination is not available. Anecdotal evidence is heard often enough to suggest a role for government would be that of investigating the existence of discrimination.

A final related market to be scrutinized is that for residential mortgage insurance. This industry has always been dominated by CMHC as a public insurer under the National Housing Act. In 1978 CMHC held 57 percent of the mortgage insurance in force (Task Force 1979, 49), although the fraction had been declining rapidly to that date. There once were three private insurance firms, but now there is one. Rather than addressing the question of whether policies are needed to deal with monopoly or oligopoly, it is more appropriate to ask whether Pareto efficiency requires a continuance of public mortgage insurance. There are two options to consider: public insurance may be maintained, or public insurance may be phased out and the industry subject to existing competition laws and existing regulations governing the insurance industry.

There are several issues bearing on whether terminating public insurance would be a Pareto improvement. Discontinuing public insurance leaves open the possibility of non-competitive behaviour, perhaps even a monopoly, causing resource misallocation. However if the market were contestable, even with a single firm, no misallocation need occur. It has been argued that the current situation of one private supplier is not indicative of what would prevail without government insurance because the situation came about through CMHC setting public insurance premiums too low. However there are reasons to argue that the industry would be highly concentrated. There are likely scale economies in one city or market area to assessing and processing applications and to portfolio management. At the same time, an insurer would try to diversify across cities in order to reduce risk, under the assumption that some factors determining default rates are uncorrelated between cities. It may be impossible to answer how many firms would exist in a purely private market, but the market would surely be very concentrated. It is also difficult to establish how contestable the market would be. The need for a firm to diversify across cities suggests new entrants might not be able to match the production conditions of an incumbent. There might be the possibility of premiums above marginal cost.

Replacing public insurance with private insurance might change the resource cost of initiating and processing insurance applications and of managing the investment portfolio. Current conventional wisdom suggests private insurance companies would be more efficient, but there is little evidence to confirm or deny this. Existing charges by CMHC for insurance initiation are likely below the true costs (Task Force 1979).

The secondary market in mortgages would develop less rapidly if public insurance were discontinued because private insurers would have different criteria for assessing insurable loans and offer less security than the government, thus making it more difficult to buy and sell packages of insured mortgages.

The continued operation of public insurance allows the possiblity of subsidies being delivered inadvertently to borrowers, as has often been the case in the past. The existing system does not differentiate borrowers by risk class. High-risk borrowers such as non-profit groups or new home purchasers receiving extensive government assistance have been insured at the regular premium. This, of course, is not to argue that the subsidization of mortgage insurance could never be an instrument of public policy. However, the role of delivering actuarially sound insurance, and the role of subsidizing insurance have become intermingled, thus preventing rational policy decision making.

If public insurance were terminated, the possible gains from more efficient operation and better assistance policies must be traded off against possible oligopoly resource misallocations and weakening of the secondary mortgage market. On balance, and recognizing the welfare costs of a transition, one might tentatively recommend the continuation of mortgage insurance. However it is extremely difficult to quantify the costs and benefits of the various results.

This discussion of the degree of competition in Canadian housing and related markets suggests there has been little misallocation of resources, and there are therefore no opportunities for Pareto improvements. This may appear to have been a lot of trouble to knock over straw men. However, over the last 20 years in Canada there have been frequent allegations of monopoly or above-normal returns in the various markets, and these have provided a justification for various housing programs. These allegations are heard less frequently now, but no doubt will be again should house prices or rents begin to rise more rapidly.

EXTERNALITIES

The second item on the list of rationales for government housing policy is externalities. The intuitive reason why these may provide a need for government intervention is obvious. The price system is successful in generating a Pareto optimum in cases where private and social costs and benefits are the same. Private decision makers acting in their own interests also act in society's interests. However if there exist technological externalities, the social costs or benefits of an action are not coincident with private costs, and these external effects are not taken into account by the decision makers. More formally, a necessary condition for a Pareto optimum is that the sum of the marginal rates substitution of all affected individuals equals the marginal rate of transformation (the sum of everyone's willingness to pay equals what must be given up). Private markets, because of free-rider problems, do not offer a mechanism for aggregating this willingness to pay, with the exception of the situation outlined by Coase (1960): if transaction costs are zero, and property rights are specified, private markets can generate an efficient resource allocation through negotiation to deal with the externality. There are numerous alleged externalities in housing matters, three of which are most important: indirect consumption externalities, externalities from home renovation, and land use externalities.

It is sometimes claimed that housing consumption generates an indirect consumption externality (to be distinguished from the direct consumption externality of chapter seven). The housing consumption of household k influences the utility of household i, not because it appears as an argument in the utility function of household i, but because the housing consumption of household k affects some other variable that is an argument in the utility function of household i. A general formulation of an indirect consumption externality is presented in equations 8.1. The utility of household i is influenced by variable D_i; let us define it for the sake of illustration as crimes committed against individual i. An increase in D_i, all other things held constant, reduces utility. The level of crimes against individual i is a function of many variables, including the housing consumption of the kth household. The remaining variables are summarized by the vector $\mathbf{E}$. If the housing

$$U_i = U_i \left(x_{i1}, x_{i2}, x_{i3}, D_i \right)$$

$$\frac{\partial U_i}{\partial D_i} < 0$$

$$D_i = f \left(x_{k2}, \mathbf{E} \right)$$

(8.1)

$$\frac{\partial D_i}{\partial x_{k2}} \begin{cases} < 0 & x_{k2} < \bar{\bar{x}}_2 \\ = 0 & x_{k2} \geqslant \bar{\bar{x}}_2 \end{cases}$$

consumption of household k increases, up to some threshold level $\bar{\bar{x}}_2$, then crimes against household i decrease, and their utility increases. There is an indirect positive externality. The literature has identified three variables of the "D" type. They are fire damage, infectious illness, and crime. Rothenberg (1967), in a careful exploration of the economics of urban renewal, provides a good discussion of them. If one household has poor housing, it is alleged, then this household is more likely to have a fire in their dwelling, and so it is more likely that a neighbour will suffer fire damage as the fire spreads. Analogously the poorly housed household is more likely to become ill, and if the illness is contagious, then neighbours are more likely to become ill. And as housing consumption increases, it is argued, the household will be more stable and less likely (especially the children) to engage in antisocial or criminal activity that hurts others.

This form of externality is similar to many pollution externalities. To illustrate let us consider the problem of acid rain, so familiar to Canadians. The emission of sulphur dioxide into the air in conjunction with a number of other variables, such as the meterological conditions and the amount of other air particles that interact with the sulphur dioxide, causes sulphuric acid to be created which falls with rain into lakes. If the lakes do not contain limestone, their waters become acidic, causing fish to die, thus reducing the utility of anglers. The emission of sulphur dioxide has a negative externality, but the relationship is indirect.

The indirect consumption externalities from housing are similar. Consider the case of low consumption of housing measured as an overcrowded apartment. This overcrowding may lead to stress, which may lead to aggressive antisocial behaviour, which may harm others outside the household. The relationship between crowding and stress, however, is a complex one. It will depend on who the other people are in the housing unit, the substitutes available for passing time in the dwelling, the layout of the dwelling, and even the cultural heritage of the inhabitants. The relationship between stress and antisocial behaviour is also a complex one. Some individuals may respond positively to stress. The amount of antisocial behaviour will also depend on the gains from that behaviour, the penality of being convicted of a crime, and the probability of being convicted.

Just as in the case of pollution externalities, we are a long way from either a full theoretical or empirical understanding of these relationships. Early empirical research was very simple, showing strong positive correlations between low housing consumption and fire, illness, and crime rates. However it was quickly recognized that these correlations did not prove the existence of the externality because there were many other variables, themselves correlated with poor housing, that might explain the fire, illness, and crime rates. More sophisticated tests are required to document and measure these externalities. Economists are divided on what conclusions to draw from existing evidence.[5]

Indirect consumption externalities are a poor basis on which to justify a government housing program in Canada for several reasons. Their existence remains conjectural. It is highly likely that the threshold level for such externalities, $\bar{x}_2$, is very low; below the housing consumption of almost all Canadians. Many other variables influence fire, illness, and crime, and a larger Pareto improvement might be achieved through policies to influence these other variables rather than housing consumption.

A second externality that may offer the possibility of a Pareto improvement is the positive externality from home maintenance or renovation. The existence of such externalities is easily shown by the fact that when people buy a house or rent an apartment they consider not only the characteristics of the dwelling unit but also the characteristics of surrounding buildings and the neighbourhood. These externalities are so evident that a synonym for externalities is neighbourhood effects. If landlords or owner-occupiers invest in maintenance or renovation, especially of the exterior and grounds of the building, they realise a benefit, but their neighbours also realise a benefit. Similarly, the maintenance decision of the neighbours will affect the landlords or owner-occupier. This form of interdependence sometimes gives rise to what is known as a prisoner's dilemma; which can be best explained through a numerical example.[6]

Suppose there are two owners, A and B, of adjacent properties. They have each made an initial investment and are contemplating renovation, but do not know whether the other will renovate or not. Both have funds, say in government bonds, which is their best alternative investment, that are just enough for the renovation (assuming only one sort of renovation project is technically feasible). Both act to maximize the return on their capital. The possible outcomes are summarized in the payoff matrix, figure 8.2.[7] In each cell of the matrix the right-hand term is the rate of return on the portfolio of owner A, and the left-hand term is the rate of return on the portfolio of owner B. If both A and B decide not to renovate, they get the return on the existing building and bonds, which is 10 percent (lower right cell). If both A and B decide to renovate they get the returns from the improvement in their own dwelling plus the positive externality from their neighbour's renova-

FIGURE 8.2
Renovation Payoff Matrix

OWNER A*

	Renovate	Do Not Renovate
Renovate (OWNER B*)	.18 .18	.08 .20
Do Not Renovate	.20 .08	.10 .10

*In each cell the right-hand term is the rate of return on the portfolio of owner A, and the left-hand term is the rate of return on the portfolio of owner B.

tion, which together yield 18 percent (upper left cell). If A were to renovate and B did not, the situation is somewhat more complicated (lower left cell). The renovation of A still yields positive gross benefits, but the return is very low because of the unrenvoated adjacent property, so the return of A's portfolio falls to 8 percent. B, on the other hand, keeps his money in bonds but enjoys a higher rate of return on his building because of the positive externalities from A's renovation: B's portfolio now has a return of 20 percent. Symmetric results hold if B were to renovate, but not A (upper right cell).

Both property owners know the payoff matrix, but not what the other will do. What will be the result? Consider the decision of owner B. He says to himself: Suppose owner A were to renovate, then the best return

I can achieve is by not renovating; and suppose owner A were to not renovate, then the best return I can get is by not renovating. Thus for each possible choice of A, the best decision for B will be no renovation. Similar logic is followed by owner A. Therefore both decide not to renovate; although both would be better off if both renovated. A Pareto improvement is possible.

This outcome relied on the fact that neither owner knew what the other would do. Of course if they were able to negotiate with one another, the more likely outcome would be that both would renovate. No Pareto improvement would be possible over the resource allocation of the private market. Alternatively a third party might buy both properties, renovate both, and so internalize the externality. However if one of the existing owners recognized the plan to jointly renovate, he might hold out for a high price and extract all the returns from the joint renovation. It is for this reason that developers assembling a large plot of land for a project often disguise their intentions from existing owners.

This discussion draws out an important idea for the analysis of how the government can improve efficiency. By definition, a Pareto improvement can help someone and hurt no one; and the potential Pareto improvement with suitable side payments can also help someone and hurt no one. Thus there are incentives in the private market to make Pareto and potential Pareto improvements. If people could co-ordinate their activities, there would be no need for government. It is only where this co-ordination fails that there may be a role for government. The method of establishing whether a potential Pareto improvement is possible is cost-benefit analysis. It is not possible to discuss cost-benefit analysis here, but the ideas are well known and there are numerous excellent treatments available.[8]

The public sector has a special role when the co-ordination of activities also involves the co-ordination of public sector investments such as roads, water mains, sewers, and schools. If a Pareto improvement is possible, the government has a number of instruments at its disposal: it can undertake the project itself (as in urban renewal); it can create instruments to foster private co-ordination (by creating local improvement districts); it can subsidize renovation; and it can compel renovation (through zoning by-laws and building standards).

This discussion has dealt with positive renovation externalities, but the spatial fixity of housing implies many other sorts of externalities as well. High-rise apartments impose negative externalities on adjacent single, detached homes; many non-residential uses, especially industrial uses, impose negative externalities on adjacent housing; a list of examples could be extended easily to great length. The analysis of where to locate a single firm that imposes negative externalities in an urban area would be relatively straightforward, but the problem of designing an efficient pattern of land use over time is extremely complex, and economic theory has produced no prescriptions on the efficient pattern of government intervention. Almost all jurisdictions have dealt with these externalities through zoning by-laws that restrict the uses of land. Certain areas are designated residential, others commercial, and yet others industrial; within residential areas the allowable densities are set out. These regulations are relatively crude instruments. They no doubt reduce negotiation costs and deal with many externalities; however they no doubt also prevent many land-use reallocations that would be Pareto improvements. It is an empirical question, as yet unanswered, whether zoning by-laws lead to a Pareto improvement over what would have existed without them.

Zoning by-laws are also part of a system of optimal local governments in a large metropolitan area. Tiebout (1956) pointed out that if people in a large metropolitan area could choose to live in one of many local government jurisdictions, each with a different pattern of taxes and local public services, they could choose the tax-expenditure package consistent with their utility maximum. People by "voting with their feet" would reveal their preferences for local public goods, and the efficient level of local public goods could be supplied. All residents of a jurisdiction consume the same level of public goods and, for efficiency, all must pay the same price. However, local governments are not allowed to use a poll tax, only a property tax to raise revenue. To ensure that all residents pay the same taxes (price), zoning by-laws are required so all properties are of equal value. Then no one can buy a small house, pay low taxes, and enjoy a high level of public services. The important implication for housing economics is that the Pareto efficient provision of local public goods requires that housing be of similar value within a jurisdiction and, assuming households have similar tastes but different incomes, implies neighbourhoods will be homogeneous by income.[9] However if local public goods are merit goods, particularly merit goods of the sort that society believes all people should have, the same level of consumption (as may be the case for primary and secondary education or police protection), then the Tiebout analysis does not hold. Rather than organizing local government to see local public goods vary by willingness to pay, local government should be organized to ensure equal levels of service. The latter seems to have motivated much local government reorganization in Canada.

UNCERTAINTY

The normative analysis of chapters six, seven, and eight, and almost all of the positive analysis of the previous chapters assumed that there was no uncertainty – all agents were equally and fully informed about current and future values of all relevant variables. Obviously, this assumption is unrealistic. There is considerable uncertainty in housing markets. This does not mean that we should throw out the previous positive and normative analysis, but rather that we should try to introduce this further complexity into models of agents' behaviour and market interaction, and that we should be cautious in applying analysis that does not recognize uncertainty.

The basic framework for the welfare analysis of uncertainty is provided by Arrow (1971). He showed that the existence of uncertainty does not necessarily imply that private markets will not achieve Pareto efficiency. If there is a full set of contingency markets, private markets will be efficient, and risk will be optimally allocated.

The real world, however, does not offer a full set of contingency markets. A number of institutional arrangements, in particular insurance and securities markets, provide some mechanisms for shifting of risk. However a complete set of insurance markets has not evolved for a number of reasons.

Potential insurers or those who would buy insurance may have wrong information. There may be high transactions costs to establishing a market. Or, information may be unequally distributed between a potential insurer and client, which gives rise to the problems of moral hazard and adverse selection. Moral hazard arises when the activities of the insured affect the liabilities of the insurance company, and the company does not have complete information about this behaviour. With insurance, the customer takes fewer precautions and the insured-against outcome increases so much that the premiums imply a lower expected utility with insurance than without. No market will exist. Adverse selection arises when individuals know their own riskiness better than the insurance company. If there are individuals of many degrees of riskiness, eventually only insurance for the most risky will exist. "It is only too clear that the shifting of risk in the real world is incomplete" (Arrow 1971, 148).

Thus, in the world of uncertainty, the proof that Pareto efficiency will be attained by private markets does not hold, and an examination is warranted to see whether government intervention might be a Pareto improvement. In housing matters, the examination usually focuses on three areas: innovation, mortgage credit rationing, and mortgage insurance markets.

An innovation can frequently be copied. The costs of developing the innovation are borne by one agent, but the benefits may be enjoyed by several. This sugests that the private market may underinvest in research and development. Government may have a role to stimulate innovation; for example, in housing design changes to increase energy efficiency, or in the design of mortgage contracts.

The phenomenon of credit rationing has been discussed in chapter five (see references to the literature there). Rationing can arise in the equilibrium of a market with rational agents when there is incomplete and asymmetric information. Most writers on rationing have not directly addressed the question of whether public lending would be a Pareto improvement, but seemed implicitly to suggest that because governments would have the same information about borrowers as private lenders, an intervention would not be Pareto improving. However a recent paper (B. Smith 1983) has presented a model in which government lending to meet all excess demand for credit at the prevailing market rate would be a Pareto improvement.

The final area of consideration is mortgage insurance markets. As already noted, insurance markets play a critical role in securing the Pareto efficient allocation of risk-bearing in an uncertain world. Is there a role for government in the mortgage insurance market, apart from dealing with the problems of securing a competitive market? Private mortgage insurance is provided, so general problems of adverse selection and moral hazard do not seem to be prevalent. However, certain classes of borrowers and more importantly certain types of mortgage contracts, for example graduated payment mortgages, are not insurable privately. The absence of private insurance is most likely due to the assessment of private lenders that if the insurance carried an appropriate premium, there would be no demand. If the public sector has different information or a different assessment of risk, there is a possibility that public provision will be a Pareto improvement. This appears to have been the rationale for NHA insurance in the 1950s.

Although it cannot be generally shown that the private market is Pareto efficient when there is uncertainty, by the same token it cannot generally be shown where government can make a Pareto improvement. Governments usually have the same information problems and costs of acquiring information as private agents. Research into welfare economics with uncertainty is just beginning, and it is probably premature to recommend specific interventions.

STABILIZATION OF FLUCTUATIONS

Neoclassical economics also recognizes a potential role for government in stabilizing fluctuations in the economy. This role is usually dealt with under the heading of macroeconomics rather than welfare economics, but fundamentally the rationale for intervention is the same. Unemployment is undesirable because the lost output reduces utility levels. Inflation is undesirable because, given existing institutional and contractual arrangements, it causes inefficient resource allocation and unintended income redistribution. Government intervention can be explored either on the basis of the Pareto criterion or the social welfare function criterion. Two sorts of fluctuations will be considered: fluctions in the entire economy, and fluctuations in the housing sector.

In order to establish a role for government in stabilizing the entire economy, it should first be shown how the economy would fluctuate in the absence of government policy. This would require analysis using a large simulation model of the economy. We will simply assume that there would be significant fluctuations, and the possibility must be considered of using fiscal and/or monetary policy to stabilize the economy and so generate a potential Pareto improvement. The fiscal or monetary policy might involve housing instruments. If the government wishes to stimulate the economy, a public house-building program, or a program to subsidize consumers or builders, or a public mortgage lending program could be adopted; or if the government wished to contract the economy these programs could be reversed. Alternatively the government may wish to adopt a monetary policy that contains offsets for sectors where investment is particularly interest elastic. Housing is such a sector, and a prolonged restrictive monetary stance with high real interest rates might be accompanied by a public mortgage lending program. This would be justified if it were the optimal monetary package in the sense of achieving a given reduction in the rate of inflation at the least increase in unemployment. Alternatively a prolonged easy monetary policy with low real rates might be paired with reductions in the base level of public mortgage lending.

Few would dispute that national income, employment, and prices would have shown instability during the postwar period in Canada in the absence of government intervention. There does, however, exist debate about the fundamental causes of these fluctuations and the efficiency of using government policy to reduce them, between the two principal competing viewpoints often labelled monetarist and Keynesian.

There are two variants of the monetarist position, both of which lead to the same conclusion about stabilization policy (Gordon 1981). The free market economy is held to be stable, or at least to be self-stabilizing, so that it naturally tends toward a relatively stable price level and full employment. There is no need for the public sector to engage in the management of aggregate demand; indeed it is claimed much of the instability of the postwar period has been caused by government policies. An alternative monetarist view accepts that shifts in private consumer spending and business investment do cause instability, but because monetary policy is powerful and fiscal policy relatively weak, because we lack precise knowledge about the magnitude and timing of their effects on aggregate demand, and because political decision makers tend to overact, the most prudent course for government is not to engage in discretionary stabilization policy. If either variant is accepted, the discussion need not proceed further. Housing instruments would not be needed as part of a policy to stabilize the economy. Any attempts to regularly intervene would make things worse.

The Keynesians deny that the free market is stable, or self-regulating, or that our knowledge of the economy is so sketchy as to rule out countercyclical policies. While perhaps unable to reach agreement about the relative effectiveness of various instruments, they agree that unemployment or inflation can be counteracted by government policy. The question becomes which instrument to use in stabilization policy.

Assuming some form of stimulative fiscal policy was desired, a number of issues govern whether expenditure changes, or tax changes, or direct lending will be the optimal government policy, and whether these changes should be focused on certain sectors. The lags between recognition of the need for stimulus and the change in target variables are important, with shorter lags being more desirable because there is less likelihood that economic conditions will have changed between decision and effect. Housing instruments would have a similar legislative lag to other fiscal instruments (although longer than monetary instruments), but would influence aggregate demand more rapidly than many public spending projects (and less rapidly than personal tax changes). Private builders usually have a "shelf" of ready housing projects, and resources move relatively easily into the housing sector. Another criterion is efficiency, defined as extra dollars of nominal GNP per dollar of deficit. The high interest elasticity of housing construction suggests mortgage programs would be relatively efficient, assuming unemployed resources were drawn into housing. Housing investment has relatively low leakages of first-round expenditure into imports, and the dollar of deficit has no leakage into savings as does a personal or corporate income tax cut. Reversibility is also a desirable quality of any fiscal instrument. Mortgage lending programs are reversible in the sense that they may be started and stopped relatively easily.

Fiscal instruments also differ in their locational and sectoral impacts. If all locations and markets always exhibited the same degree of excess supply or excess demand (after standardizing for structural differences), the specific impact of fiscal policy would not matter. However regions, product, and input markets do not all move together. The national economy may be contracting or growing more slowly, and there may be downward pressure on the rate of price change, and yet individual industrial sectors may be expanding, and experiencing rising prices. Fixed capital and certain types of labour are relatively immobile between sectors in the short run, and so different sectors may exhibit considerable differences in excess capacity. Fiscal stimulus might yield the largest output increase for a given increase in prices if the initial stimulus were applied in markets with falling prices or prices that have been rising at a less rapid rate over time. This assertion seems plausible, but there is little empirical evidence to verify it. Alternatively stimulus could be applied to a sector, like housing, into which resources move easily and thus will be less likely to raise prices. In any event some choice must be made because stimulus cannot be evenly applied across all sectors in the first round.

Another issue influencing the choice of a housing-related instrument of stimulus will be whether it increases or decreases the housing fluctuations. If the housing and business cycles are in phase, a housing program would reduce fluctuations in the housing cycle and tend to reduce long-run average costs. However if the cycles were out of phase, long-run average costs might be increased.

On balance, a housing intervention might be the optimal instrument of a stimulative fiscal policy, if at the time stimulus was required, housing was a relatively depressed sector.

The other possibility, one that has been suggested for the situation in the early 1980s in Canada and the United States, is to use a mortgage market intervention in conjunction with monetary restraint. When monetary policy is restrictive and raises interest rates, new construction declines more than output in most other sectors because of its higher interest elasticity. It has been argued that an optimal monetary policy would combine general restraint with offsetting policies to shelter the mortgage market, but again evidence is lacking to assess the optimality of such a policy.

It is sometimes argued that it would be a potential Pareto improvement to stabilize the fluctuations in new housing construction without reference to general macroeconomic policy. It is alleged that fluctuations have meant the housing sector is undercapitalized, has not invested in research, or adopted new technologies, and that input costs are higher to compensate for dislocation and unemployment. Reductions in housing fluctuations could therefore reduce long-run average costs of housing production. While at first intuitively appealing, there is little empirical evidence to support these arguments. It was once felt that factory-produced components for mass-production housing would yield substantial savings. These technologies have been tried, and few savings materialized. Housing production was revealed to be intrinsically different in time, place, and dwelling type. It was also found that consumers value heterogeneity. As renovation becomes an increasing fraction of housing investment, the opportunities for scale economies become correspondingly reduced. Also, labour and other factors move relatively easily in and out of residential construction, commanding little premium for the dislocation.

Even if savings were realisable from stabilizing housing starts, two other problems must be addressed. To achieve the desired result, a government must possess sufficient economic expertise to recognize turning points in the housing cycle, and sufficient political will to adopt an appropriate response, including, of course, holding housing starts in an expansion below what they otherwise would have been. The evidence of the last ten years makes one reluctant to recommend a policy of sectoral fine tuning.[10]

Further, it is possible that stabilization of the housing sector would work against stabilization of the entire economy and on balance would not be Pareto improving. It should be emphasized that what is being considered here is an intervention focusing only on the housing sector independent of other concerns, not a macroeconomic policy with sector-specific components.

The examination of the role of government in housing markets is now completed. Throughout chapters six, seven, and eight, the view of Davis and Whinston (1961, 105) has been adopted. "The role of the economist in the formation of social policy may be compared to that of the consultant to an industrial firm. The consultant to a firm serves two functions. First, given the goals of the firm, he tries to find the best or most efficient means of achieving these goals. The second function of the consultant is equally important; he must try to clarify vague goals by pointing out possible inconsistencies, and determining implications in order that re-evaluations and explicit statements can be made." In these three chapters, there has been almost no mention of actual government policies, because the concern was with the design of optimal policies. The next chapter describes actual housing policies in Canada, and the final chapter examines their effects.

SUGGESTIONS FOR FURTHER READING

Clemhout, S. (1981) "The Impact of Housing Cyclicality on the Construction of Residential Units and Housing Costs," *Land Economics* 57: 609–23.

Davis, O. A., and A. B. Whinston (1961) "The Economics of Urban Renewal," *Law and Contemporary Problems* 26: 105–17.

HUD (1976) *Housing in the Seventies Working Papers* (Washington: U.S. Department of Housing and Urban Development).

Markusen, J. R., and D. T. Scheffman (1977) *Speculation and Monopoly in Urban Development: analytical foundations with evidence for Toronto* (Toronto: University of Toronto Press for the Ontario Economic Council).

9 | Housing Policy in Canada[1]

The first National Housing Act (NHA) was passed by the Government of Canada in 1938,[2] but it was not until after 1945, when Central Mortgage and Housing Corporation, CMHC (now called Canada Mortgage and Housing Corporation) was created as a Crown corporation to administer the federal National Housing Act, that housing interventions began as we know them now. Since then, there have been hundreds of different programs and hundreds of revisions. Because of the number and complexity of housing programs, one is often overwhelmed by detail. This chapter attempts to provide perspective on current policy and its evolution to the present, while being sufficiently specific about the instruments of policy to permit an analysis of their effects in the chapter following. First there is an overview of federal programs and then an overview of provincial programs.[3]

FEDERAL HOUSING POLICY

The involvement of the federal government in housing matters since 1954 can be usefully divided into three periods. These periods can be characterized according to the main preoccupation of government, or according to – and this may amount to the same thing – the public's attitude to the role of government. In thinking about the evolution of housing policy it is useful to place it in this broader perspective of all government activity, because housing policy was shaped by this context. The first period from 1954 to 1963 was concerned with stabilization and growth; the second, from 1964 to 1977, with equity and affordability; and the third, from 1978 to 1983, with stagflation and restraint.

The first era was a time when the government was applying the theories of Keynes to stabilize fluctuations in the national economy, and was encouraging and accommodating economic growth. The accepted role of government was "to make the private market work," rather than to substantially alter its outcome. In welfare economic terms, the emphasis was stabilization and efficiency, not equity. The issue in housing policy was to ensure mortgage funds and serviced land so that housing, especially single-family housing in the suburbs, could be built. There had been little housing constructed during the depression and the Second World War. Incomes were rising, and the children of the baby boom were arriving. It was obvious that high levels of new construction were implied, and the government sought to create a strong building industry and to remove any bottlenecks to the smooth flow of resources into housing.

The cornerstone of policy in this era was public mortgage insurance, established in 1954. Public insurance is still provided and remains important today. Central Mortgage and Housing Corporation acted as an insurer of mortgage loans made by approved lending institutions. The insurance premium was paid by the borrower, about one percent of the loan, which was below what lenders implicitly were charging for self-insurance. The insurance premium was added to the mortgage and amortized with the loan. Central Mortgage and Housing Corporation would then cover any interest or capital losses of lenders on defaulted loans. Central Mortgage and Housing Corporation established the criteria for eligible loans. Currently, a maximum loan is set, differing by region; the term is established, usually 5 years (originally it was 25 to 40 years), with an amortization period of from 25 to 40 years; loan-to-value ratios may be as high as 0.95 for mortgages financing home purchase; and principal, interest, and property taxes cannot exceed 30 percent of the borrower's allowable gross income. The maximum allowable loans are rather low, and in major metropolitan areas are well below the average house price, so NHA insured financing is now mainly used for condominiums and townhouses. The interest rate is now free to be established in the financial markets, although this was not always the case. Until 1966, the rate on NHA-insured mortgages was set by the government provided the rate was not more than 2 1/2 percent above the government long-term bond yield. The balancing of borrower pressure to reduce interest rates against the realities of the financial markets, which required mortgage rates to increase with other rates if the supply of mortgage credit was to be maintained, was not an easy task for the government. Often, changing conditions in the financial markets sharply altered the relative attractiveness of NHA mortgage loans, although the government had not changed the terms for eligibility. Table 9.1 shows the amounts insured over the period, and reveals the fluctuations. From 1966 to 1969, the mortgage rate was tied to the average yield on long-term government bonds of the previous quarter. The maximum NHA rate was first 1 1/2 percent and then 2 1/4 percent above this bond yield. In 1969, the rate was freed.[4]

The motivation for public insurance seems to have been that the federal government held a different view of the risks of mortgage lend-

TABLE 9.1
Mortgage Lending and Mortgage Insurance Activities of CMHC 1954 – 1963 ($ millions)

	1954	1955	1956	1957	1958	1959	1960	1961	1962	1963
Mortgage Lending Programs										
Federal-Provincial Housing	11.9	12.4	4.0	11.1	10.7	7.6	6.2	6.0	4.2	10.8
Entrepreneurs[1]	16.1	9.9	10.5	30.6	49.2	35.5	11.0	25.5	9.0	14.6
Other Direct Lending[2]	–	–	–	198.7	324.4	308.6	150.1	237.9	154.3	281.2
Student Housing	–	–	–	–	–	–	–	9.6	24.2	24.4
Mortgage Insurance Programs										
Insured Mortgage Loans by Approved Lenders	378.2	600.7	387.5	261.0	510.0	283.0	231.9	439.4	383.9	364.5
Insured Home Improvement Loans by Approved Lenders	–	27.3	29.7	30.6	39.7	37.5	30.1	42.6	38.0	36.7

1. Program was also called Limited Dividend Housing.
2. Program was also called Residual Lending.

SOURCE: Fallis (1980, 14).

ing than private lenders or potential insurers. Ex post the government's view proved correct; as the insurance fund could maintain adequate reserves against insurance in force. National Housing Act mortgage insurance reduced and almost removed (there was a small amount of co-insurance) the risk of default on mortgage loans. Mortgages became a more attractive investment for intermediaries, and the flow of mortgage credit was increased.

From the beginning of public insurance, the majority of NHA insured loans were used to finance the construction of new, detached, single-family houses (the mortgages were then assumed by the purchaser). In 1959, loans for rental construction became eligible, and in 1969 loans to finance purchases of existing housing became eligible. During the 1950s, life insurance companies and chartered banks were the main source of funds; in the 1960s, trust companies emerged as a major source; and in the 1970s, banks and trust companies increased their involvement, while the share of life insurance companies showed a decline.

A second insurance system, NHA Home Improvement Loan Insurance, was also instituted during this period and remains in effect. It was intended to promote the modernization and repair of existing houses. Insurance was available on small loans, often secured as a second mortgage, made by approved lenders, to be used by owner-occupiers or landlords for home improvements. The program does not appear to involve a subsidy, because the insurance fund covers costs and maintains adequate reserves against insurance in force. A small but steady flow of loans was insured until the early 1970s when a decline began. In the last several years, federal and provincial subsidies have been available for home rehabilitation, and the decline has been very steep.

The other major program of the era was the lending of public funds by CMHC as mortgages to finance new construction. This program was intended to be rather small; it was to be residual, supplying mortgage funds to creditworthy borrowers who for some reason were not serviced by private lenders. However from 1957 until the mid-1970s, the power to make direct loans was used in an attempt to increase the total volume of mortgage credit, and in an attempt to reduce fluctuations in housing construction, and in the level of general economic activity. Far from being residual, these loans were a major source of mortgage credit, and financed almost twenty percent of new construction between 1957 and 1970. The annual lending is presented in table 9.1.

There were several other programs operating during this period but, as table 9.1 indicates, they were rather small. There were few initiatives to directly increase the housing consumption of low-income households. The situation of the poorest households was of some concern, but it was felt that their living conditions would improve substantially through the "filtering-down" process. Partly as it was recognized that despite filtering-down, many low-income households continued to inhabit very poor housing, and partly because there was a desire "to spread the benefits of the affluent society" (Carver 1975, 164), the focus of housing policy began to shift.

The second era of housing policy, from 1964 to 1977, was a time when governments were confident that the economy could be stabilized and would grow. There was affluence, the prospect of increasing affluence, and governments intervened to ensure a fairer distribution of the pie. The emphasis shifted from stabilization and efficiency to equity concerns. This was the era when the welfare state was put in place. The federal government in 1973, "adopted the principle that [says] it is a fundamental right of Canadians, regardless of their economic circumstances, to enjoy adequate shelter at reasonable cost" (Hansard 1973).[5]

Lending and insurance under the various programs of this era are reported in table 9.2. There was an almost continual expansion of government housing activity. Not only did the annual amount of subsidies and loans advanced grow, but, more importantly, the sorts of households eligible for assistance expanded. At first low-income renters were the main recipients. Later, programs emerged to assist middle-income renters and middle-income home buyers. In 1970 almost 30 percent of

TABLE 9.2
Mortgage Lending and Mortgage Insurance Activities of CMHC
1966 – 1977 ($ millions)

	1966	1967	1968	1969	1970	1971	1972	1973	1974	1975	1976	1977
Mortgage Lending Programs												
Public Housing	60.9	114.3	128.5	170.5	235.4	277.0	238.0	199.7	177.4	296.2	350.4	153.4
Federal-Provincial Housing	14.6	34.3	41.0	27.9	29.0	31.5	39.1	51.8	58.1	96.2	99.5	104.8
Non-Profit Corporations	–	–	–	31.0	72.9	79.3	42.9	95.1	124.7	159.0	288.0	157.4
Co-operatives	–	–	–	–	–	–	–	7.6	19.8	44.4	40.3	62.8
Entrepreneurs	19.9	30.6	86.4	146.0	241.2	231.9	94.7	59.5	74.5	235.2	9.2	5.6
Assisted Home Ownership	–	–	–	–	–	–	–	133.1	435.2	458.2	80.0	23.7
Assisted Rental	–	–	–	–	–	–	–	–	–	–	137.5	320.8
Student Housing	53.2	56.6	73.8	55.5	41.0	36.7	14.4	3.8	4.0	0.4	–	7.7
Other Direct Lending	451.1	512.7	251.9	163.1	361.5	202.5	110.0	38.2	39.6	13.6	13.8	10.8
Residential Rehabilitation	–	–	–	–	–	–	–	–	4.2	14.9	61.0	101.3
Mortgage Insurance Programs												
Insured Mortgage Loans by Approved Lenders	191.2	355.8	832.2	711.0	937.0	1866.4	2150.4	1930.1	1370.0	3576.5	4461.0	6213.7
Insured Home Improvement Loans by Approved Lenders	35.9	35.2	23.9	22.1	16.9	19.0	19.0	16.2	18.6	15.8	10.5	8.8

SOURCE: Fallis (1983c)

housing starts were CMHC financed, and throughout the period over 15 percent were CMHC financed.

The programs of the first era were continued in the second, although with some changes. The main thrust of change was to reduce government regulation of the financial markets. The interest rate on NHA-insured mortgages was freed to be market-determined; the minimum term on NHA-insured mortgages was reduced from twenty-five to five years; the banks were permitted to make conventional mortgage loans; and the interest ceiling on bank loans was removed.

The second era began with NHA amendments in 1964 containing new arrangements for financing public housing – housing that is owned by the public sector, and on which the rents charged to households are set according to ability to pay rather than to cover resource costs. The program grew rapidly until in 1970, over ten percent of the housing starts in Canada were public housing.

There had been a public housing program in the 1954–1963 period, provided through a federal-provincial partnership agreement: the federal government provided seventy-five percent of the capital cost and operating losses. The provincial government provided the balance, and could request that a municipality assume a portion of the provincial share. Because the program required joint ownership rather than outright provincial ownership of public housing projects, it remained small.

Under the 1964 NHA amendments the old federal-provincial terms remained, but alternative terms became available and constituted what is normally termed public housing. The program proved popular with the provinces because the federal government had no ownership in the projects. Construction or acquisition loans for up to 90 percent of the total cost of the project were available from CMHC. The term of the loan could be for as long as fifty years, and there was a preferred interest rate, sometimes as much as 2 percentage points below the private mortgage rate. Provinces supplied the remaining 10 percent of capital costs. The federal government provided 50 percent of the annual operating losses incurred in the operation of public housing projects; the other 50 percent was provided by the province, or the province and the municipality in which the project was located. Tenants were charged a rent geared to their income, usually about 25 percent of their income, although the lowest income tenants paid a lower percentage. Most tenant households were families or senior citizens.

As public housing grew it became the object of strong criticism. Because it concentrated assisted households in one place, it was said to stigmatize tenants, to increase crime and vandalism, and to impose negative externalities on the surrounding neighbourhood. It offered tenants little choice of location and often meant they lived far from their jobs, friends, and the social services they used. Furthermore, the assistance was enormously expensive because the actual rent charged was low compared to the cost of the housing provided (which was expensive because it was new housing). In other words, the benefit per household was large. But only a lucky few of the eligible households participated in the program.

The criticism led to two reform thrusts. The first was to disperse assisted households, and mix them with households of different incomes. The Rent Supplement Program was created in the 1970s, under which government makes an agreement with a private landlord to rent an apartment to tenants from the public housing waiting list. The government pays the landlord the market rent, and the tenants pay the government a rent geared to their income. No more than twenty-five percent of the units in any one building can be under a rent supplement agreement. Recipients are thus dispersed and mixed. The level of subsidy remains about the same as public housing because relatively new buildings are used; the new buildings, which were financed under the other rental programs described below, often included rent supplement units. The second reform thrust was to assist the rehabilitation of older housing under the Residential Rehabilitation Assistance Program. This meant that the increase in housing consumption enjoyed by the recipient was much lower, that the subsidy per household was lower, and that the same amount of money could be spread among more people. Accompanying this scheme was the Neighbourhood Improvement Program which subsidized improvements to roads, public utilities, and community facilities. This reflected a belief that the housing conditions of households must be conceived more broadly than simply the condition of the dwelling unit, and the belief that further private renovation would occur without subsidy only if the conditions of the neighbourhood were improved.

A much discussed but not yet implemented program that would combine these two reform thrusts is a shelter or housing allowance, under which recipients receive cash assistance to increase their housing consumption in the private market.[6] While the public housing program shrank in response to criticism, the rent supplement and rehabilitation programs did not grow rapidly, with the result that new commitments to assisting low-income households declined after the early 1970s. The absolute level of government assistance continued to rise because the cost of supporting the existing tenants in public housing rose.

Throughout this period another group of rental programs operated; all intended to produce housing that would rent for slightly less than equivalent private sector housing built without any government assistance. In the late 1960s and early 1970s these programs grew significantly (see table 9.2). Those enjoying the lower rents were mainly moderate-income households. The first program was the Limited Dividend Program, which had been in existence during the 1950s, although never large then, and later called Entrepreneurial Housing. It was intended to encourage non-government organizations to become involved in the provision of assisted housing; but it was used mainly by private firms. Because private developers moved in and out of this program depending upon the profitability of the investment compared to unassisted buildings, and because it was felt that agents primarily concerned with housing assistance rather than profit should deliver housing assistance, the federal government began making more loans to co-operatives and non-profit groups. These comprised the so-called third sector, after the government and the private sector. After 1973, housing assistance to lower-middle-income renters was delivered by the third sector under the Co-operative and Non-profit Programs.[7]

While differing importantly in detail, the instrument of intervention under all of these rental programs was a public mortgage loan on attractive terms – a higher loan-to-value ratio, a longer amortization period, and a lower interest rate than market mortgage loans. Regulations either on rates of return or rents insured that the benefits of the attractive terms were passed on in reduced rents. Often loans were made with an agreement that one-quarter of the units be available to the rent supplement program.

A final rental program that existed for several years at the end of this era was the Assisted Rental Program. It assisted developers of moderate rental buildings, enabling them to charge rents comparable to existing buildings rather than the rents that would have been required given the high interest rates. There were no restrictions on rates of return or the incomes of tenants, and it can be viewed as a program to stimulate rental construction. In 1975, the program offered cash subsidies. By 1976, this was changed to a system of annual assistance loans secured as a second mortgage. The maximum annual loan in the first year was $1,200 per unit, and interest free up to ten years. The annual loan was decreased by one-tenth of the original amount each year. The rate of interest at the end of ten years was the NHA direct lending rate.

There also emerged programs directed at middle-income home buyers. At times in the late 1960s and early 1970s, house prices rose faster than incomes, and there developed the idea that first-time home buyers faced an affordability problem. The federal government (and several provinces) began programs to subsidize home purchases. The federal program, called the Assisted Home Ownership Program (AHOP), began in 1973. This marked an important change in housing policy. Although in the past much of CMHC's effort and direct lending had been intended to facilitate homeownership, there had always been the belief that the intervention was "to make the private market work." The Assisted Home Ownership Program on the other hand supplied direct cash subsidies in addition to loans.

Under the original 1973 version of AHOP, CMHC provided a mortgage of up to 95 percent of the lending value of the house, for a five-year term, with an amortization period of thirty-five years. The Central Mortgage and Housing Corporation would then reduce the interest rate from that written on the mortgage down to eight percent, or until payments of principal, interest, and taxes reached 25 percent of income. If payments still exceeded 25 percent, a grant of up to $300 per year was available to reduce monthly payments to the 25-percent figure (by June 1975 this grant had been increased to $600 per annum). Those eligible for assistance had to have incomes below a certain level, had to be purchasing a house priced below a certain level, which varied by city, and had to have one or more dependent children.

A 1976 revision of AHOP offered an annual interest reduction loan rather than a grant, to bring the interest rate to eight percent, to households with private first mortgage money. Annual loans were available in the first five years of occupancy and were interest-free. The initial amount of the loan was reduced by one-fifth each year. The loans were a second mortgage on which payments began after five years. Immediate repayment was required if the property was sold or if a new first mortgage was obtained for an increased amount. If purchasers made use of the maximum interest reduction loan, and had at least one dependent child, and were still paying more than twenty-five percent of their gross household income on mortgage payments and municipal taxes, they were eligible for an AHOP subsidy. The maximum subsidy was $750 in the first year of occupancy, then reduced over five years. Often provinces offered still further assistance which enabled relatively modest income households to purchase a home.

This second era began with concern for the least-well-off members of our society, but gradually expanded to consider the problems of moderate-income households. It was not so much that these households would have had inadequate housing in the absence of government help, indeed they would have been quite well-housed; rather these programs were attempts to deal with what were called housing affordability problems. A major provincial initiative – rent controls – discussed in more detail below, can also be viewed as a response to the affordability issue. House prices were rising, mortgage interest rates were rising, causing monthly carrying costs to rise; and rents were rising. All were rising more rapidly than in the past, but it was often forgotten that incomes were rising even more rapidly than the price of housing. It was not a time of rapid increase in the relative price of housing, but rather a time of inflation – a rising, unanticipated and unpredictable inflation – and many of our institutions, especially the mortgage contract, had not adjusted to this new inflation. Until the late 1970s, this situation was met by subsidy programs to a larger and larger group of people.

In the third period of federal housing policy, from 1978 to 1983, the response to inflation changed. The Assisted Rental and Assisted Home Ownership Programs were altered in 1978, so that no subsidy was offered, and in effect the programs offered a graduated payment mortgage with public funds. A series of declining annual payment reduction loans produced a five-percent annual increase in the borrower's net mortgage payments. The loan advances continued for five years, at the end of which time the loan and accrued interest had to be amortized using level payments. These loans were available for a transitional period until private lenders began to offer graduated payment mortgages that had become insurable under the National Housing Act. No public loans are now made under the AHOP program.

Macroeconomic policy was also changing at the beginning of this era. In the late 1970s and early 1980s Canada had been faced with stagflation – the simultaneous occurrence of high and rising unemployment with high and rising rates of inflation. The response at the federal level on the fiscal side was a restraint of expenditure, which in practice meant no new programs or commitments were made, but existing programs continued; and on the monetary side a gradualist policy, which meant a slow reduction in the rate of growth of the money supply consistent with a falling rate of inflation. Nominal mortgage interest rates remained high, but not until inflation fell sharply in 1983 did real rates become high. As well there was a general reappraisal of the welfare state and of the role of government in the economy.

These changes in macroeconomic policy and in the attitude to government had strong repercussions for housing policy. Fiscal restraint could be relatively easily implemented in the housing sector. Few new housing programs were implemented, and none that were primarily to deal with equity or affordability issues. Public lending for housing was slashed: in 1978 CMHC made loans totalling $1.18 billion, while in 1979 it made only $350 million in loans. Annual lending and insurance under the various programs are summarized in table 9.3. Annual expenditures by CMHC however continued to rise rapidly because of commitments to households already participating under past programs.

The desire for restraint led to the combining of public housing, non-profit housing, and co-operative housing into one program called the new non-profit program. Provincial or municipal housing agencies, private non-profit groups, and co-operatives could all receive assistance on roughly the same terms: public loans from CMHC were no longer available, but privately arranged loans could be NHA insured, and CMHC would subsidize the interest costs down to the equivalent of two percent. Public borrowing in the capital markets was thus reduced, consistent with the goal of restraint. The data in table 9.3 on CMHC lending thus overstate the extent of federal withdrawal because of the shift from public lending to interest subsidization. The terms of the subsidy were rather complex but resulted in buildings that were rented to moderate-income households at rents below resource costs but equal to "equivalent" private housing; and also rented to some low-income households

TABLE 9.3
Mortgage Lending and Mortgage Insurance Activities of CMHC 1978 – 1982 ($ millions)

	1978	1979	1980	1981	1982
Mortgage Lending Programs					
Public Housing	176.1	21.8	21.6	16.8	14.1
Federal-Provincial Housing	125.7	105.8	113.5	96.0	98.3
Non-Profit Corporations	120.6	4.6	4.9	3.3	0.6
Co-operatives	36.9	2.5	1.4	0.1	0.2
Entrepreneurs	1.9	–	–	–	–
Assisted Home Ownership	1.8	–	–	–	290.9[1]
Assisted Rental	96.2	0.4	–	35.6	165.1[2]
Student Housing	6.4	–	–	–	–
Other Direct Lending	11.0	11.0	12.1	20.4	10.5
Residential Rehabilitation	150.1	124.7	132.9	126.3	149.9
Mortgage Insurance Programs					
Insured Mortgage Loans by Approved Lenders	4455.9	4157.0	3333.4	3107.9	3417.3
Insured Home Improvement Loans by Approved Lenders	4.2	3.8	2.9	1.8	1.0

1. This figure includes loans under the Canadian Homeownership Stimulation Plan.
2. This figure includes loans under the Canada Rental Supply Plan.

SOURCE: Fallis (1983c)

on a rent-geared-to-income basis. About one-quarter of the tenants in any one building could be of low income. There are still unresolved controversies surrounding this program. A mixing of tenants of various income groups has been achieved, but middle-income households are receiving substantial subsidies under the program, and for every low-income family assisted, there are three moderate-income families assisted.

The monetary side of the macroeconomic strategy also had housing repercussions. The gradualist monetary policy meant high nominal interest rates, while measures to redress the tilt problem were only slowly introduced. This reduced the demand for ownership housing and the supply of rental housing.[8] Also, low rates of economic growth and high unemployment reduced housing demand. As a result of these factors and the restraint of housing programs, housing starts fell from 200,000 in 1977 to 125,000 in 1981, a fall of almost forty percent. Few other sectors of the economy suffered such shrinkage. There were some initiatives to offset this. Additional assistance for home renovation, loans to finance new rental construction, and $3,000 grants to home buyers were offered for a time in 1982 and 1983. These are best considered as part of a broadly defined macroeconomic policy rather than a housing policy.

Overall during the 1978–1983 period, the approach of federal housing policy seems to have shifted back to what it had been in the first era. Stabilization and efficiency were central again. The emphasis was on making the private market work, rather than on the housing problems of low- and middle-income households.

So far, this overview of housing policy has included only programs that are explicitly related to housing. If one wishes to take a comprehensive approach and describe those activities of the federal government that have a substantial impact on housing matters – housing output, prices, and the housing consumption of households – the coverage has been too narrow. Macroeconomic policies have been alluded to although not dealt with in detail; but they certainly belong in the more comprehensive approach. And there are many other activities as well. Immigration policy affects the demand for housing services, especially in certain cities, because most immigrants to Canada have chosen to live in Montreal, Toronto, or Vancouver. Similarly transportation expenditures, regional development grants, and equalization payments influence the spatial distribution of the demand for housing.

Of particular importance is the income security system. No attempt will be made to detail the income security system in Canada,[9] but an awareness of some of its dimensions is important, because more low-income Canadians increase their housing consumption as a result of income transfers than as a result of explicit housing programs. In 1977–1978, the system made payments of almost $17 billion, with almost 1.2 million Canadians dependent on assistance payments. The assistance is delivered through a number of programs; principally at the federal level, they are: the Old Age Security program and its supplements, family allowances, unemployment insurance, and the Canada Pension Plan; and at the provincial level: welfare, workers' compensation, and various add-on programs complementary to federal programs.

Another item to include in a comprehensive look at federal involvement in housing matters is the income tax system. Not only is its influence on housing consumption, prices, and output enormous, but also it is often used in pursuit of housing goals.

When thinking about income taxes as a policy instrument one begins from a standard of what the base of the income tax should be. Economists usually adopt a Haig-Simons definition of income as "the algebraic sum of (1) the market value of rights exercised in consumption and (2) the change in the value of the store of property rights between the beginning and the end of the period in question" (Simons 1938, 50). This is a comprehensive definition including net income whether unrealised or realised, net capital gains whether realised or unrealised, and income in kind. Once this normative tax base is set out, then any income that is exempted from the base, or any income that is taxed at a lower rate than other sources, has received preferential treatment. In principle, this preferential treatment could be achieved either through the tax system or by direct expenditure financed by a uniform rate of tax on all income. For this reason, the preferential tax treatment is sometimes referred to as a tax expenditure.[10]

There are three main tax expenditures that relate to owner-occupied housing. The first and most controversial is the exemption of net imputed income from the tax base. Savings held in financial assets yield monetary returns, and these are included in taxable income (except the first $1,000 of interest earnings or dividends from Canadian corporations, which are exempt from taxation). However, savings held as real assets yield returns as a flow of services in-kind or imputed income (for example, the services of living in a house), and these returns are exempt from income taxation. One form of income from savings is taxed, and the other form is not. A household with some savings has an incentive to place these savings in a house (or any real asset) rather than placing them in financial assets. This incentive to own housing is even greater because of a second tax expenditure that exempts the capital gains realised on the sale of a principal residence. All capital gains receive preferential treatment because they are taxed on a realised rather than an accrual basis, and because only fifty percent of the gains are taxable. But none of the gains on a principal residence are taxable.

The third ownership tax expenditure benefits those who are saving to buy a house, not those who already own houses. Every taxpayer is allowed to establish one Registered Home Ownership Savings Plan in their lifetime. Up to a maximum of $1,000 per year, to a cumulative total of $10,000 may be contributed to this plan, and the contributions are deductible from taxable income. When the plan is terminated and the proceeds are used to buy a house, the contributions and any interest earnings on them are not taxed. The tax savings each year are equivalent to a government grant to help buy a house and, as is the case with all tax expenditures, the savings are larger the higher the marginal tax rate of the household.

Owners of rental residential buildings also enjoy tax expenditures, although the foregone revenues are much smaller, and some of the benefits are passed on in reduced rents. The allowable deduction for depreciation exceeds the true economic depreciation, which reduces the taxable income of the owner in that year. When allowable depreciation has been exhausted, true depreciation exceeds the allowable depreciation. The effect of the provision is to postpone paying the full tax, and has a value equal to an interest-free loan on the postponed tax. There are a number of other provisions regarding the timing of cost deductions, the pooling of assets when computing depreciation, and whether real estate losses created by depreciation deductions can be deducted against income from other sources. These have been changed numerous times over the last fifteen years, and when the changes have been unanticipated have significantly altered the levels of residential housing construction. Historically the returns from investment in rental real estate were subject to many preferential provisions, but the trend has been to remove these and treat different forms of investment income more neutrally. It has not however been an uninterrupted trend. As a provision was removed, the supply of new rental housing fell, and often, following a political uproar, the provision was restored or another preferential provision introduced.

If the tax expenditure is measured as the tax revenue that would have been collected if the item had been included in the tax base, or if the income were taxed at full rates (and assuming no change in the behaviour of economic agents), then federal tax expenditures on housing in 1979 totalled $5.35 billion (Canada 1979). When juxtaposed against explicit housing assistance, which totalled only $288 million under the public housing, co-operative, and non-profit programs, foregone tax revenue is enormous. Most provincial governments accept the federal definition of taxable income, and so the provincial governments also have tax expenditures under these provisions.

This more comprehensive look at federal involvement in housing can be completed with a brief discussion of the regulation of financial markets and of CMHC lending to finance what might be termed community development; lending that is apart from but complementary to its housing subsidies.

In the main, the regulation of the capital markets has not been used to increase the flow of mortgage credit. Indeed the period since 1950 has been marked by a gradual removal of regulations on financial markets and the integration of the mortgage market with other credit markets. The latter was mainly achieved by gradually admitting the chartered banks into mortgage lending. The banks were first permitted to make mortgage loans in 1954, provided the loans were insured under NHA insurance. The six-percent rate ceiling on bank lending sometimes curtailed their mortgage lending, but this ceiling was removed in the 1967 Bank Act revision. As well, banks were permitted in 1967 to enter the conventional mortgage market, thus greatly widening the potential source of funds. Banks may only lend up to 75 percent of the property value, but they have mortgage affiliates that supply the remainder up to 90 percent. In 1967, banks were permitted to issue debentures, and when the five-year renewable mortgage became insurable under the National Housing Act in 1969, a matching of the terms of assets and liabilities became feasible. Coupled with the removal of controls on the NHA mortgage interest rate in 1969, a clear pattern of deregulation and increasing competition in the mortgage market is revealed.[11]

One instrument that has been used to affect mortgage credit is moral suasion. In the mid-1970s, lending institutions were asked to direct additional funds into financing low and moderately priced housing, and to provide high-ratio lending to such housing. Recently, banks have been asked to give special consideration to households having to refinance their mortgages at much higher interest rates.

Community development programs have offered public loans to finance urban renewal, land assembly, sewage treatment plants, and neighbourhood improvements. Most provinces have programs to support such activities as well. Table 9.4 shows lending by CMHC from 1955 to 1982. Urban renewal loans were used to finance the demolition and clearance of blighted or substandard residential areas for a redevelopment project, usually part of which was public housing. Although the subject of much controversy, the program was never large in Canada. Lending was restricted under the program following the Task Force on Housing and Urban Development (Canada 1969), and the 1973 amend-

TABLE 9.4
Other Lending Activities of CMHC
1955 – 1982 ($ millions)

Year	Urban Renewal	Land Assembly	Sewage Treatment	Neighbourhood Improvement
1955	1.8			
56	3.5			
57	1.1			
58	0.0			
59	3.4			
1960	4.5			
61	2.9		39.5	
62	3.5		43.4	
63	3.7		35.9	
64	10.3		26.2	
65	n.a.		n.a.	
66	1.1		34.1	
67	9.4		31.2	
68	6.6		39.5	
69	14.5	17.2	50.2	
1970	4.0	24.5	77.7	
71	15.0	21.3	113.7	
72	13.4	74.4	114.8	
73	0.8	185.2	153.8	
74	–	101.4	171.9	3.0
75	0.7	80.2	183.3	10.6
76	0.1	86.4	302.6	17.5
77	–	44.3	247.0	15.4
78	4.1	32.2	290.3	16.2
79	–	17.5	2.6	–
1980	2.2	12.0	10.1	–
81	–	10.0	3.3	–
82	–	6.6	–	–

SOURCE: Fallis (1983c).

ments to the National Housing Act eliminated all loans for urban renewal. Funds for site clearance became available, however, under the Neighbourhood Improvement Program in 1973, but these have since been discontinued.

Central Mortgage and Housing Corporation made loans and grants to provinces and municipalities to finance trunk sewers, water mains, and sewage and water treatment facilities. It advanced over $100 million annually from 1971 to 1978, but now has stopped altogether. The provision of such facilities is clearly a natural monopoly that is normally dealt with by having the public sector provide them. These loans formed part of our system of intergovernmental fiscal arrangements that attempted to balance the revenue raising and borrowing capabilities with the expenditure responsibilities of the various levels of government.

The land-assembly program was intended to ensure an adequate supply of serviced residential land, "to stabilize and where possible reduce land prices, and to promote a high standard of residential development" (CMHC 1976, 14). It was often claimed that public land banking could reduce long-run land prices; but this claim became muted as it was discovered that land was not supplied monopolistically, and that at best public banking could raise prices as the land was acquired, and lower prices as the land was sold; while at worst, seriously disrupt the land market, even raising prices in the long run. Subsequently the more emphasized goals were land-use control and the advance acquisition of land for assisted housing.

Under the Neighbourhood Improvement Program (NIP), the federal government contributed fifty percent of the cost of acquiring and clearing land for social or recreational facilities or housing, of constructing social or recreational facilities, and twenty-five percent of the cost of improving municipal and public utilities in run-down neighbourhoods. Loans were also available for improvement of commercial enterprises.

PROVINCIAL HOUSING POLICIES

Now let us turn to consider the activities of the provinces. Many of the federal programs already described were in fact shared-cost programs, with both Ottawa and the provinces contributing loans and/or grants. Sometimes a province would enter into a special agreement with CMHC to tailor the program to provincial priorities. However, the specific legislation was federal, and the driving force in these shared endeavours was usually CMHC, so they have been treated under the heading of federal housing policy in the previous section. In this section will be considered those activities of the provinces or municipalities that did not involve the federal government. This sort of independent provincial role in Canadian housing policy emerged only in the 1970s.

It is perhaps an impossible task to summarize satisfactorily, provincial activities of any sort. The voices of the regions are constantly reminding us of their differentness, and resisting attempts to define the average situation. In housing this is further complicated because there is no clearing house gathering comparable data or program descriptions, and almost no secondary sources dealing with the provinces. Notwithstanding these problems, an attempt will be made to summarize housing policies.

As a preliminary, it is worthwhile to consider the allocation of responsibility for housing policy under the Constitution Act, 1982 (formerly the British North America Act, 1867). The distribution of powers followed the general principle that areas of general interest were allocated to the federal level, while areas of particular or local interest were assigned to the provinces (Dawson 1964, 82). Basically, Ottawa is responsible for legislation concerned with finance and banking, trade and commerce, defence, national services (post office and census taking), criminal law, international trade and relations, and more generally, for legislation to assure peace, order, and good government. Provincial responsibilities are for hospitals, prisons, education, local works, and property and civil rights. Not surprisingly, housing policy is not mentioned explicitly. The federal government's position follows from responsibility for mortgage markets as part of banking and finance, and responsibility for income redistribution which has been presumed to flow from the peace, order, and good government clause. The provincial position follows from housing being of a local nature, and from the responsibility for property rights.

The provinces first began to participate actively in housing policy under the 1964 amendments to the National Housing Act. In order to exploit the new NHA terms, provincial governments created special agencies. The first to be created was the Ontario Housing Corporation in 1964, which immediately embarked on an ambitious public housing program. In 1967, the Alberta Housing and Urban Renewal Corporation, the Quebec Housing Corporation, and the Manitoba Housing and Renewal Corporation were begun, and the duties of the Nova Scotia Housing Commission were extended to permit usage of the new terms. By 1968, all but two provinces had established their own administrative instruments. The British Columbia Housing Management Commission was operational in 1970, and the Saskatchewan Housing Corporation in 1973. In the late 1960s, these housing agencies were still mainly involved in the public housing program with the federal government and had few independent programs.

The establishment of these agencies was important because a body of administrative and technical skills was developed that would permit the launching of independent provincial programs. These emerged mainly through the 1970s. The first, in 1967, were the Home Ownership Made Easy Plan (Ontario) and the Provincial Home Acquisition Program (British Columbia). The former involved the provision of low-priced building lots for lease, and the latter assisted buyers of their first home with down payments.

The same instruments used by the federal government have been used by the provinces in their housing programs with the exception of mortgage insurance. The provincial programs have involved direct lending, either as first or second mortgages, to finance the purchase of existing houses or the construction of new housing. The mortgages were often at a lower interest rate, and had a longer term and amortization period, and higher loan-to-value ratio than a conventional mortgage loan. There have been grants to subsidize housing expenditures by both owners and renters often operating as a deduction of a portion of property taxes paid from taxable personal income. There have been mortgage loans and grants to finance renovation of older housing, and to assist households and builders in small communities and rural areas.

A uniquely provincial instrument, rent controls, was used in all jurisdictions during national wage and profits controls, and remains in some provinces. The exact system of control differs from province to province, but the principal characteristics are similar. Rents are allowed to rise a certain percentage each year; greater increases are permitted subject to regulatory approval. Cost increases, including some of the increases in financing costs, can be passed through. Reductions in the level of service or maintenance can mean lower rent increases. New units, extensively renovated units, and sometimes relatively high-rent units are exempt from controls.

With the exception of rent control, the rationale for almost all provincial programs has been to provide housing assistance to specific groups. There has not been a sense at the provincial level that all housing construction or all housing consumption ought to be subsidized, or that the private flow of mortgage finance was inadequate, or that private markets were restricting the supply of new construction. A possible exception might be Alberta. There has been special emphasis on assisting low- and medium-income households with the purchase of a house, especially those households who are buying their first house. Here the exception is Quebec which has not promoted home ownership to the same extent.

The most comprehensive documentation of provincial housing programs was prepared for a study of "Future Fiscal Arrangements for Housing in Canada." A statistical addendum (Alberta 1981) described housing activity from 1971 to 1981 in each of the provinces. However even this study was filled with caveats (see Alberta [1981] for details), and concluded the section on data sources with the following statement: "As a result of these limitations readers should be very cautious in using the updated tables for inter-provincial comparisons. The information contained herein goes only part way in providing a consistent and comprehensive housing activity data base by province." Nevertheless, this is by far the best source available, and permits the broad patterns of provincial housing activity since 1971 to be sketched with some confidence.

The statistical addendum reported the number of dwelling units (and hostel beds) that had been assisted under federal programs, federal/provincial programs, and purely provincial programs. The data are summarized in table 9.5 (data were not available for Quebec and Nova Scotia). The federal and federal/provincial programs were described and discussed in the previous section, and are pooled together in table 9.5. It should be remembered that the level of assistance per assisted dwelling unit varies greatly under the various programs, and that the number of assisted dwelling units does not measure the net additions to total housing starts as a result of government housing programs. Table 9.5 shows the pattern of federal activity already discussed: a high level of involvement until 1977, and then sharp contraction from 1978 to1981. In 1977, almost 40 percent of all housing starts were federally assisted, but by 1981 this had fallen to 11 percent. Provincial housing involvement does not follow the same pattern. It was high in the mid-seventies, then was sharply cut back, but then expanded dramatically in 1980 and 1981. Thus overall government activity, while at its height in 1977, had not contracted significantly in 1981. It seems, very roughly, that the provinces cut back when federal involvement was large in 1976 and 1977, and then expanded to counteract federal restraint in 1980 and 1981.

The summary table, however, masks substantial variation between provinces. Table 9.6 reports the percentage of starts in each province that were assisted under purely provincial programs. On average over the period, Alberta and Saskatchewan had substantial independent provincial programs; Ontario, New Brunswick, and Prince Edward Island had moderate involvement; while British Columbia, Manitoba, Quebec, Nova Scotia, and Newfoundland had few independent pro-

TABLE 9.5
Assisted Starts[1] as a Percentage of Total Starts, 1973 – 1981

	1973	1974	1975	1976	1977	1978	1979	1980	1981
Federal and Federal/Provincial Programs	23	17	27	26	39	21	14	18	11
Provincial Programs	6	9	12	6	5	3	4	17	26
All Government	29	26	39	32	44	24	18	35	37

1. Excluding Quebec and Nova Scotia in all years, and excluding Ontario in 1973.

SOURCE: Fallis (1983c)

TABLE 9.6
Provincially Assisted Starts as a Percentage of Housing
Starts in that Province, 1971 – 1981

Province	1971	1972	1973	1974	1975	1976	1977	1978	1979	1980	1981	Average
British Columbia	0	0	0	0	0	0	0	0	0	14	2	2
Alberta	2	4	9	13	15	18	16	10	15	47	47	21
Saskatchewan	n.a.	n.a.	46	25	25	15	8	5	2	5	11	16
Manitoba	0	0	0	0	0	0	0	0	0	0	0	0
Ontario	n.a.	n.a.	n.a.	11	16	4	1	0	0	0	34	8
Quebec							n.a.					
New Brunswick	1	3	2	3	5	5	5	7	8	17	19	8
Nova Scotia							n.a.					
Prince Edward Island	n.a.	n.a.	20	8	0	10	17	13	11	7	5	10
Newfoundland	n.a.	n.a.	5	7	0	0	0	0	1	4	13	3
All Canada[1]	–	–	6	9	12	6	5	3	4	17	26	10

1. Excluding Quebec and Nova Scotia in all years, and Ontario in 1971, 1972, and 1973.

SOURCE: Fallis (1983c)

grams.[12] The trends over time also show substantial variation. Alberta, Quebec, New Brunswick, and Nova Scotia have been increasing their purely provincial involvement, while Saskatchewan, Ontario (with the exception of 1981), and Prince Edward Island have been cutting back.[13]

The activities so far described are those that are usually taken to constitute the housing policy of a province. They would be carried out by a housing ministry or a specially created housing agency. Other provincial activities have an equal or even greater influence on housing markets, although they usually are not considered part of housing policy. Many of these activities are actually carried out by local government, but local governments only have authority insofar as it has been delegated to them by the provinces, and therefore all of these activities will be discussed under the heading of provincial policy.

The provinces establish the structure of local government, specifying the responsibilities, spatial boundaries, and financing arrangements of the units created.[14] These form the institutional arrangements within which housing markets operate. There is enormous variation between the provinces in the structures that have been adopted, especially with respect to the degree of provincial control retained over local affairs. In the main, however, municipal governments are responsible for the provision of roads, transit, sewers, water purification and distribution, garbage collection and disposal, and police and fire protection. These are by far the largest expenditure categories. Other smaller categories are parks, recreational facilities, libraries, public health, housing assistance, and welfare payments. While giving rise to relatively little expenditure, municipal land-use regulation is of significant influence on housing. Primary and secondary education are usually local responsibilities, but which are provided by a specially created system of government – the school board – rather than by municipal governments. All these activities, individually and collectively, affect the price, type, and spatial distribution of housing in a city, and as hedonic pricing equations indicate, also affect the price of an individual house or apartment. Of course the housing consumption of individuals is also influenced.

Land use regulation in particular has a very direct influence on housing markets. Again, although interprovincial variation is great, a composite picture can be composed. Most local governments establish an official plan that sets out the allowable uses of land and the allowable intensity of the land use – for example, a parcel may be designated for residential use provided that the floor area of the building is not more than twice the area of the lot. The official plan is given force through a system of zoning by-laws. Most official plans and zoning by-laws were implemented long after the land was developed. The laws are not retroactive, and permit legal, non-conforming uses, but do govern any alterations to the land use. During most of the postwar period, the most significant land-use regulation occurred through the subdivision approval process. Any new residential development had to be approved, and was subject to extensive regulation regarding lot size, street size, and layout, and the provision of land for schools and parks.

The motivations for this land-use regulation are several. In the terminology of economics some of it was externality zoning – regulation to locate land uses with negative externalities so that resources are efficiently allocated. Some of it was fiscal zoning – regulation to ensure that all residents of a community had the same value of houses, so that all paid the same in taxes for the common level of public services. But much of it was zoning to ensure a "well-planned" or "desirable" community. The development should conform to well-established planning practices. There is no term for this in welfare economics except perhaps to say that the social welfare function of the planner was imposed on the development.

SUGGESTIONS FOR FURTHER READING

Carver, H. (1975) *Compassionate Landscape* (Toronto: University of Toronto Press).

Dennis, M., and S. Fish (1972) *Programs in Search of a Policy* (Toronto: Hakkert Press).

Fallis, G. (1983c) *Governments and the Residential Mortgage Market II: Programs and Evaluation* Discussion Paper No. 240 (Ottawa: Economic Council of Canada).

Wolman, H. L. (1975) *Housing and Housing Policy in the U.S. and the U.K.* (Lexington, Mass.: Lexington Books).

10 | The Effects of Policies

The purpose of this chapter is to study the effects of different housing programs: on consumers, on producers, and on the market equilibrium. It draws together the analysis of all the previous chapters. For example, to examine the effects of a housing price subsidy to consumers, we begin from the model of household choice and econometric estimates of the price elasticity of demand for housing services in order to establish the shift in the market demand curve for housing services. Then the model of market equilibrium, and econometric estimates of the price elasticity of the supply curve, are used to establish the effect of the housing subsidy on the price of housing services and the quantity exchanged. The chapter is positive in orientation, but the ideas can be used in normative research. In order to choose the optimal policy, one must know the effects of each policy, so that the effects can be judged against the objectives.

This chapter examines five housing programs. They have been selected to encompass the main sorts of programs that have existed in Canada, and to illustrate the application of the techniques and results of the previous chapters. There is a general discussion of each program and its effects, followed by a more detailed look at particular issues that have been central to the analysis of that program. The ideas developed could also be applied in the study of other programs.

In any policy analysis using formal economic models, the minute details of a specific program must be glossed over because the theoretical models cannot accommodate programs with complex terms. This is even more true in this chapter where "typical" programs presented in a stylized form are examined, rather than actual programs. However, the importance of these minute details should not be forgotten. Often the effects of programs on specific people are determined by these details. A complete program analysis would contain both general and detailed elements.

The technique of analysis will be comparative statics. An initial equilibrium is established. Then an exogenous factor is changed – the government program is introduced. And a new equilibrium is characterized. The effect of the program is the movement from the old to the new equilibrium. It is essential in such work to recognize that any government program must be financed either by increased taxation, a reduction in other expenditure, or by increased borrowing. In certain cases the financing can be ignored: for example, if it is a regulatory program that employs few regulators; or if it is a small expenditure program concentrated on a few beneficiaries that is financed by taxing all taxpayers. However, it should always be remembered that a housing program must be financed, and the full effect is the effect of both program and financing.

SHELTER ALLOWANCES

Although not widely used in Canada, many regard shelter allowances as the best program to increase the housing consumption of the poor, and predict their adoption over the next few years. Shelter allowances provide cash assistance to households for the purpose of housing expenditure. A common type is the percent-of-rent sort, under which the transfer received is some fraction, s, of rent expenditure (equation 10.1).

$$T = s\, p_2 x_2 \tag{10.1}$$

To acquire some level of housing services, x_2, the household must now spend only $p_2 x_2 - s p_2 x_2$ of their own money. In effect, the price of housing services that is perceived by the household has fallen to $p_2 (1 - s)$. For any given market price, the recipient household will wish to consume more housing services. Assuming that the price elasticity of demand for housing services is -0.8 (see chapter two), and the shelter allowance reduced the perceived price by 20 percent, the household would desire 16 percent more housing services at any given market price. The demand curve for these households, when drawn on axes that have the *market* price as the vertical axis, will shift to the right by 16 percent at each price.

Now let us suppose that there are two equal-sized groups of households in this housing market – the poor and the rich – and that the poor receive the shelter allowance, but the rich do not. The market demand curve for housing services is the horizontal addition of the market demands of these two groups. Assuming that at every price the rich demand three times as much housing as the poor, the market demand curve has shifted four percent to the right; see equation 10.2. The greater the share of the poor in total housing consumption, the larger the shift in the market demand curve.

$$\frac{0.16 p_2 x_{2p}}{p_2 x_{2p} + 3 p_2 x_{2p}} = 0.04 \tag{10.2}$$

What is the effect of this program on housing prices? Let us assume that the medium-run price elasticity of supply is 3 (see chapter three); and we will use the simple algebraic model of a housing market presented in chapter four, equations 4.1 to 4.3. The new equilibrium price of housing services is equation 10.3, where θ is the price elasticity of

$$p_2 = (1.04)^{\frac{1}{\theta - \alpha}} \left[\frac{Ay^\beta}{B} \right]^{-\frac{1}{\theta - \alpha}} \tag{10.3}$$

the market supply curve, α is the price elasticity of the market demand curve ($\alpha < 0$), and the bracketed term to the exponent, on the right-hand side, is the original price of housing services. The market price of housing services rises by $(1.04)^{1/(3 + 0.8)}$, or about one percent.

After the market has adjusted, the poor perceive the price of housing services to have fallen by 19 percent, and consume 15.2 percent more housing services. The price of housing services paid by the rich (the market price) has risen by one percent, and the rich consume 0.8 percent less housing. The poor are made better off and the rich worse off (see below for how to measure the income equivalent of a price change). The total production of housing services increases by slightly over three percent.

The effect of a shelter allowance can also be illustrated graphically. In figure 10.1 the poor's demand curve, AB, and the demand curve of the rich, CD, form the market demand curve CEF. The shelter allowance shifts the demand curve of the poor to $A'B$ (recalling that a straight line demand curve does not have a constant price elasticity) and the market demand curve to $CE'F$.

Thus far this analysis has assumed that the rich do not contribute to the financing of the subsidy – their demand curve was unchanged. But the effects of the financing must also be analysed. Suppose that the shelter allowance was financed by a poll tax on the rich. If the government's budget constraint is to be exactly met – the revenues from the poll tax exactly equal the expenditures through the housing subsidy – then the amount of the tax and the amount of the price reduction cannot be established a priori, but are interdependent and depend upon the operation of the housing market. However, the qualitative impact of the financing is obvious. The demand curve of the rich will shift to the left. The market demand curve may or may not shift out as the net result of shelter allowance and financing; it could even shift inwards. The shelter allowance program will have relatively little influence on the price of housing services and the quantity supplied. The poor will get the full benefit of the reduction in the price of housing services implied by the terms of the shelter allowance; and the rich will suffer because of a loss of income, but not from a rise in the price of housing services.[1]

The graphical model of figure 10.1 assumed that there was one market for the homogeneous commodity, housing services. The shifts in demand curves of the rich or the poor affected the price paid by both rich and poor alike. However in a market of heterogeneous housing, the results may be different. Suppose there were housing of different qualities. A shelter allowance financed by a tax on the rich would increase the demand for low-quality housing and decrease the demand for high-quality housing. The maintenance levels on each would be affected. The new equilibrium would have to be determined using a model like that of Rosen (1974) or Sweeney (1974) described in chapter four. If the price elasticity of supply of low-quality housing were relatively low, there might be a significant increase in the price of low-quality housing and a slight decline in the price of high-quality housing. In such a world, a shelter allowance would not increase the housing con-

FIGURE 10.1
Shelter Allowance for the Poor

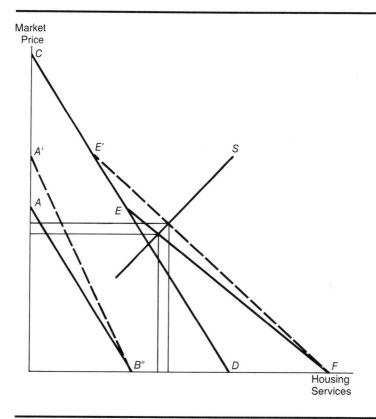

sumption of the poor very much. Unfortunately, although the possibility of such an outcome is central to our understanding of the effects of shelter allowances, we do not have econometric estimates of maintenance functions disaggregated by quality levels.

DIRECT MORTGAGE LENDING

In order to study a supply-side program, let us consider the effects of public mortgage loans at reduced interest rates to builders of new apartment buildings. The focus on new construction suggests that the stock-flow model (used in chapter five) is appropriate. Assume that the rental market is independent of the ownership market – for some reason the population may be divided into owners and renters, and dwelling units cannot be shifted from one market to the other. The original equilibrium in the rental market is depicted in figure 10.2. The demand curve for rental housing services (= housing stock) and the perfectly inelastic supply curve of existing stock determine the price of housing stock, P_1. The price of housing stock and the supply curve of new construction determine the flow supply of new housing stock, C_1. It is assumed that one unit of stock produces one unit of service, and that there is a constant rate of stock depreciation. In equilibrium as in figure 10.2, the price of housing stock is such that new housing construction just matches depreciation of the existing stock – the long-run level of stock and the price of stock are constant. Now suppose that the government offers mortgage loans to builders of rental units at less than the market rate of interest. Mortgage credit is a significant determinant of the profitability of an apartment given a rent level over time (or the price of rental stock), and therefore the CC curve shifts down to C^*C^*. This assumes that government loans are available to all builders. In the first period of the program, housing construction increases significantly from C_1 to C_1^*. Smith (1974) estimated an equation for multiple-housing starts and found the interest elasticity of multiple starts (evaluated at the means of variables) was -2.19. For the time being, any effects of the financing of the program will be ignored. This stimulative effect of a subsidized mortgage loan program has always attracted much attention. However, this is only the first period of the program. In the next period, assuming that subsidized loans are still available to all builders, the price of housing stock will fall below P_1 to P_2, and new construction will be less than C_1^* at C_2. Eventually a new equilibrium will be reached in which new construction just matches the depreciation of the somewhat larger existing stock. The increase in the new steady state stock will depend upon the price elasticity of demand, the rate of depreciation, the price elasticity of the CC curve, the interest elasticity of new construction, and the size of the reduction in the mortgage rate of interest.

FIGURE 10.2
Public Mortgage Lending Program: Universal

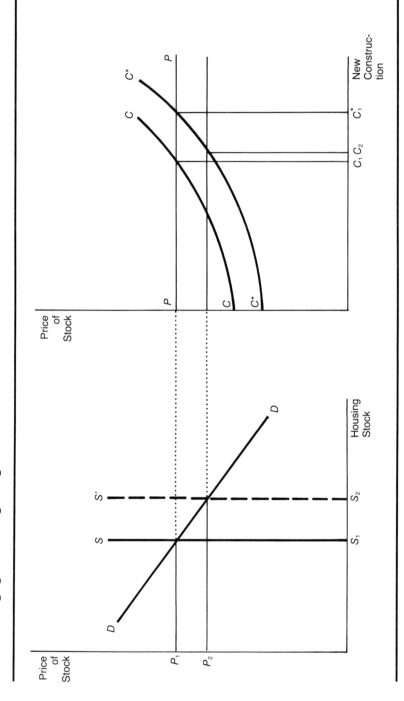

Consider the following algebraic example. The demand for rental stock is as in equation 10.4; the supply of new construction function, as in equation 10.5, is assumed to have constant price and interest rate

$$Q_D = AP_2^\alpha \qquad (\alpha < 0) \qquad\qquad (10.4)$$

$$NC = CP_2^a\, r_m{}^b \qquad (a > 0, b < 0) \qquad\qquad (10.5)$$

elasticities; and the depreciation rate is d. These are the exogenous factors in the market. For an equilibrium, conditions as in equations 10.6 and 10.7 must hold (suppressing the dynamic aspect of the model), where S is the housing stock. Equation 10.6 says supply equals demand in the market for housing stock. Equation 10.7 says that in equilibrium,

$$S = AP_2^\alpha \qquad\qquad (10.6)$$

$$dS = CP_2^a r_m{}^b \qquad\qquad (10.7)$$

new construction equals depreciation of the existing stock. The solution for the steady state stock is as in equation 10.8; and the elasticity of stock with respect to the mortgage rate of interest is as in equation 10.9. As the interest elasticity of the new construction supply curve in-

$$S = \left[\frac{C}{d} A^{-\frac{a}{\alpha}}\right]^{\frac{\alpha}{\alpha - a}} r_m{}^{\frac{b\alpha}{\alpha - a}} \qquad\qquad (10.8)$$

$$\frac{dS}{dr_m} \cdot \frac{r_m}{S} = \frac{b\alpha}{\alpha - a} \qquad\qquad (10.9)$$

creases (in absolute value), the stock elasticity increases (in absolute value); as the price elasticity of new construction increases, the stock elasticity declines (in absolute value); and as the price elasticity of demand for housing services rises (in absolute value), the stock elasticity rises (in absolute value). Taking plausible values of the parameters ($\alpha = -0.8$, $a = 0.5$, $b = -2$), the equilibrium stock increases by 1.23 percent with a one-percent decline in the mortgage rate of interest; compared to a two-percent increase in construction in the first period.

This treatment of public mortgage lending has assumed it was available to all builders, and was permanent. It was equivalent to a permanent, universal mortgage interest subsidy. As expected, a reduction in the price of a factor of production increased the long-run stock and decreased the long-run price. However, public mortgage lending programs have been neither permanent nor universal.

Suppose the mortgage lending program lasted only one period. In the first period new construction would increase from C_1 to C_1^*, and the stock would increase from S_1 to S_2. In the next period, the price of housing stock would be P_2, and because the new construction curve would have shifted back to CC, the level of construction would fall below C_1 (see figure 10.2). New construction is not sufficient to replace the depreciation of the housing stock. Over time the stock will shrink, the price will rise, new construction will increase until the original steady state is realised, and new construction matches depreciation. Therefore a temporary mortgage lending program does not alter the long-run price or quantity of housing services. This is often forgotten. It appears that the program has added a durable good, and that the economy will have this extra housing until it is torn down. But this extra stock reduces the price, reduces unsubsidized construction next period, and so the original level of stock is restored. Only a permanent subsidy will increase the long-run level of services available.

Now suppose that the public lending is not perfectly elastically supplied, but is available only to a certain group of builders. This is usually the case. The government plans to make a certain volume of subsidized loans, and this volume is far less than annual private sector loans. The effects of such a program depend upon a complexity of factors; importantly, the reasons why the CC curve slopes upward. Let us first suppose that the sole reason why the CC curve slopes upward as the level of new construction expands is that mortgage interest rates rise; all other inputs are perfectly elastically supplied to the construction industry, and firms have constant returns to scale. Assume that the volume of mortgage lending is directly proportional to the flow of new construction. Now suppose, as shown in figure 10.3a, that the volume of budgeted public lending will finance C_g of new construction. These loans are at an interest rate below the market rate of interest. The CC curve becomes perfectly elastic until starts reach level C_g, as in figure 10.3a. To this level there is no demand for private mortgage credit, and so the private mortgage interest rate remains unchanged. After level C_g is reached, increases in starts again raise mortgage interest rates: CC has shifted right by distance C_g to $C'EFC'$. As indicated in figure 10.3a, the volume of new construction increases in the first period by the full amount that can be financed by public lending. Over time a permanent program will have less effect on annual construction, and a temporary program will have no effect in the long run. Again the effects of financing have been ignored for the time being.

However if the reason why the CC curve slopes upward is rising prices of other inputs such as land, labour, and materials, while mortgage credit is elastically supplied, the effects of the program are quite different. The subsidized mortgage interest rate lowers the CC curve to $C'E$, up to the level of housing construction C_g, as in figure 10.3b. The portion $C'E$ slopes upward because other factor prices are rising. At levels of construction beyond C_g, the factor prices and mortgage interest

FIGURE 10.3
Public Mortgage Lending Program: Non-Universal

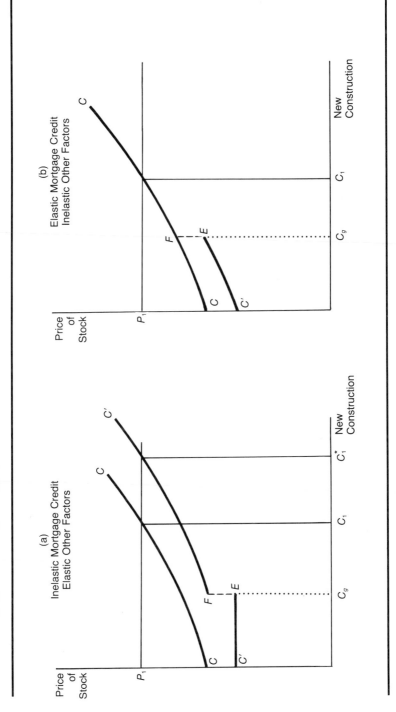

rate remain exactly as in the world of no government intervention. Thus the government lending program will have no effect on the level of housing construction and no effect on housing prices, if the P_1 line intersects $C'EFC$ to the right of C_g. Some inframarginal units have been subsidized, but the benefits of the subsidy flow to the inframarginal producer.[2]

These analyses of different public lending programs have assumed that the builders who received the loans were able to charge the market rent on the dwelling units. But public loans are often accompanied by controls on the rents that the landlord may charge – the combination of controlled rent and subsidized mortgage yielding a rate of return slightly higher than that available using private financing. A new housing sector is established in which rents are not market determined. The program influences both demand and supply curves in the subsidized and unsubsidized sectors; and a proper analysis must consider the simultaneous equilibria in the two sectors. Households leave the private market for the subsidized sector, and the demand curve in the private sector shifts to the left. The supply functions of the two sectors will depend on how factor prices change with increases in total construction, and on how builders respond to the slightly higher rate of return in the subsidized sector.

We may summarize the above analysis by stating: public sector lending usually stimulates new construction initially, but over time the effects are reduced. And these stimulative effects are further reduced when account is taken of the financing of the program. Here we turn to macroeconomic models for an analysis of the package of housing program plus financing, on general economic conditions. If the loans are financed by increased taxes, the balanced budget intervention would be mildly stimulative. But it is more likely that public mortgage lending is financed by increased public sector borrowing. If the bonds were bought by private intermediaries, the interest rate would rise and reduce private investment, both housing and non-housing. Some economists believe that the interest rate rises sufficiently that private investment falls to fully offset the government-subsidized investment. Private investment is "crowded out." Regardless of how complete the crowding out is, the stimulative effect of the government mortgage lending on new construction is partly offset by a fall in non-subsidized starts and a fall in other investment. If the financing is through bond sales to the central bank, and there is an accommodating increase in the money supply, the program will be stimulative, and its effects will depend upon the nature of the aggregate supply curve.[3]

PUBLIC HOUSING

Public housing has always been in Canada the major program providing housing assistance to very-low-income households. Under almost all public housing programs, a household is offered a dwelling unit, with a rent below the market level. The price on one specific apartment is reduced; the tenant is not offered a price reduction on any amount of housing he wishes to consume, as with a percent-of-rent shelter allowance. The alteration of the household's set of feasible choices is shown in figure 10.4. Given the household's income and the market price of the composite good and of housing services, the feasible choices lie along line AB, the budget line. The public housing program offers the household one additional point: point E in figure 10.4. The point is outside the original budget line and has been selected to lie above U_1, the indifference curve attained without public housing, in order that the household would voluntarily participate in the program. The household in the program consumes x_1^2 of the composite good and x_2^2 of housing services (more of both goods than before), and reaches utility level U_2.

FIGURE 10.4
Public Housing and Household Choice

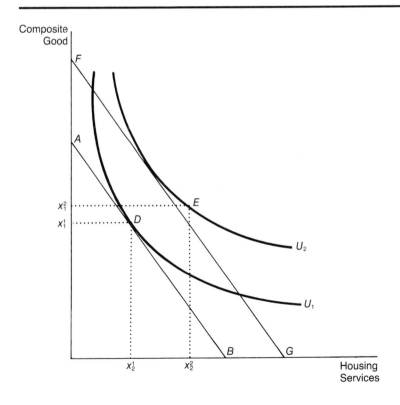

Depending on the objective of the program, the government may be interested in how much the household's housing consumption has expanded $(x_2^2 - x_2^1)$, or by how much their real income or utility has increased $(U_2 - U_1)$ (see chapter seven). But regardless of the objective, an important issue in a positive analysis of the effects of public housing is how much the real income of the beneficiary has increased. Stated more formally: what increase in income, in lieu of participating in public housing, would leave the household on the indifference curve attained when participating in the program? This is an equivalent cash grant or Hicksian consumer's surplus measure of the benefits of public housing. Graphically, the measure is easily shown. The line FG, parallel to AB and tangent to U_2, is the budget line that would permit the household to reach U_2, while paying market prices for both commodities. Measured in units of the composite good, the equivalent cash grant is AF; by appropriate definition of units, the distance AF is equal to the cash grant.[4]

The measure can also be computed algebraically. Assume that the tenant has a Cobb-Douglas utility function (equation 10.10). Given income y and prices p_1 and p_2, the demand functions are as shown in equation 10.11 and 10.12. For any income level, given market prices,

$$U = A\, x_1^{\alpha}\, x_2^{1-\alpha} \tag{10.10}$$

$$x_1 = \frac{\alpha y}{p_1} \tag{10.11}$$

$$x_2 = \frac{(1-\alpha)y}{p_2} \tag{10.12}$$

$$U = A\left(\frac{\alpha y}{p_1}\right)^{\alpha}\left(\frac{(1-\alpha)y}{p_2}\right)^{1-\alpha} \tag{10.13}$$

the household will attain the utility level as shown in equation 10.13. Under public housing, the household achieves utility level U_2 as in equation 10.14, where y_0 is original income, and $\bar{p}_2$ is the implicit price of housing services under public housing. The actual rent paid equals $\bar{p}_2 x_2^2$. The income that would let the household realise utility level U_2,

$$A\left(\frac{y_0 - \bar{p}_2 x_2^2}{p_1}\right)^{\alpha}(x_2^2)^{1-\alpha} = U_2 \tag{10.14}$$

paying market prices, is the solution to equation 10.15, which may be expressed as in equation 10.16, where $p_2 x_2^2$ is the market value of the

$$A\left(\frac{\alpha y}{p_1}\right)^{\alpha}\left(\frac{(1-\alpha)y}{p_2}\right)^{1-\alpha} = A\left(\frac{y_0 - \bar{p}_2 x_2^2}{p_1}\right)^{\alpha}(x_2^2)^{1-\alpha} \tag{10.15}$$

public housing unit. The cash equivalent transfer is thus $y^* - y_0$.

$$y^* = \left(\frac{y_0 - \overline{p}_2 x_2^2}{\alpha}\right)^\alpha \left(\frac{p_2 x_2^2}{1 - \alpha}\right)^{1 - \alpha} \qquad (10.16)$$

In order to estimate the effect of public housing on the real income of tenants, equation 10.16 can be used. The researcher will need to know the income of the tenant, the actual rent paid, the market value of the public housing unit, and the parameters of the household's utility function. Fallis (1980) examined the distribution of benefits to tenants under the Ontario public housing program in 1970.[5] In order to deal with the financing side of the public housing program, it was assumed that a program, equal in total cost, that paid benefits in proportion to income, was substituted for the public housing program. The differential benefits and the differential incidence (the ratio of benefits to income) were computed (see table 10.1). The lower-income tenants were made worse off by the substitution of the alternative program, and the higher-income tenants made better off. The incidence results show that the public housing program has a more progressive pattern of benefits than one that distributes benefits in proportion to income.

So far we have looked at the effect of public housing on the individual tenant. But what of its effects on the private housing market? Public housing removes tenants from the private market, and so the market demand curve shifts down and to the left. There may be a slight shift left of the supply curve if the construction and operation of public housing raises the price of some inputs to private housing. The new equilibrium likely has a lower price of housing services and a smaller quantity of services supplied.

And finally again, the financing of the public housing deficit must be considered. If it is to be financed by increased taxes, this will shift the private market demand curve further left and further reduce the price and stock of private rental housing. Overall, public housing re-

TABLE 10.1
Differential Benefits of Ontario Public Housing, 1970

Income Class ($)	Distribution of Participants (%)	Differential Benefits ($)	Differential Incidence
0–1,999	24	−282	−.163
2,000–3,999	25	−71	−.023
4,000–5,999	46	438	.092
6,000–7,999	5	889	.132
8,000	–	–	–

SOURCE: Fallis (1980)

duces rents significantly for participants, reduces private rents slightly, and reduces the incomes of taxpayers. The major effect of public housing is on income distribution and the housing consumption of participants rather than on private market prices or stock.

RENT CONTROLS

The details of the laws and regulations of any rent control system, particularly those governing how the allowable rent increase is calculated, significantly shape the effects of the system. Here, however, we will examine a rather stylized conception of controls. The standard analysis is presented in figure 10.5. There is an initial equilibrium in the rental market at R_1 and Q_1. Implicitly, the assumptions are made ensuring the rental market is independent of the ownership market. Controls establish a rent R_c (price per unit of housing service), which is below the equilibrium R_1; supply contracts to Q_c, and there is excess demand in the rental market of AB. The amount of excess demand depends upon the price elasticities of the supply and demand functions and the difference $R_1 - R_c$.

This standard analysis is logically correct, but cannot be applied to the study of actual control regimes because of its many unrealistic assumptions. For example, the analysis assumes that there is no negotiation between landlords and tenants, or between a sitting tenant and a prospective tenant. However under controls, there is excess demand for housing services. Households are willing to pay more than the controlled rent to secure a dwelling unit. Tenants may make side payments over and above the rent. These payments are very hard to police because both parties to the exchange are better off, and therefore have no incentive to report it. If side payments are made to landlords, the true rent under controls is above R_c, and the effects on supply are less. If side payments are made between tenants, the income redistribution as a result of controls is altered (see Cheung [1974], [1975]).

The standard analysis assumes that the regulators can actually control the price per unit of housing service. However, a unit of housing service and the price of this unit are unobservable constructs, and it is more likely that regulators control the total rent on a dwelling unit. The controlled rent on a particular dwelling unit is set at $\overline{R}$; this rent is the product of the price per unit of housing service and the quantity of housing services yielded by the dwelling unit. At the moment controls are imposed, the quantity of services from a dwelling unit is fixed, and thus the reduction of the rent on the dwelling unit is a reduction in the price of housing services received by the landlord. If over time the landlord reduces the level of services from a dwelling and the controlled rent remains at $\overline{R}$, the price of services received by the landlord has risen. Most control regimes try to prevent reductions in service levels,

FIGURE 10.5
Standard Analysis of Rent Controls

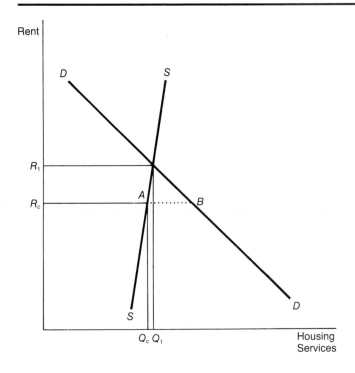

or if they occur, to adjust $\bar{R}$ accordingly; but full monitoring and adjustment is unlikely. It is even possible that output levels can be so reduced that a rent-control regime raises the price of housing services, and permits landlords to earn above-normal profits (see Frankena [1975]).

And finally, the standard analysis assumes that the controls cover all rental units. But almost all regimes exempt some units. Sometimes newly constructed units are exempt, or units renting above some maximum amount, or government-subsidized units, or units in small buildings. Sometimes units are decontrolled at each turnover of tenants. Let us consider the most common and important of these exemptions: the exemption for units built after controls were imposed. This discussion is based on Fallis and Smith (1984).

One of the most obvious and undesirable effects of a universal system of rent controls is that the level of new construction is reduced. To prevent this, most control regimes provide an exemption for new units. There are then two rental markets: the controlled and the uncontrolled. Figure 10.6 shows the equilibrium before controls, the equilibria in the

FIGURE 10.6
Rent Controls with a New Unit Exemption

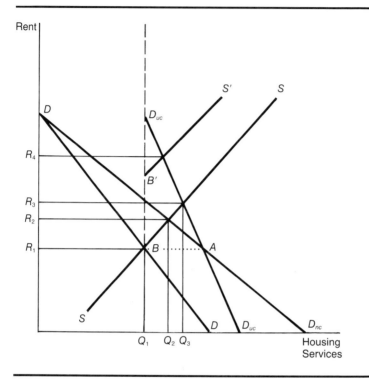

controlled and uncontrolled markets, and what the equilibrium would have been had controls not been imposed.

The initial equilibrium is at R_1 and Q_1, where the market supply curve SS and market demand curve DD intersect. Assume that the rental market is independent of the ownership market. And suppose for some reason, to be discussed below, the market demand curve shifts to DD_{nc}. To prevent rents from rising to R_2 the government imposes rent controls – setting the price per unit of housing service at R_1, but exempting new construction. At the moment controls come in, there is excess demand in the controlled market; prices do not ration the existing stock, Q_1. The rationing mechanism for the controlled stock is simply that tenants occupying units before controls were imposed, occupy them after as well.

It is helpful in modelling the uncontrolled market to consider the reason why the market demand curve shifted from DD to DD_{nc}. Suppose that the shift occurred because new households moved into the community. The controlled stock is already occupied, and therefore the new entrants are forced into the uncontrolled market (assuming no side payments pass between new and original households). All the increase· in demand spills into the uncontrolled market. The market demand and supply curves of the uncontrolled market can be drawn on the axes of figure 10.6. A vertical line through Q_1 is the price axis of the un-controlled market, and the quantity supplied-demanded is measured along the horizontal axis to the right of Q_1. The supply curve of un-controlled housing is the upper BS portion of the original market supply function, assuming that suppliers of new housing do not believe that rent controls are now more likely to be extended to their new units at some time in the future. The relationship between rent and quantity supplied continues as before. The demand curve for uncontrolled hous-ing is $D_{uc}D_{uc}$: it intersects the DD_{nc} curve at A because DD_{nc} is the horizontal addition of DD and $D_{uc}D_{uc}$. The uncontrolled market rent is R_3, and the quantity supplied is $Q_3 - Q_1$.

In the controlled market, the demand curve is DD. The supply curve is the lower portion of the original supply curve SB, assuming the costs of controlled landlords are unaffected by the level of supply in the uncontrolled market. The controlled market rent is the regulated level R_1; the quantity supplied is Q_1. There is no excess demand.

This stylized sort of control has a startling result. Rent in the con-trolled market is less than rent in the uncontrolled market ($R_1 < R_3$), and lower than rent in the absence of controls ($R_1 < R_2$), as would be expected. But rent in the uncontrolled market is higher than rent in the absence of controls ($R_3 > R_2$). And furthermore, the total quantity of housing services supplied under controls with exemptions is higher than without controls ($Q_3 > Q_2$). Some tenants are made worse off, and the quantity supplied has increased.

This outcome however is unlikely to occur. Once controls have been imposed on some dwellings, suppliers are likely to believe controls are more likely to be extended to new construction. Expected future rents are reduced. The supply curve of uncontrolled housing shifts up and left to $B'S'$. Uncontrolled rents rise to R_4, and the quantity supplied decreases. Also, the above model assumed that controlled landlords earned normal profits at the controlled rent. Usually controls do not permit a normal return, and so the supply of controlled stock would diminish.

The effects of controls with exemptions thus depend on the return allowed controlled landlords, the formation of expectations about fu-ture rents by builders of new housing, and the mechanism of rationing the controlled stock. In the example above, the demand curve shifted out as a result of new entrants – this made clear how the controlled stock was rationed. If the market demand curve shifted because of an increase in the incomes of existing tenants or other reasons, the ra-tioning would be different. The final outcome depends upon the sequence of moves within the controlled market, and from the controlled to the uncontrolled market.

The analysis predicts that rents in the uncontrolled market will be higher than rents in the controlled market: a prediction that is intuitively appealing but that cannot be directly verified. Observed uncontrolled rents may be higher, but uncontrolled apartments are newer, and may be larger, or better designed, or better located, or provide more facilities, and so on. Housing is a heterogeneous commodity and dwelling units in the two markets are quite different. The theory of hedonic pricing offers a way to deal with this problem. For example, Fallis and Smith (forthcoming) gathered data on the rent and characteristics of a sample of controlled and uncontrolled apartments in the metropolitan Toronto housing market in 1982. On average, uncontrolled rents were 48 percent higher than controlled rents; but uncontrolled buildings had more rooms, were better equipped, newer, in better neighbourhoods, although further from the centre of the city. Clearly some of the difference between controlled and uncontrolled rents is explained by the higher quality of uncontrolled units. Linear hedonic price functions, as in equation 10.17, were estimated by regressing rent on ten char-

$$R = \beta_0 + \beta_1 z_1 + \beta_2 z_2 + \beta_3 z_3 + \ldots + \beta_{10} z_{10} \qquad (10.17)$$

acteristics. Separate equations were estimated for the controlled and uncontrolled markets.[6]

Comparison of the two markets can be made by using two price indices as in equations 10.18 and 10.19, evaluated at the mean characteristic value in each market. Index I evaluates the average apartment

$$I = \frac{\beta_0^{uc} + \beta_1^{uc} z_1^c + \beta_2^{uc} z_2^c + \ldots + \beta_{10}^{uc} z_{10}^c}{\beta_0^c + \beta_1^c z_1^c + \beta_2^c z_2^c + \ldots + \beta_{10}^c z_{10}^c} \qquad (10.18)$$

$$II = \frac{\beta_0^{uc} + \beta_1^{uc} z_1^{uc} + \beta_2^{uc} z_2^{uc} + \ldots + \beta_{10}^{uc} z_{10}^{uc}}{\beta_0^c + \beta_1^c z_1^{uc} + \beta_2^c z_2^{uc} + \ldots + \beta_{10}^c z_{10}^{uc}} \qquad (10.19)$$

unit of the controlled market at the hedonic prices of the uncontrolled market and expresses this as a ratio of the average controlled unit at controlled hedonic prices. Index I equalled 1.149. Thus the average controlled unit would cost 15 percent more if evaluated at uncontrolled prices. Index II repeats the same procedure only using the average uncontrolled unit. Index II equalled 1.24. Thus the average uncontrolled unit costs 24 percent more when evaluated at uncontrolled as opposed to controlled prices. This application of hedonic pricing and index number techniques suggests rents are 15 to 24 percent higher in the uncontrolled market as a result of controls. The rest of the difference in observed rents is attributable to differences in quality.

INCOME TAXATION

When discussing government housing programs, emphasis is usually placed on the programs of housing ministries and housing agencies. However, the income tax system – by specifying what income is subject to tax, what deductions are permitted, and what rate is applied to taxable income – significantly influences the housing market. Here we will take a detailed look at the exemption for imputed income under the personal income tax law. Let us postulate that under the income tax system to be used as a normative standard, the gross imputed income from owning and occupying a house would be taxable – that is, the market value of the flow of services from the housing stock would be subject to tax. In a system of perfect, competitive markets this would equal the rental that the house could command in the market. Deductions of expenses incurred to earn this imputed income would be allowed. Property taxes, insurance premiums, depreciation, and maintenance would be deductible. The homeowner is a landlord who rents the house to himself. The normative income tax system would tax owner-occupying "landlords" just as it taxed landlords who rent their buildings in the private market. The Canadian income tax system, however, exempts imputed income (and does not allow deductions).

Table 10.2 helps to draw out the nature of this exemption. There are three households, each with incomes of $30,000 and savings from past periods of $20,000, and they live in identical houses worth $100,000.

TABLE 10.2
Comparison of Identical Households:
Net Imputed Income Exempt[1]

	Renter ($)	Owner: $10,000 down $90,000 mortgage ($)	Owner: $20,000 down $80,000 mortgage ($)
Income			
Earned income	30,000	30,000	30,000
Bond interest	2,000	1,000	–
Taxable Income	27,000	26,000	25,000
Taxes	5,400	5,200	5,000
Disposable Income	26,600	25,800	25,000
Housing Expenditures			
Rent	12,000	–	–
Mortgage Interest	–	9,000	8,000
Operating Expenses	–	2,000	2,000
After-housing, disposable income	14,600	14,800	15,000

1. For assumptions underlying calculation, see text.

One household rents the house and places their savings in a government bond with an interest rate of 10 percent. This interest income is taxed (the exemption for the first $1,000 of interest is ignored). The house rents for $12,000 per year (10% return on $100,000 plus $2,000 in operating costs). The second household purchases the house using $10,000 of savings and a $90,000 mortgage at 10 percent, and invests the remaining $10,000 of savings in a government bond. The third household buys the house using an $80,000 mortgage and all his savings. The after-tax, after-housing income of the three households is calculated in Table 10.2, assuming all households have $5,000 in deductions and a tax rate of 20 percent. It is assumed there are no capital gains, in order to isolate the effect of the imputed income exemption. These are identical households – they have the same income, same savings, and consume the same housing. Under the normative standard, the households would be similarly well off after tax. Under the Canadian income tax system, they are not. Households with savings find they are more favourably treated if the savings are placed in housing equity of a house they occupy. Of course households with no savings are not influenced by this provision, and also households that do not pay tax.

Let us start from the basic standard commodity model and build from there to analyse the effect of the exemption for imputed income on the housing market. Assume there is a market for housing services and that for some a priori reason households may be divided into owners and renters. The market demand curve for housing services DD is the horizontal sum of the demands of owners DD_O and of renters DD_R, as in figure 10.7. In chapter two (see figure 2.4), it was demonstrated that the imputed income exemption is equivalent to a reduction in the price of housing services for owners using savings from price P_2 $(r_m + c)$ to $P_2[r_m(1 - t) + c]$; and equivalent to an income transfer equal to $r_m E t$ for owners using a mortgage. Assume for the moment that all owners finance their house purchase in part with a mortgage. The income elasticity of demand for housing services is positive; assume it to be 0.8. The owners' demand curve for housing services shifts to the right by $0.8 \times (r_m E t / y_O) \times 100$ percent to DD_O', where y_O is the income of owners. The market demand curves shifts to DD' (a lesser percentage shift). The price of housing services rises to p_2' and the quantity produced to Q_2'. Renters pay higher prices and consume less housing. Owners face higher housing prices and consume more housing services and on balance are better off.

But what of the financing of the exemption? Let us suppose that it is financed by an increase in tax on all other sources of income. The market housing demand curves of both owners and renters shift left. The actual pattern of redistribution will depend upon the income elasticity of housing demand by owners and the pattern of taxation.

FIGURE 10.7
Exemption for Imputed Income

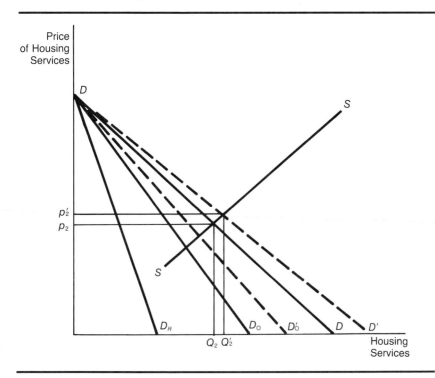

SOURCE: Based on White and White (1977)

The tax treatment of owner-occupied housing is somewhat different in the United States than Canada. Not only is imputed income not included in taxable income, but also property taxes and mortgage interest may be deducted from taxable income. The foregone tax revenue is considerably larger than for Canadian taxpayers. For a United States homeowner using either savings or a mortgage to purchase the marginal unit of housing stock, the tax provisions result in a reduction in the price of housing services.

Rosen (1979) estimated housing demand and tenure choice functions for the United States, and with them simulated the removal of all the favourable tax provisions for owners, accompanied by a proportional reduction of marginal tax rates to maintain total tax revenues. The distribution of income by income class remained about the same; but housing demand fell, average house prices fell, and the percentage of households that were homeowners declined about four percentage points.[7]

Slemrod (1982) developed a more sophisticated simulation model incorporating the intertemporal consumption decisions of households, a growth model of a two-sector economy, and capital market constraints requiring downpayments for home purchase. He simulated the effect of alternative tax policies on the economy in steady state growth. He found that reducing the allowed deduction of mortgage interest by one-half decreased owned housing stock, increased rented-housing stock, and overall total housing stock declined. Non-housing capital increased slightly, but total capital stock declined. The return to capital fell slightly and to labour rose slightly; which is what one would expect from the two-sector, general equilibrium model (see chapter four), because resources are leaving the relatively capital-intensive housing sector. Renters consumed more housing services across the life-cycle, while households that rent early in life and then own, consumed more as renters (saving for a downpayment was reduced) and less as owners later in life. The percentage of households owning housing dropped from 70 to 67.1 percent.

There are no empirical estimates of the effects of the Canadian income tax laws; likely the qualitative effect is the same as in the United States, but quantitatively the effects will be smaller.

SUGGESTIONS FOR FURTHER READING

Aaron, H. J. (1972) *Shelter and Subsidies* (Washington, D.C.: The Brookings Institution).

Cheung, S. N. S. (1975) "Roofs or Stars: The Stated Intents and Actual Effects of a Rents Ordinance," *Economic Inquiry* 13: 1–21.

De Salvo, J. S. (1971) "A Methodology for Evaluating Housing Programs," *Journal of Regional Science* 11: 173–85.

Rosen, H. S. (1979) "Housing Decisions and the U.S. Income Tax," *Journal of Public Economics* 11: 1–23.

Notes

CHAPTER 1: **Introduction**

1. These problems are not unique to housing analysis. For some commodities the issue of heterogeneity can be dealt with by analysing the markets for separate homogeneous commodities that are close substitutes for one another. The market for pens could be broken down into the market for fountain pens, ballpoint pens, and quill pens. However the heterogeneity of housing is too great for this to be a useful approach in most cases.
2. In a similar fashion, much labour economics abstracts from the heterogeneity of labour through the construct of an efficiency unit of labour.
3. Equation 1.2 is from the point of view of a single household, and is not a market equilibrium. This cost can be negative; and consumers would hold infinite stocks to reap infinite gains.
4. This approach is set out in more detail for housing in Fallis (1983a) and for durable goods in general in Deaton and Muellbauer (1980).
5. If there are no transactions costs, no taxes, and perfect capital markets, the user cost to owners will equal the price of services to renters in equilibrium. For further discussions of the cost to owners see Gillingham (1983) and Hendershott (1980).

CHAPTER 2: **The Demand for Housing**

1. Kent (1983) points out that estimated price and income elasticities have been based on data that include one, two, or all three of these decisions. He solves for price and income elasticities on each choice, examines their relationships, and suggests how this might explain some of the diversity of empirical estimates.
2. The determinants of household formation are only beginning to be explored. Clearly, the price of housing services will be important. A purely economic model would analyse household formation as the outcome of utility maximizing behaviour in the tradition of Becker (1976) and (1981).
3. See Stigler (1954) for a discussion.
4. The utility function that lies behind this demand function has not been made explicit.
5. This list of explanations is by no means exhaustive. The econometric work has the usual difficulties of sample selection, specification error, and definition of variables.
6. For discussion of some of the problems with these approaches see Gillingham (1975).
7. Demand analysis of housing as a standard commodity has been extended in a number of ways. Demographic variables have been aded to the utility function and so the demand function as in Awan et al. (1982). Transactions costs have been indirectly incorporated by considering demand as a stock

adjustment process as in Hanushek and Quigley (1979), (1980) and Cronin (1982).

8. A number of variants of this multiple characteristic model have been developed to formally model both the heterogeneity and durability of housing. See Sweeney (1974) and Arnott (1981).

9. See Kain and Quigley (1975), King (1976), Straszheim (1975), and a survey in McDonald (1979).

10. This greatly complicates the analysis, and much beyond the introduction of future prices and incomes. These future prices and incomes are unknown, so a formal model will have to represent how consumers formulate expectations about future events, and how they feel about uncertainty or risk.

11. For a good survey of life-cycle analysis see Beach et al. (1981) and Blinder (1974).

12. For a full discussion of the comparative statics of a two-period, single-good model see Deaton and Muellbauer (1980).

13. There is a large literature on the relative price of housing services under ownership or rental, although it is not explicitly based on an equilibrium in the housing services and housing stock markets. Examples of the literature are Shelton (1968), Laidler (1969), Rosen and Rosen (1980), Diamond (1978), and Johnson (1981).

14. Papers discussing these explanations of tenure choice in greater detail are Shelton (1968), Laidler (1969), Bossons (1978), Weiss (1978), Artle and Varaiya (1978), Ioannides (1979), and Henderson and Ioannides (1983). Goldberg (1983) reports a survey of homeowners' transaction costs.

15. See for example Bossons (1978), Rosen (1979), and Struyk (1976.)

16. See Frankena (1979) for a discussion of the valuation of travel time.

17. The equation is a differential equation that has a solution that is unique up to an arbitrary constant. Some initial condition is needed for the solution, which is provided in a full spatial model. See chapter four.

18. Empirical work on the demand for housing in a spatial context is just beginning. Straszheim (1973) and (1975) and Quigley (1976) estimated demand functions using data from a single city and allowed the price of housing (or its components) to vary across the city according to the spatial relationship of a house to a number of workplaces.

19. McDonald (1979) surveys spatial models of housing markets and indicates which assumptions have been altered in each model.

20. For example see Oates (1969) and Chinloy (1978).

CHAPTER 3: **The Supply of Housing**

1. These are preliminary 1982 national accounts data as reported in CMHC (1982, 20). It is conceptually very difficult to separate expenditures that are part of operating costs in producing output, and expenditures that are reinvestment in capital stock. The repairs and maintenance category has been treated as pure investment in stock.

2. See Smith (1974, 41) and Land Task Force (1978). There is considerable variation across cities and within a city.

3. See Land Task Force (1978) for a study of land markets and the role of government.

4. See Muller (1978), and also for a study of the industrial organization of the housing industry.

5. Muth (1969) used 0.05 as the share of land, and Maclennan (1982) reports it is between 0.1 and 0.15 in Britain.

6. Bromwich (1976) provides a very accessible discussion of the investment decision, which was used in preparing this section.
7. Hirshleifer (1958) provides a graphical analysis of the investment decision.
8. See Bromwich (1976) for a discussion of the internal rate of return rule and how it can differ from the present value rule.
9. See for example Pyhrr and Cooper (1982).
10. See Bromwich (1976) for a discussion of these generalizations.
11. The role of risk in housing demand analysis was mentioned briefly in note 10 of chapter two in the context of intertemporal choice. Chapter four offers some discussion of the analysis of housing markets with risk. While the decision making of a single demander or single supplier when confronted with uncertainty may be analysed alone, usually the market demand and market supply cannot be developed independently in a world with risk. See Hey (1981).
12. See Sandmo (1974).
13. There is a literature of the effect of land use controls on land and housing prices; see Ohls et al. (1974) and Peterson (1974).
14. The discussion below is a simplified case study of the general issues that arise in considering the effect of age on the services from capital goods and the role of maintenance. See Hall (1968) and for its application to housing see Margolis (1981), Dildine and Massey(1974), and Moorehouse (1972).
15. Muth (1976) and Anas (1978) present "putty-clay" models of housing services production.
16. For more detailed analysis of maintenance, where housing stock has both a quality and quantity dimension, see Sweeney (1974) and (1975), Ingram and Oron (1977), and Arnott (1981).
17. Sirmans, Kau, and Lee (1979) explicitly tested whether the production function was constant elasticity of substitution and rejected this functional form in favour of a variable elasticity of substitution.
18. Widely cited supply elasticity estimates of this sort are Muth (1969) and Smith (1976). Muth (1969) calculated the supply elasticity per unit of land to be around 14, using a share of land of 0.05 and an elasticity of substitution of 0.75. Smith (1976) allowed for housing quality variation in his estimate of the supply per unit of land. The quantity elasticity was estimated to be 5.27, and the quality elasticity was 3.75, indicating an elasticity of 9.02 for a standardized commodity.

CHAPTER 4: Models of the Housing Market

1. Hey (1979) and (1981) offer an excellent survey of the literature and of the techniques used in the economics of uncertainty and information. Maclennan (1982) surveys the work on housing search models.
2. When a market does not clear, it is sometimes said that the market is in disequilibrium. Bowden (1978) provides a clear introduction to the concept, as background to discussion of econometric problems associated with markets in disequilibrium. A good deal of this section is based on Bowden.
3. Smith (1974b) found a relationship between rents and vacancy rates in Canada. Blank and Winnick (1953), Maisel (1963), and Fair (1972) suggested such a relationship should exist, but Eubank and Sirmans (1979) were unable to detect the relationship in the United States. Rosen and Smith (1983) through specification of the natural vacancy rate were able to show the relationship.

4. Rosen (1974) characterized the equilibrium and outlined the determination of the equilibrium $p(z)$ function in the restricted case of housing with only one characteristic (a quality index). The equilibrium determination was not general but for a specific set of utility and production functions, and there was no comparative statics analysis.

5. The theory provides no a priori reason why the function should be linear or semilog. Halvorsen and Pollakowski (1981) fitted a general form containing these as special cases, and their data rejected these forms. Butler (1982) showed that the bias from using a restricted set of variables was likely small.

6. The hedonic prices can be used to estimate demand functions when both producers and households differ, by using a simultaneous equation framework, assuming data can be obtained on why producers and households differ.

7. Examples of such studies are Harrison and Rubinfeld (1978), Nelson (1978), and Blomquist and Worley (1981). These contain citations of much of the literature.

8. Davies (1978) and Maclennan (1982) survey the literature on filtering. Important writers in this field, what has sometimes been called the old urban economics in contrast to the spatial model of the new urban economics, are Hoyt (1939), Grigsby (1963), and Smith (1970). More recently, filtering has been analysed in large simulation models of a spatial housing market such as those of Lowry (1964), the NBER model reported in Kain, Apgar, and Ginn (1976), and Ohls (1975). Sweeney (1974) provides the most fully articulated theoretical model. It explicitly incorporates both durability and heterogeneity.

9. Comparative statics analysis of more complex models is available in Henderson (1977). Mills (1972b) presents a clear exposition of a closed-city model.

10. For surveys of the new urban economics see Anas and Dendrinos (1976), and Richardson (1977). Henderson (1977) and McDonald (1979) set out and explain the framework with rigour and in detail. Solow (1972) is an example of a model with endogenous congestion, and Muth (1976), an example of a vintage housing stock model.

11. Clear statements of some of the conflicting views are found in Richardson, Solow, and Mirrlees (1973). McDonald (1979), chapter one, discusses the methodological issues relating to empirical tests of the spatial housing model.

CHAPTER 5: Housing and Mortgage Markets in the National Economy

1. Henderson (1977) develops a model that links separate, individually modelled markets into a system of interdependent markets. The analysis of the incidence of the residential property tax, for example in Mieszkowski (1972), considers the economy as a system of interdependent housing markets.

2. Summaries of the literature, all of which support this conclusion, are Grebler and Maisel (1963), Hadjimatheou (1976), Fromm (1973), and Fair (1973).

3. Some of the most rigorous work in this area, and most of the work using Canadian data has been done by Smith, gathered together in Smith (1974), on which much of the following is based.

4. Long-run cycles are discussed in Hansen (1964), Duesenberry (1958), and Abromovitz (1964).

5. Arcelus and Meltzer (1973a) (1973b) argue that availability is not an issue;

Swan (1973) disagrees. Jaffee and Rosen (1979) find their measure of credit availability (the real flow of funds to thrift institutions) important in explaining single and multiple starts. Hendershott (1980) grants it little role in explaining the 1979–80 recession in the United States and thinks it will unlikely be a major factor now that U.S. mortgage markets are largely integrated into the capital market.

Theoretical analyses of credit rationing are offered by Jaffee and Russell (1976), Fried and Howitt (1980), Keeton (1979), and Stiglitz and Weiss (1981). Originally the existence of this behaviour had simply been asserted, but not explained; for example Guttentag (1961). The empirical work has been quite separate from the theory, and has been confined to testing the significance of proxy variables for credit availability in estimated equations explaining housing starts. Various proxies for credit availability have been used. Maisel (1963) used the treasury bill rate, Alberts (1962) the ratio of mortgage to bond yields, Suits (1962) the difference between FHA and bond yields, Smith (1974) the difference between the average of the conventional and NHA mortgage rate and the bond yield, and Jaffee and Rosen (1979) used the flow of funds to thrift institutions. The presumption of credit rationing disequilibrium in the mortgage market presents fundamental econometric problems that are ignored in these articles. See Fair (1972), Fair and Jaffee (1972), Fair and Kelejian (1974), and Bowden (1978).

6. For Canada see Fallis (1983b), and for the United States see Grebler and Burns (1982).

7. It has the added advantage for being representable graphically. For extensive graphical treatment of the two-sector model, see Johnson (1971), Johnson and Krauss (1974), and Baldry (1980).

8. See any intermediate macroeconomic text, for example Dornbusch and Fischer (1981).

9. This is not a demand curve of the usual sort. A usual demand curve takes the price of housing services as given and implicitly assumes, recognizing that increases in mortgage credit are accompanied by increases in demand for housing services, that the supply of housing services is perfectly elastic.

10. For a more detailed look at the supply side of the Canadian mortgage market see Smith (1974), Hatch (1975), and Poapst (1962).

11. For further discussion of the behaviour of intermediaries, see Tobin (1958), Lintner (1965), and Smith (1974).

12. For an analysis of default risk see von Furstenberg (1969), (1970a), and (1970b).

13. Mortgage credit is a heterogeneous commodity and can be studied using the framework of Rosen (1974). Aaron (1972), Baltensperger (1976), and Keeton (1979) have applied it to the study of credit markets.

14. For further discussion of the tilt problem and alternatives to the LPM, see Lessard and Modigliani (1975), Pesando (1977); and Carr and Smith (1983), from which this section draws heavily.

15. For a more formal analysis see Alm and Follain (1982), and Schwab (1982). Kearl (1979) examined the effects of the tilt problem in a macroeconomic context but did not supply the microfoundations.

16. See Capozza and Gau (1983) for a study of the effects of the terms of mortgage contracts on both parties to the contract.

CHAPTER 6: The Economic Rationale for Housing Policy

1. Welfare economics is treated briefly in most introductory economics and intermediate microeconomics texts. A more detailed introduction to the

ideas is available in Layard and Walters (1978), Atkinson and Stiglitz (1980), or as applied to urban problems in Walker (1981). Normative analysis of housing policy is presented in Aaron (1972), HUD (1976), Smith (1978), and Task Force (1979).

2. The figure and the discussion that follows are based on Atkinson and Stiglitz (1980).

3. Musgrave (1959) first used the term merit good but offered only a vague definition, which in part explains the subsequent confusion. Pazner (1972), and Hillman (1980) use the term in a manner similar to that used in this chapter. See also the discussion in Tobin (1970) of specific egalitarianism.

4. For this reason and because people care not only about efficiency but also about distribution, the adoption of the Pareto criterion by economists has proven much more controversial than they supposed.

5. This of course is very like the procedure using the social welfare function adopted in this book.

6. The theorems of welfare economics will not be presented here. Readers seeking a formal discussion might refer to the works cited in note one. Stigler (1975) provides insightful essays about how economists have used welfare economics.

7. Condition (v) on the list is stated as a tautology. "If there are no macroeconomic problems, there will be no problems requiring government intervention." A more careful statement of the condition would be that there is a full equilibrium in all markets, or rather set out the conditions that must hold in order for there to be a full equilibrium.

8. Bish and Nourse (1975) offer a good introduction to the optimal government problem.

9. Good surveys of the public choice literature are available in Hartle (1976), and Mueller (1976) and (1979).

CHAPTER 7: Policies to Achieve Equity

1. Osberg (1981) has a discussion of the determinants of the distribution of income and the effect of government on the distribution of income. See also Gillespie (1980) for estimates of the net effect of government.

2. Aaron and von Furstenberg (1971) measured the inefficiency of a price subsidy as the difference between the cost of the price subsidy and the cost of a cash grant to achieve the same utility level, divided by the cost of the price subsidy. Inefficiency decreased as the price elasticity of demand for housing fell (in absolute value). Inefficiency increased with the percentage price reduction of the price subsidy.

3. It can be shown that for certain quite general social welfare functions and utility functions, there exist cases where an optimally designed system of in-kind transfers yields a higher level of social welfare than an optimally designed linear cash transfer.

4. It is interesting to note that practitioners of applied economics recognized that an income tax (which is not a lump-sum tax) cannot be shown in general to be superior to an excise tax. Little (1951) and Friedman (1953) provided proof of this proposition. The choice of cash versus in-kind subsidies is analogous, but a preference for cash transfers remains.

Boadway (1979) contains a good introduction to the optimal tax literature. Sandmo (1976) sets out the optimal tax problem in the way the optimal transfer problem has been set out here. Atkinson and Stiglitz (1976) have proven that if the utility function is separable between goods and leisure, the optimal tax system will not require excise taxes. Presumably an analogous result holds for the optimal distribution problem, but it is of little interest here because housing services and leisure are obviously complementary.

5. The existence of housing subsidies is also consistent with many other things besides housing as a merit good. It is consistent with the contention that society desires the benefits of a transfer payment be shared equally by all members of the household, especially the children. It is consistent with the contention that utility functions are interdependent. Indeed the idea of a merit good is very analogous to the idea of interdependent utilities (donor preferences), as will be discussed later in the chapter. It is also consistent with a public choice analysis that shows that the housing industry is an especially effective lobby group.

6. Building codes could be interpreted as laws to enforce a minimum level of housing consumption.

7. Atkinson (1977) derives an optimal housing subsidy but does not compare it with other policy instruments. A very general treatment of the notion of merit goods and optimal government policies is that of Hillman (1980).

8. A percent-of-rent housing allowance is a program of this type. Housing allowances have often been recommended as a response to merit good concerns. See Friedman and Weinberg (1982), or Bradbury and Downs (1981).

9. This evidence is consistent not just with donor preferences but with many other hypotheses as well. See note 5.

CHAPTER 8: Policies to Achieve Pareto Efficiency

1. Several sections of this chapter are extensively based on Fallis (1983b), and many passages have been taken directly from the same source. That monograph focused on the possible role for government in mortgage markets; here there is a broader concern with a possible role for government in housing and housing-related markets.

2. The third item on the list from chapter six – public goods – will be omitted, because they can be considered a special case of externalities, and because there do not appear to be any public goods justifications for housing policy. It might be argued there are positive externalities from home ownership. These are not considered.

3. Markets with high transactions costs cannot in general be shown to be efficient; however nor can Pareto improvements through government intervention be shown generally to be possible. High transactions costs may redistribute income, but this is an equity issue, discussed in chapter seven.

4. The market for construction labour is likely not competitive because of labour unions; and the markets for many building materials probably are concentrated on the supply side. These markets have not been dealt with.

5. See for example the survey by Kasl (1976), Muth (1976b), and Rothenberg (1976).

6. This discussion is based on Davis and Whinston (1961).

7. The numerical example has been selected to generate a prisoner's dilemma outcome. It is an empirical question whether the true externalities are of these dimensions.

8. See for example Layard (1972), and Dasgupta and Pearce (1978), Rothenberg (1967) presents a cost-benefit analysis of urban renewal.

9. The Tiebout paper (1956) has spawned a large literature. See a collection of recent papers on resource allocation in the local public sector, and the

citations therein – Epple and Zelenitz (1981), Oates (1981), and Yinger (1981b).
10. For further discussion of housing fluctuations, see Jaffee and Rosen (1978), Clemhout and Neftci (1981), and Clemhout (1981).

CHAPTER 9: Housing Policy in Canada

1. Several sections of this chapter are extensively based on Fallis (1983c), and many passages have been taken directly from that source. That monograph describes the role of Canadian governments in mortgage markets; here there is a broader concern with government housing programs of all types.
2. The public sector had been involved before this – lending $10 million between 1919 and 1923 for the construction of modest housing, building some housing for veterans of the First World War, and building houses for the poor in Toronto – but the involvement was sporadic (Rose 1980, 2), and Task Force (1979).
3. Other surveys of housing policy are available, but somewhat diverse in orientation: some are restricted to certain periods, some provide economic analysis of the policies, and some are more institutional. Other surveys include Canada (1962), Rose (1969), Canada (1969), CMHC (1976), Smith (1974), (1977), (1981), Dennis and Fish (1972), Fallis (1980), and Rose (1980). Simple listings of programs and the details of the assistance provided under them are usually available from CMHC and provincial housing agencies.
4. See Smith (1974) for a more detailed discussion of the evolution of the mortgage insurance program.
5. While the government declared all were entitled to adequate housing, it did not attempt to publicly provide housing for everyone or even for all the needy. It did not adopt what is sometimes called a social service philosophy in housing matters. See Wolman (1975) for a comparison of housing policy in the United Kingdom and the United States, and the relative importance of the social service philosophy in the two countries. Donnison (1967) characterizes three types of housing policy: an assisted free market approach; social housing programs combined with free market production; and comprehensive housing policies. Canada adopted the second sort, while such countries as Sweden and Germany followed the third.
6. For a discussion of shelter allowances and a large American experiment with such programs see Bradbury and Downs (1981), and Friedman and Weinberg (1982).
7. Non-profit groups always in principle had been eligible for loans under the limited dividend program, and building co-operatives could use NHA direct lending. From 1964 to 1969, non-profit groups were dealt with under a separate NHA section, then were merged again with entrepreneurial housing until 1973.
8. See Schwab (1982) for a discussion of the impact of inflation on the demand for housing, given a standard level payment mortgage. He concludes that low rates of inflation have little effect, but high rates reduce demand.
9. A good survey is available in the Interprovincial Task Force (1980).
10. The concept of a tax expenditure was applied in the United States by Surrey (1973), and by Smith (1979) in Canada. The federal Department of Finance first published an estimate of taxes foregone under special tax provisions in 1979 (Canada 1979). The journal *Canadian Taxation* has presented nu-

merous articles on the concept and its application in Canada, including its application to housing. See also Smith (1977), and Canadian Tax Foundation (1977).

11. For a description of the evolution of financial regulation, see Binhammer and Williams (1976).

12. The characterizations of Quebec and Nova Scotia are based on available expenditure data rather than on numbers of assisted dwelling units (Alberta 1981).

13. These data relate to new units assisted in that year. Actual expenditures for housing programs may be rising each year, reflecting payments that must be made under assistance commitments begun in previous years.

14. For citations of the literature and a discussion of local government structure in Canada, see Tindall and Tindall (1984), and of local property taxation, see Bird and Slack (1983).

CHAPTER 10: The Effect of Policies

1. During the 1970s in the United States, there was a large social experiment to study the effects of shelter allowances, called the Experimental Housing Allowance Program. For a description of its effects see Bradbury and Downs (1981), especially Hanushek and Quigley (1981); and Friedman and Weinberg (1982).

2. Notice how the original analysis in figure 10.2 implicitly assumed that there was a perfectly elastic supply of subsidized government mortgages, and that the CC curve sloped upward due to rising prices of non-credit inputs.

3. For further analysis of direct lending by CMHC, see Smith (1974); and of lending in the U.S., see Aaron (1972).

4. There is a literature evaluating the benefits of public housing. See for example De Salvo (1971), Murray (1975) and (1978), and other work cited therein.

5. Fallis (1980) also estimated consumer's surplus measures of benefit for a wide range of housing programs in Ontario.

6. In the controlled market there is likely excess demand; the observed data are not an equilibrium of the sort analysed by Rosen (1974). The observed data do generate a set of implied characteristics prices, although another unit of the characteristic may not be available at this price. Marks (1984) conducted similar hedonic analysis using Vancouver data with similar sorts of results.

7. Econometric estimates by Rosen and Rosen (1980) also showed that United States tax provisions increased homeownership by four percentage points.

References

Aaron, H. (1972) *Shelter and Subsidies* (Washington, D.C.; The Brookings Institution).

Aaron, H., and G. von Furstenberg (1971) "The Inefficiency of Transfers in Kind: The Case of Housing Assistance," *Western Economic Journal* 9: 184–91.

Abromovitz, M. (1964) *Evidences of Long Swings in Aggregate Construction Since the Civil War* (Princeton, N.J.: Princeton University Press for the National Bureau of Economic Research).

Alberta (1981) *Statistical Addendum to the Report Entitled "Future Fiscal Arrangements for Housing in Canada"* (Alberta: prepared for Alberta Housing and Public Works by Clayton Research Associates).

Alberts, W. W. (1962) "Business Cycles, Residential Construction Cycles, and the Mortgage Market," *Journal of Political Economy* 70: 263–81.

Alm, J., and J. Follain (1982) "Alternative Mortgage Instruments: Their Effects on Consumer Choices in an Inflationary Environment," *Public Finance Quarterly* 10: 134–57.

Anas, A. (1978) "Dynamics of Urban Residential Growth," *Journal of Urban Economics* 5: 66–87.

Anas, A., and D. Dendrinos (1976) "The New Urban Economics: A Brief Survey," in G. Papageorgiou, ed., *Mathematical Land Use Theory* (Lexington, Mass.: D.C. Heath).

Arcelus, F., and A. H. Meltzer (1973a) "The Markets for Housing and Housing Services," *Journal of Money, Credit and Banking* 5: 78–99.

——— (1973b) "A Reply to Craig Swan," *Journal of Money, Credit and Banking* 5: 973–78.

Arnott, R. (1981) *Rent Control and Options for Decontrol in Ontario* (Toronto: Ontario Economic Council).

Arrow, K. J. (1951) *Social Choice and Individual Values* (New York: John Wiley).

——— (1971) *Essays in the Theory of Risk-Bearing* (Chicago: Markham Publishing Company).

Artle, R., and P. Varaiya (1978) "Life Cycle Consumption and Homeownership," *Journal of Economic Theory* 18: 38–58.

Atkinson, A. B. (1977) "Housing Allowances, Income Maintenance, and Income Taxation," in M. S. Feldstein, and R. P. Inman, eds., *The Economics of Public Services* (London: Macmillan).

Atkinson, A. B., and J. E. Stiglitz (1976) "The Design of Tax Structure: Direct Versus Indirect Taxation," *Journal of Public Economics* 6: 55–75.

——— (1980) *Lectures on Public Economics* (Maidenhead, England: McGraw-Hill [UK] Ltd.).

Awan, K., J. C. Odling-Smee, and C. M. E. Whitehead (1982) "Household Attributes and the Demand for Private Rental Housing," *Economica* 49: 183–200.

Baldry, J. C. (1980) *General Equilibrium Analysis: An Introduction to the Two-Sector Model* (London: Croom Helm).

Baltensperger, E. (1976) "The Borrower-Lender Relationship, Competitive Equilibrium, and the Theory of Hedonic Prices," *American Economic Review* 66: 401–05

Bank of Canada (various years) *Bank of Canada Review* (Ottawa: Bank of Canada).

Baumol, W. (1982) "Contestable Markets: An Uprising in the Theory of Industry Structure," *American Economic Review* 72: 1–15.

Beach, C. M., with D. E. Card and F. Flatters (1981) *Distribution of Income and Wealth in Ontario: theory and evidence* (Toronto: University of Toronto Press for the Ontario Economic Council.)

Becker, G. (1976) *The Economic Approach to Human Behavior* (Chicago: The University of Chicago Press).

––––––– (1981) *A Treatise on the Family* (Cambridge, Mass.: Harvard University Press).

Binhammer, H. H., and J. Williams (1976) *Deposit-Taking Institutions: Innovation and the Process of Change* (Ottawa: Economic Council of Canada).

Bird, R., and N. E. Slack (1983) *Urban Public Finance in Canada* (Toronto: Butterworths).

Bish, R., and H. Nourse (1975) *Urban Economics and Policy Analysis* (New York: McGraw-Hill).

Blank, D. M., and L. Winnick (1953) "The Structure of the Housing Market," *Quarterly Journal of Economics* 67: 181–203.

Blinder, A. S. (1974) *Toward an Economic Theory of Income Distribution* (Cambridge, Mass.: The MIT Press).

Blomquist, G., and L. Worley (1981) "Hedonic Prices, Demands for Urban Housing Amenities, and Benefit Estimates," *Journal of Urban Economics* 9: 212–21.

Boadway, R. (1979) *Public Sector Economics* (Cambridge, Mass.: Winthrop Publishers, Inc.).

Bossons, J. (1978) "Housing Demand and Household Wealth: Evidence for Homeowners," in L. Bourne and J. Hitchcock, eds., *Urban Housing Markets: Recent Directions in Research and Policy* (Toronto: University of Toronto Press).

Bowden, R. (1978) *The Econometrics of Disequilibrium* (Amsterdam: North Holland).

Bradbury, K. L. and A. Downs (1981) *Do Housing Allowances Work?* (Washington, D.C.: The Brookings Institution).

Bromwich, M. (1976) *The Economics of Capital Budgeting* (Harmondsworth, England: Penguin Books).

Browning, E. K., and J. Browning (1979) *Public Finance and the Price System* (New York: Macmillan).

Buchanan, J. (1968) "What Kind of Redistribution Do We Want?" *Economica* 35: 185–90.

Butler, R. V. (1982) "The Specification of Hedonic Indices for Urban Housing," *Land Economics* 58: 96–108.

Canada (various years) *Census of Canada* (Ottawa: Statistics Canada).

––––––– *National Income and Expenditure Accounts* (Ottawa: Statistics Canada).

––––––– *The Consumer Price Index* (Ottawa: Statistics Canada).

––––––– *Survey of Consumer Finances* (Ottawa: Statistics Canada).

_____ Family Expenditure in Canada (Ottawa: Statistics Canada).

_____ (1962) Report of the Royal Commission on Banking and Finance (Ottawa: Queen's Printer).

_____ (1969) Report of the Task Force on Housing and Urban Development (Ottawa: Queen's Printer).

_____ (1978) Report of the Royal Commission on Corporate Concentration (Ottawa: Minister of Supply and Services).

_____ (1979) Government of Canada Tax Expenditure Report (Ottawa: Department of Finance).

CMHC (1976) A Catalogue of Housing Programs (Ottawa: Central Mortgage and Housing Corporation).

_____ (1981) Background Document on Social Housing (Ottawa: Canada Mortgage and Housing Corporation).

_____ (1982) (Various years) Canadian Housing Statistics (Ottawa: Canada Mortgage and Housing Corporation).

Canadian Tax Foundation (1977) Proceedings of the 1977 Corporate Management Tax Conference (Toronto: The Foundation).

Capozza, D., and G. Gau (1983) "Optimal Mortgage Instrument Designs," in G. Gau and M. Goldberg, eds., North American Housing Markets into the Twenty-First Century (Cambridge, Mass.: Ballinger Publishing Company).

Carliner, G. (1973) "Income Elasticity of Housing Demand," Review of Economics and Statistics 55: 528–32.

Carr, J., and L. B. Smith (1983) "Inflation, Uncertainty and Future Mortgage Instruments," in G. Gau and M. Goldberg, eds., North American Housing Markets into the Twenty-First Century (Cambridge, Mass.: Ballinger Publishing Company).

Carver, H. (1975) Compassionate Landscape (Toronto: University of Toronto Press).

Cheung, S. N. S. (1974) "A Theory of Price Control," Journal of Law and Economics 17: 53–71.

_____ (1975) "Roofs or Stars: The Stated Intents and Actual Effects of a Rents Ordinance," Economic Inquiry 13: 1–21.

Chinloy, P. (1978) "Effective Property Taxes and Tax Capitalization," Canadian Journal of Economics 11: 740–50.

Clemhout, S. (1981) "The Impact of Housing Cyclicality on the Construction of Residential Units and Housing Costs," Land Economics 57: 609–23.

Clemhout, S., and S. N. Neftci (1981) "Policy Evaluation of Housing Cyclicality: A Spectral Analysis," Review of Economics and Statistics 63: 385–94.

Coase, R. (1960) "The Problem of Social Cost," Journal of Law and Economics 1–44.

Cronin, F. J. (1982) "Estimation of Dynamic Linear Expenditure Functions for Housing," Review of Economics and Statistics, 64, 97–103.

Dasgupta, A. K., and D. W. Pearce (1978) Cost-Benefit Analysis: Theory and Practice (London: Macmillan).

Davies, G. (1978) "Theoretical Approaches to Filtering in the Urban Housing Market," in L. Bourne and J. Hitchcock, eds., Urban Housing Markets: Recent Directions in Research and Policy (Toronto: University of Toronto Press).

Davis, O. A., and A. B. Whinston (1961) "The Economics of Urban Renewal," Law and Contemporary Problems 16: 105–17.

Dawson, R. M. (1964) The Government of Canada (Toronto: University of Toronto Press).

Deaton, A., and J. Muellbauer (1980) Economics and Consumer Behaviour (Cambridge: Cambridge University Press).

de Leeuw, F. (1971) "The Demand for Housing: A Review of Cross-Section Evidence," *Review of Economics and Statistics* 53: 1–10.

de Leeuw, F., and N. Ekanem (1971) "The Supply of Rental Housing," *American Economic Review* 61: 806–17.

Dennis, M., and S. Fish (1972) *Programs in Search of a Policy* (Toronto: Hakkert Press).

De Salvo, J. S. (1971) "A Methodology for Evaluating Housing Programs," *Journal of Regional Science* 11: 173–85.

Diamond, D. B. (1978) "A Note on Inflation and Relative Tenure Prices," *American Real Estate and Urban Economics Association Journal* 6: 438–45.

Dildine, L. L., and F. A. Massey (1974) "Dynamic Model of Private Incentives to Housing Maintenance," *Southern Economic Journal* 40: 631–39.

Donnison, D. V. (1967) *The Government of Housing* (Harmondsworth, England: Penguin).

Dornbusch, R., and S. Fischer (1981) *Macroeconomics* (New York: McGraw-Hill).

Duesenberry, J. S. (1958) *Business Cycles and Economic Growth* (New York: McGraw-Hill).

Economic Council of Canada (1976) *Efficiency and Regulation: A Study of Deposit Institutions* (Ottawa: E.C.C.).

Edelstein, R. (1983) "The Production Function for Housing and Its Implications for Future Urban Development," in G. Gau and M. Goldberg, eds., *North American Housing Markets into the Twenty-First Century* (Cambridge, Mass.: Ballinger).

Epple, D., and A. Zelenitz (1981) "The Roles of Jurisdictional Competition and of Collective Choice Institutions in the Market for Local Public Goods," *American Economic Review*, Papers and Proceedings 71: 87–92.

Eubank, A. A., and C. F. Sirmans (1979) "The Price Adjustment Mechanism for Rental Housing in the United States," *Quarterly Journal of Economics* 93: 163–83.

Fair, R. C. (1972) "Disequilibrium in Housing Models," *Journal of Finance* 27: 207–21.

Fair, R. C. (1973) "Monthly Housing Starts," in R. B. Ricks, ed., *National Housing Models* (Lexington, Mass.: Lexington Books).

Fair, R. C., and D. M. Jaffee (1972) "Methods of Estimation for Markets in Disequilibrium," *Econometrica* 40: 497–514.

Fair, R. C., and H. H. Kelejian (1974) "Methods of Estimation for Markets in Disequilibrium: A Further Study," *Econometrica* 42: 177–90.

Fallis, G. (1980) *Housing Programs and Income Distribution in Ontario* (Toronto: University of Toronto Press for the Ontario Economic Council).

—— (1983a) "Housing Tenure in a Model of Consumer Choice: A Simple Diagrammatic Analysis," *American Real Estate and Urban Economics Association Journal* 11: 30–45.

—— (1983b) *Governments and the Residential Mortgage Market I: A Normative Analysis*, Discussion Paper No. 239 (Ottawa: Economic Council of Canada).

—— (1983c) *Governments and the Residential Mortgage Market II: Programs and Evaluation*, Discussion Paper No. 240 (Ottawa: Economic Council of Canada).

Fallis, G., and L. B. Smith (1984) "Uncontrolled Prices in a Controlled Market: The Case of Rent Control," *American Economic Review* 74: 193–200.

—— (forthcoming) "Price Effects of Rent Control on Controlled and Uncontrolled Housing in Toronto: An Hedonic Index Approach," *Canadian Journal of Economics*.

Financial Publishing Company (1966) *Monthly Payments for Mortgage Amortization* (Boston: Fin. Pub.).

Frankena, M. (1975) "Alternative Models of Rent Control," *Urban Studies* 12: 303–08.

―――― (1979) *Urban Transportation Economics* (Toronto: Butterworths).

Fried, J., and P. Howitt (1980) "Credit Rationing and Implicit Contract Theory," *Journal of Money, Credit and Banking* 12: 471–87.

Friedman, J., and D. H. Weinberg (1982) *The Economics of Housing Vouchers* (New York: Academic Press).

Friedman, M. (1953) *Essays in Positive Economics* (Chicago: University of Chicago Press).

―――― (1957) *A Theory of the Consumption Function* (Princeton: Princeton University Press).

Fromm, G. (1973) "Econometric Models of the Residential Construction Sector: A Comparison," in R. B. Ricks, ed., *National Housing Models* (Lexington, Mass.: Lexington Books).

Gillespie, W. I. (1980) *The Redistribution of Income in Canada* (Ottawa: Gage Publishing Limited in association with the Institute of Canadian Studies, Carleton University, Ottawa).

Gillingham, R. (1975) "Place-to-Place Rent Comparisons," *Annals of Economic and Social Measurement* 4: 153–73.

―――― (1983) "Measuring the Cost of Shelter for Homeowners: Theoretical and Empirical Considerations," *Review of Economics and Statistics* 65: 254–65.

Goldberg, M. (1983) *The Housing Problem: A Real Crisis?* (Vancouver: University of British Columbia Press).

Gordon, R. (1981) *Macroeconomics* (Boston: Little, Brown).

Grebler, L., and S. Maisel (1963) "Determinants of Residential Construction: A Review of Present Knowledge," in *Impacts of Monetary Policy*, Commission on Money and Credit (Englewood Cliffs, N.J.: Prentice-Hall).

Grebler, L., and L. Burns (1982) "Construction Cycles in the United States Since World War II," *American Real Estate and Urban Economics Association Journal* 10: 123–51.

Grieson, R. (1973) "The Supply of Rental Housing: Comment," *American Economic Review* 63: 433–36.

Grigsby, W. G. (1963) *Housing Markets and Public Policy* (Philadelphia: University of Pennsylvania Press).

Guttentag, J. M. (1961) "The Short Cycle in Residential Construction 1946–1959," *American Economic Review* 51: 275–98.

Hadjimatheou, G. (1976) *Housing and Mortgage Markets* (London: Saxon House).

Hahn, F. A. (1973) "On Optimum Taxation," *Journal of Economic Theory* 6: 96–106.

Hall, R. E. (1968) "Technical Change and Capital from the Point of View of the Dual," *Review of Economic Studies* 35: 25–46.

Halvorsen, R., and H. O. Pollakowski (1981) "Choice of Functional Form for Hedonic Price Equations," *Journal of Urban Economics* 10: 37–49.

Hansard (1973) "Speech by the Hon. Ron Basford" (Ottawa: Queen's Printer).

Hansen, A. J. (1964) *Business Cycles and National Income* (New York: Norton).

Hanushek, E. A., and J. M. Quigley (1979) "The Dynamics of the Housing Market: A Stock Adjustment Model of Housing Consumption," *Journal of Urban Economics* 6: 90–111.

―――― (1980) "What is the Price Elasticity of Housing Demand?" *Review of Economics and Statistics* 62: 449–54.

―――― (1981) "Consumption Aspects," in K. L. Bradbury, and A. Downs, eds.,

Do Housing Allowances Work? (Washington, D.C.: The Brookings Institution).

Harrison, D., and D. L. Rubinfeld (1978) "Hedonic Housing Prices and the Demand for Clean Air," *Journal of Environmental Economics and Management* 5: 81–102.

Hartle, D. G. (1976) *A Theory of the Expenditure Budgetary Process* (Toronto: University of Toronto Press for the Ontario Economic Council).

Hatch, J. E. (1975) *The Canadian Mortgage Market* (Toronto: Queen's Printer for Ontario).

Hendershott, P. H. (1980) "Real User Costs and the Demand for Single Family Housing," in W. C. Brainard and G L. Perry, eds., *Brookings Papers on Economic Activity* (Washington, D.C.: The Brookings Institution).

Henderson, J. V. (1977) *Economic Theory and the Cities* (New York: Academic Press).

Henderson, J. V., and Y. M. Ioannides (1983) "A Model of Housing Tenure Choice," *American Economic Review* 73: 98–113.

Hey, J. D. (1979) *Uncertainty in Microeconomics* (Oxford: Martin Robertson).

_____ (1981) *Economics in Disequilibrium* (Oxford: Martin Robertson).

Hillman, A. L. (1980) "Notions of Merit Want," *Public Finance/Finances Publiques* 35: 213–25.

Hirshleifer, J. (1958) "On the Theory of the Optimal Investment Decision," *Journal of Political Economy* 66: 329–52.

Hochman, H. M., and J. D. Rogers (1969) "Pareto Optimal Redistribution," *American Economic Review* 59: 542–47.

Hoyt, H. (1939) *The Structure and Growth of Residential Neighbourhoods in American Cities* (Washington, D.C.: Government Printing Office).

HUD (1976) *Housing in the Seventies Working Papers* (Washington, D.C.: U.S. Department of Housing and Urban Development).

Ingram, G K. (1979) "Simulation and Econometric Approaches to Modeling Urban Areas," in P. Mieszkowski and M. Straszheim, eds., *Current Issues in Urban Economics* (Baltimore: The Johns Hopkins University Press).

Ingram, G. K., and Y. Oron (1977) "The Production of Housing Services from Existing Dwelling Units," in G. K. Ingram, ed., *Residential Location and Urban Housing Markets* (Cambridge, Mass.: Ballinger).

Interprovincial Task Force (1980) *The Income Security System in Canada* (Ottawa: Canadian Intergovernmental Conference Secretariat).

Ioannides, Y. (1979) "Temporal Risks and the Tenure Decision in Housing Markets," *Economics Letters* 4: 293–97.

Jaffee, D. M. and T. Russell (1976) "Imperfect Information and Credit Rationing," *Quarterly Journal of Economics* 90: 651–66.

Jaffee, D. M. and K. T. Rosen (1978) "Estimates of the Effectiveness of Stabilization Policies for the Mortgage and Housing Markets," *Journal of Finance* 33: 933–46.

_____ (1979) "Mortgage Credit Availability and Residential Construction," in *Brookings Papers on Economic Activity 2* (Washington, D.C.: The Brookings Institution).

Johnson, H. G. (1971) *The Two-Sector Model of General Equilibrium* (London: Allen and Unwin).

Johnson, H. G. and M. B. Krauss (1974) *General Equilibrium Analysis: A Micro-Economic Text* (London: Allen and Unwin).

Johnson, M. S. (1981) "A Cash Flow Model of Rational Housing Tenure Choice," *American Real Estate and Urban Economics Association Journal* 9: 1–17.

Kain, J. F., and J. M. Quigley (1975) *Housing Markets and Racial Discrimination* (New York: National Bureau of Economic Research).

Kain, J. F., W. C. Apgar Jr., and J. R. Ginn (1976) "Description of the NBER Simulation Model," in HUD (1976b) *Simulation of the Market Effects of Housing Allowances Vol. 1* (Washington, D.C.: U.S. Department of Housing and Urban Development).

Kasl, S. (1976) "Effects of Housing on Mental and Physical Health," in HUD (1976) *Housing in the Seventies Working Papers* (Washington, D.C.: U.S. Department of Housing and Urban Development).

Kearl, J. R. (1979) "Inflation, Mortgages and Housing," *Journal of Political Economy* 87: 1115–139.

Keeton, W. R. (1979) *Equilibrium Credit Rationing* (New York: Garland Publishing, Inc.).

Kent, R. J. (1983) "The Relationships Between Income and Price Elasticities in Studies of Housing Demand, Tenure Choice, and Household Formation," *Journal of Urban Economics* 13: 196–204.

King, A. (1976) "The Demand for Housing: A Lancastrian Approach," *Southern Economic Journal* 43: 1077–87.

Laidler, D. (1969) "Income Tax Incentives for Owner-Occupied Housing," in A. C. Harberger and M. J. Bailey, eds., *The Taxation of Income from Capital* (Washington, D.C.: The Brookings Institution).

Land Task Force (1978) *Down to Earth Vol. 1*, Report of the Federal-Provincial Task Force on the Supply and Price of Serviced Residential Land (Toronto: David Greenspan, Chairman).

Layard, R. (1972) *Cost Benefit Analysis: Selected Readings* (Harmondsworth, England: Penguin).

Layard, R., and A. Walters (1978) *Microeconomic Theory* (New York: McGraw-Hill).

Lee, T. H. (1968) "Housing and Permanent Income: Tests Based on a Three-Year Reinterview Survey," *Review of Economics and Statistics* 50: 480–90.

Leigh, W. A. (1980) "Economic Depreciation of the Residential Housing Stock of the United States, 1950–1970," *Review of Economics and Statistics* 62: 200–06.

Lessard, D., and F. Modigliani (1975) "Inflation and the Housing Market: Problems and Solutions," in F. Modigliani and D. Lessard, eds., *New Mortgage Designs for Stable Housing in an Inflationary Environment* (Boston: Federal Reserve Bank of Boston).

Lintner, J. (1965) "Valuation of Risk Assets and the Selection of Risky Investments in Stock Portfolios and Capital Budgets," *Review of Economics and Statistics* 47: 13–37.

Little, I. M. D. (1951) "Direct Versus Indirect Taxes," *Economic Journal* 61: 557–84.

Lowry, I. (1964) *A Model of Metropolis* (Santa Monica, Calif.: RAND Corporation).

McDonald, J. F. (1979) *Economic Analysis of an Urban Housing Market* (New York: Academic Press).

——— (1981) "Capital-Land Substitution in Urban Housing: A Survey of Empirical Estimates," *Journal of Urban Economics* 9: 190–211.

McFadyen, S., and R. Hobart (1978) "An Alternative Measure of Housing Costs and the Consumer Price Index," *Canadian Journal of Economics* 11: 105–11.

Maclennan, D. (1982) *Housing Economics* (London: Longman).

Maisel, S. J. (1963) "A Theory of Fluctuations in Residential Construction Starts," *American Economic Review* 53: 359–83.

Maisel, S. J., J. B. Burnham, and J. S. Austin (1971) "The Demand for Housing – a Comment," *Review of Economics and Statistics* 53: 410–13.

Margolis, S. E. (1981) "Depreciation and Maintenance of Houses," *Land Economics* 57: 91–105.

Marks, D. (1984) "The Effects of Rent Controls on the Price of Rental Housing," *Land Economics* 60: 81–94.

Markusen, J. R., and D. T. Scheffman (1977) *Speculation and Monopoly in Urban Development: analytical foundations with evidence for Toronto* (Toronto: University of Toronto Press for the Ontario Economic Council).

Mieszkowski, P. (1972) "The Property Tax: An Excise Tax or a Profits Tax?" *Journal of Public Economics* 1: 73–96.

Mills, E. S. (1972a) *Studies in the Structure of the Urban Economy* (Baltimore: The Johns Hopkins Press for Resources for the Future, Inc.).

—— (1972b) *Urban Economics* (Glenview, Illinois: Scott Foresman).

Mishan, E. J. (1981) *Introduction to Normative Economics* (Oxford: Oxford University Press).

Moorehouse, J. C. (1972) "Optimal Housing Maintenance Under Rent Control," *Southern Economic Journal* 4: 93–106.

Mueller, D. C. (1976) "Public Choice: A Survey," *Journal of Economic Literature* 14: 396–433.

—— (1979) *Public Choice* (Cambridge: Cambridge University Press).

Muller, R. A. (1978) *The Market for New Housing in the Metropolitan Toronto Area* (Toronto: Ontario Economic Council).

Murray, M. P. (1975) "The Distribution of Tenant Benefits in Public Housing," *Econometrica* 43: 771–88.

—— (1978) "Methodologies for Estimating Housing Subsidy Benefits," *Public Finance Quarterly* 6: 161–92.

Musgrave, R. (1959) *The Theory of Public Finance* (New York: McGraw-Hill).

Muth, R. (1960) "The Demand for Non-Farm Housing," in A. C. Harberger, ed., *The Demand for Durable Goods* (Chicago: University of Chicago Press).

—— (1964) "The Derived Demand Curve for a Productive Factor and the Industry Supply Curve," *Oxford Economic Papers* 16: 221–34.

—— (1969) *Cities and Housing* (Chicago: University of Chicago Press).

—— (1971) "The Derived Demand for Urban Residential Land," *Urban Studies* 8: 243–54.

—— (1976) "A Vintage Model of Housing Production," in G. Papageorgiou, ed., *Mathematical Land Use Theory* (Lexington, Mass.: D. C. Heath).

—— (1976b) "The Rationale for Government Intervention in Housing," in HUD (1976) *Housing in the Seventies Working Papers* (Washington, D.C.: U.S. Department of Housing and Urban Development).

Nelson, J. P. (1978) "Residential Choice, Hedonic Prices, and the Demand for Urban Air Quality," *Journal of Urban Economics* 5: 357–69.

Oates, W. (1969) "The Effects of Property Taxes and Local Public Spending on Property Values: An Empirical Study of Tax Capitalization and the Tiebout Hypothesis," *Journal of Political Economy* 77: 957–71.

—— (1981) "On Local Finance and the Tiebout Model," *American Economic Review* 71: 93–98.

Ohls, J. (1975) "Public Policy Toward Low Income Housing and Filtering in Housing Markets," *Journal of Urban Economics* 2: 144–71.

Ohls, J. C., R. Welsberg, and M. I. White (1974) "The Effect of Zoning on Land Value," *Journal of Urban Economics* 1: 428–44.

Olsen, E. O. (1969) "A Competitive Theory of the Housing Market," *American Economic Review* 59: 612–22.

Osberg, L. (1981) *Economic Inequality in Canada* (Toronto: Butterworths).

Ozanne, L., and R. Struyk (1978) "The Price Elasticity of Supply of Housing Services," in L. Bourne and J. R. Hitchcock, eds., *Urban Housing Markets:*

Recent Directions in Research and Policy (Toronto: University of Toronto Press).

Pazner, E. A. (1972) "Merit Wants and A Theory of Taxation," *Public Finance/ Finances Publiques* 27: 460–72.

Pesando, J. (1977) *The Impact of Inflation on Financial Markets in Canada* (Montreal: C. D. Howe Research Institute).

Peterson, G. E. (1974) *The Influence of Zoning Regulations on Land and Housing Prices* (Washington, D.C.: The Urban Institute).

Poapst, J. V. (1962) *The Residential Mortgage Market* (Ottawa: Royal Commission on Banking and Finance).

Polinsky, A. M. (1977) "The Demand for Housing: A Study in Specification and Grouping," *Econometrica* 45: 447–61.

Polinsky, A. M., and D. T. Ellwood (1979) "An Empirical Reconciliation of Micro and Grouped Estimates of the Demand for Housing," *Review of Economics and Statistics* 61: 199–205.

Pyhrr, S. A., and J. R. Cooper (1982) *Real Estate Investment* (New York: John Wiley and Sons).

Quigley, J. M. (1976) "Housing Demand in the Short Run: An Analysis of Polytomous Choice," *Explorations in Economic Research* 3: 76–102.

_____ (1979) "What Have We Learned About Urban Housing Markets?" in P. Mieszkowski and M. Straszheim, eds., *Current Issues in Urban Economics* (Baltimore: The Johns Hopkins University Press).

Rawls, J. (1971) *A Theory of Justice* (Cambridge, Mass.: Harvard University Press).

Reid, M. (1962) *Housing and Income* (Chicago: The University of Chicago Press).

Richardson, H. (1977) *The New Urban Economics: and Alternatives* (London: Pion).

Richardson, H. W., R. S. Solow, and J. A. Mirrlees (1973) "Comments on Some Uses of Mathematical Models in Urban Economics," *Urban Studies* 10: 259–70.

Rose, A. (1969) "Canadian Housing Policies," in M. Wheeler, ed., *The Right to Housing* (Montreal: Harvest House Limited).

_____ (1980) *Canadian Housing Policies 1935–1980* (Toronto: Butterworths).

Rosen, H. S. (1979) "Housing Decisions and the U.S. Income Tax," *Journal of Public Economics* 11: 1–23.

Rosen, H. S., and K. T. Rosen (1980) "Federal Taxes and Homeownership: Evidence from Time Series," *Journal of Political Economy* 88:59–75.

Rosen, K. T., and L. B. Smith (1983) "The Price-Adjustment Process for Rental Housing and the Natural Vacancy Rate," *American Economic Review* 73: 779–86.

Rosen, S. (1974) "Hedonic Prices and Implicit Markets: Product Differentiation in Pure Competition," *Journal of Political Economy* 82: 34–55.

Rothenberg, J. (1967) *Economic Evaluation of Urban Renewal* (Washington, D.C.: The Brookings Institution).

_____ (1976) "A Rationale for Government Intervention in Housing: The Externalities Generated by Good Housing," in HUD (1976) *Housing in the Seventies Working Papers* (Washington, D.C.: U.S. Department of Housing and Urban Development).

Rowe, A. (1981) "The Financing of Residential Construction in Newfoundland," *Canadian Public Policy* 7: 119–22.

Sandmo, A. (1974) "Two Period Models of Consumption Decisions Under Uncertainty: a survey," in J. Dreze, ed., *Allocation Under Uncertainty: Equilibrium and Optimality* (London: Macmillan).

_____ (1976) "Optimal Taxation – an Introduction to the Literature," *Journal of Public Economics* 6:37–54.

Scheffman, D. (1978) "Some Evidence on the Recent Boom in Land and House Prices," in L. Bourne and J. Hitchcock, eds. *Urban Housing Markets: Recent Directions in Research and Policy* (Toronto: University of Toronto Press).

Schwab, R. (1982) "Inflation Expectations and the Demand for Housing," *American Economic Review* 72:143–53.

Shelton, J. P. (1968) "The Cost of Renting vs. Owning a Home," *Land Economics* 44:59–72.

Simons, H. C. (1938) *Personal Income Taxation* (Chicago: University of Chicago Press).

Sirmans, C., J. Kau, and C. Lee (1979) "The Elasticity of Substitution in Urban Housing Production: a VES Approach," *Journal of Urban Economics*, 6: 407–15.

Slemrod, J. (1982) "Down-Payment Constraints: Tax Policy Effects in a Growing Economy with Rental and Owner-Occupied Housing," *Public Finance Quarterly* 10: 193–217.

Smith, B. (1976) "The Supply of Urban Housing," *Quarterly Journal of Economics* 40: 389–405.

―――― (1983) "Limited Information, Credit Rationing, and Optimal Government Lending Policy," *American Economic Review* 73: 305–18.

Smith, B., and J. M. Campbell (1978) "Aggregation Bias and the Demand for Housing," *International Economic Review* 19: 495–505.

Smith, L. B. (1974) *The Postwar Canadian Housing and Residential Mortgage Markets and the Role of Government* (Toronto: University of Toronto Press).

―――― (1974b) "A Note on the Price Adjustment Mechanism for Rental Housing," *American Economic Review* 64: 478–81.

―――― (1977) *Anatomy of a Crisis* (Vancouver: The Fraser Institute).

―――― (1978) "Federal Housing Programs and the Allocation of Credit and Resources," *Government in Canadian Capital Markets* (Montreal: C. D. Howe Research Institute).

―――― (1981) "Canadian Housing Policy in the Seventies," *Land Economics* 57: 338–52.

―――― (1984) "Household Headship Rates, Household Formation, and Housing Demand in Canada," *Land Economics* 60: 180–88.

Smith, R. S. (1979) *Tax Expenditures: An Examination of Tax Incentives and Tax Preferences in the Canadian Federal Income Tax System* (Toronto: Canadian Tax Foundation).

Smith, W. F. (1970) "Filtering and Neighbourhood Change," in M. Stegman, ed., *Housing and Economics* (Cambridge, Mass.: MIT Press).

Solow, R. (1972) "Congestion, Density and the Use of Land in Transportation," *The Swedish Journal of Economics* 74: 161–73.

Stigler, G. J. (1954) "The Early History of Empirical Studies of Consumer Behaviour," *Journal of Political Economy* 62: 95–113.

―――― (1975) *The Citizen and the State* (Chicago: University of Chicago Press).

Stiglitz, J., and A. Weiss (1981) "Credit Rationing in Markets with Imperfect Information," *American Economic Review* 71: 393–410.

Straszheim, M. H. (1973) "Estimation of the Demand for Urban Housing Services from Household Interview Data," *Review of Economics and Statistics* 55: 1–8.

―――― (1975) *An Econometric Analysis of the Urban Housing Market* (New York: National Bureau of Economic Research).

Struyk, R. (1976) *Urban Homeownership* (Lexington, Mass.: D. C. Heath).

Suits, D. B. (1962) "Forecasting and Analysis in an Econometric Model," *American Economic Review* 52: 104–32.

Surrey, S. S. (1973) *Pathways to Tax Reform: The Concept of Tax Expenditures* (Cambridge, Mass.: Harvard University Press).

Swan, C. (1973) "The Markets for Housing and Housing Services – a Comment," *Journal of Money, Credit and Banking* 5: 960–72.

Sweeney, J. L. (1974) "A Commodity Hierarchy Model of the Rental Housing Market," *Journal of Urban Economics* 1: 288–323.

_____ (1975) "Housing Unit Maintenance and Mode of Tenure," *Journal of Economic Theory* 8: 111–38.

Task Force (1979) *Report on the Canada Mortgage and Housing Corporation* (Ottawa: Canada Mortgage and Housing Corporation).

Tiebout, C. M. (1956) "A Pure Theory of Local Expenditures," *Journal of Political Economy* 64: 416–24.

Tindall, C. R., and S. Nobes Tindall (1984) *Local Government in Canada* (Toronto: McGraw-Hill Ryerson).

Tobin, J. (1958) "Liquidity Preference as Behavior Towards Risk," *Review of Economic Studies* 67: 65–86.

_____ (1970) "On Limiting the Domain of Inequality," *Journal of Law and Economics* 13: 263–77.

von Furstenberg, G. M. (1969) "Default Risk on FHA-Insured Home Mortgages as a Function of the Terms of Financing: A Quantitative Analysis," *Journal of Finance* 24: 459–77.

_____ (1970a) "Risk Structures and the Distribution of Benefits Within the FHA Home Mortgage Insurance Program," *Journal of Money, Credit and Banking* 2: 302–22.

_____ (1970b) "The Investment Quality of Home Mortgages," *Journal of Risk and Insurance* 37: 437–45.

Walker, B. (1981) *Welfare Economics and Urban Problems* (London: Hutchinson).

Weiss, Y. (1978) "Capital Gains, Discriminatory Taxes, and the Choice Between Renting and Owning a House," *Journal of Public Economics* 10: 45–55.

Wheaton, W. C. (1974) "A Comparative Static Analysis of Urban Spatial Structure," *Journal of Economic Theory* 9: 223–37.

_____ (1979) "Monocentric Models of Urban Land Use: Contributions and Criticisms," in P. Mieszkowski and M. Straszheim, eds., *Current Issues in Urban Economics* (Baltimore: The Johns Hopkins University Press).

White, M. J., and L. J. White (1977) "The Tax Subsidy to Owner-Occupied Housing: Who Benefits?" *Journal of Public Economics* 3: 111–26.

Winger, A. R. (1968) "Housing and Income," *Western Economic Journal* 6: 226–32.

Wolman, H. L. (1975) *Housing and Housing Policy in the U.S. and the U.K.* (Lexington, Mass.: Lexington Books).

Yinger, J. (1981a) "A Search Model of Real Estate Broker Behavior," *American Economic Review* 71: 591–605.

_____ (1981b) "Capitalization and the Median Voter," *American Economic Review*, Papers and Proceedings 71: 99–103.

Index